EDWARDIAN MURDER

EDWARDIAN MURDER

IGHTHAM AND THE MORPETH TRAIN ROBBERY

DIANE JANES

SUTTON PUBLISHING

First published in the United Kingdom in 2007 by
Sutton Publishing Limited · Phoenix Mill
Thrupp · Stroud · Gloucestershire · GL5 2BU

British Library Cataloguing in Publication Data
A catalogue record for this book is available from the British Library.

Hardback ISBN 978-0-7509-4780-0
Paperback ISBN 978-0-7509-4781-7

Typeset in Sabon.
Typesetting and origination by
Sutton Publishing Limited.
Printed and bound in England.

For Watson and Clouseau

Contents

List of Illustrations

Maps

Acknowledgements

Various libraries and record repositories have proved invaluable in the process of researching this work, including the Centre for Kentish Studies at Maidstone, Sevenoaks Library, the Northumberland County Archives at Morpeth, the Local Studies Department at Newcastle City Library, London Metropolitan Archives, the Family Record Centre, the National Archives at Kew, the Newspaper Section of the British Library at Colindale, BBC Archives and the Royal Norfolk Regimental Museum.

A list of published sources appears in the bibliography, but I would like separately to acknowledge the valuable work done by Monty Parkin in preserving the oral history on the Luard case and for allowing me to quote from his book *The Seal Chart Murder*, and Countryside Books for kindly giving permission for the quotation from W.H. Johnson's *Kent Tales of Mystery and Murder*.

John Endicott and David Hooper, my contacts at the Kent Police Museum, went above and beyond the call of duty for me; Louise Smith went to some trouble on my behalf when the Northumberland County Archive was about to close for several months; and Pauline Green of the *Kent Messenger* also deserves a mention on grounds of sheer enthusiasm.

I owe a particular debt to Mr and Mrs John Lewis, the current owners of Frankfield, who generously invited me into their home, guided me to the sight of the Casa and lent me their personal file of cuttings about the case. This book would have been the poorer without their help.

Acknowledgements

I am also grateful to various people who scoured their photographic collections, including members of the Dickman, Willink and Cropper families.

Peter Woolley not only read the manuscript, but transformed my garbled instructions and pathetic scribblings into beautiful maps, diagrams and sketches, effectively saving the day when it became apparent that some century-old newspaper photographs could not be reproduced.

Sincere thanks are also due to Margaret and Eric Thomas, to Peter Hyland who offered interest and encouragement, and to Erica Woolley – the best friend anyone could hope for, whether engaged on a project like this one or not.

Finally, thank you to my husband Bill, whose love and support made the whole thing possible, whose technical expertise I could not do without – and who accidentally demonstrated that it *is* possible to become so engrossed in your newspaper on the Newcastle to Morpeth line that you can miss your stop.

1

A Pair of Postcards

On the postcard stand in the National Trust gift shop at Ightham Mote, one particular card stands out. Sitting among the various photographic views is a reproduction of a Victorian engraving called *Parts of Ightham Mote*. Few if any of the visitors who choose this card will realise that the original artist was a major figure in one of the most sensational murders of the twentieth century. His name does not even appear on the postcard, although he is credited when this same engraving is reproduced in the guide-book[1] – C.E. Luard – or, to give him his full title, Major General Charles Edward Luard late of the Royal Engineers, Justice of the Peace, Fellow of the Royal Geographical Society, founder member of the Patriotic Society and long-serving member of Kent County Council: eminently respectable, well connected, and husband to Mrs Caroline Mary Luard, the victim in a murder case which so gripped the public imagination in 1908 that an enterprising local photographer turned a snapshot of the crime scene into postcards and sold hundreds of copies.

The Edwardian postcard inspired by Mrs Luard's murder shows the side of a bungalow surrounded by woodland. A flower border is just discernible below the picture window and on the left-hand side of the building there is some sort of veranda, with what might be clematis trailing along the edge of its roof. It is the sort of rustic scene which was a popular subject for postcards of the period: only the title, *Scene of Sevenoaks Murder*, betrays the macabre rationale behind the production of this particular card.

The murder of Mrs Luard has been variously described as the Sevenoaks Murder, the Seal Chart Murder, the Ightham Murder, the

1

Fish Ponds Wood Murder and, somewhat romantically, the Summer-house Murder. It created an enormous sensation in 1908 and a century later the case retains its fascination: a curiously English murder, involving golf clubs, afternoon tea, and an unbreakable alibi; just the kind of story which might have sprung from the pen of Sir Arthur Conan Doyle, or Dame Agatha Christie. Moreover, it has become inextricably linked with a second murder: that of John Innes Nisbet, who was murdered on a train as it steamed through the Northumberland countryside in the spring of 1910. Here, too, is a story which bore the hallmarks of detective fiction and enthralled the general public, who knew it as the Train Murder – a case whose progress was followed and argued over the length and breadth of the land.

Divorced from sepia costume drama, both cases represent the brutal killing of an entirely innocent person. Both left families bereaved, communities shocked and sent a shiver through respectable society. Caroline Luard's killer was never brought to trial, but one John Alexander Dickman was tried, found guilty and executed for John Nisbet's murder. Crucially, each case left questions unanswered: it has been claimed that the name of Caroline Luard's killer was known, that Dickman was an innocent man and that the two cases were linked – notwithstanding that the victims had apparently never met and were killed 18 months and over 300 miles apart.

Any overview of the story begins on a summer day in 1908. Edwardian summers are often described as 'golden', but August 1908 had been an unusually wet month, marred by high winds, low temperatures and thunderstorms.[2] The afternoon of Monday 24 August was a welcome exception: warm, dry and suitable for walking. Major General and Mrs Luard were prodigious walkers and thought nothing of a round trip of half a dozen miles or more, in spite of their advancing years. The General was approaching his seventieth birthday, while Mrs Luard was a mere three days short of her fifty-eighth.

As the Luards intended to depart for a short holiday the following day, the main purpose of their walk that afternoon was to collect the General's golf clubs. These were usually kept at the Wildernesse Golf Club, to save his carrying them to and fro on foot every time he played. The couple left home at about 2.30 with their dog Scamp, intending that Mrs Luard would go only part of the way, returning home ahead of her husband as a visitor was expected for tea. There was no direct route from their house to the Wildernesse Golf Club and a variety of lanes and footpaths they could have taken. In the event, the Luards decided on one of their favourite routes which included a short cut through some private woodland belonging to friends, where they had permission to walk whenever they wished. This route took them past a summerhouse known as La Casa, which by 24 August had been locked and deserted for several weeks because the owners were away from home.

A few minutes beyond the summerhouse, the private path intersected with a public bridleway and here the couple parted, Mrs Luard returning the way they had come, while the General continued towards the Wildernesse clubhouse at Godden Green, taking Scamp their Irish terrier with him. Up till then the Luards had not encountered anyone since leaving home, but once back on the public highway the General and his dog were observed by a series of witnesses, both going to and returning from the golf links.

After collecting his clubs the General took a slightly easier route home through Seal Chart Woods, thereby avoiding the private woodland he'd come through earlier. When he reached the main road, he was overtaken by a local clergyman, who gave him a lift in his motor car for the remainder of the journey, dropping the General off at his gate at 4.30.

On arriving home the General found that although the expected visitor had arrived and was waiting in the drawing room, there was no sign of his wife. He instructed the servants to bring in afternoon tea, explaining to his guest that he expected Mrs Luard to return at any moment. When tea was finished and Mrs Luard had still not appeared, he decided to go in search of her, and his visitor Mrs Stewart volunteered to accompany him. Together with the dog they retraced the route of the earlier walk, up to the point where the

Luards had originally entered their neighbours' woods. Here Mrs Stewart excused herself on the grounds that she now needed to get home in time for an expected visitor.

Thus the General and his dog entered the woods alone. As they approached the summerhouse Scamp ran on ahead; when the General followed the dog on to the veranda he discovered the body of his wife. She had been shot twice in the head.

General Luard ran to the nearest dwelling, which was a cottage on the edge of the wood where his friends' coachman Frederick Wickham lived with his family. On finding only Wickham's wife Anna at home, the General hastened to the main complex of buildings on the estate, where he located the coachman in the stables. The coachman fetched Herbert Harding the butler, and he accompanied the General back to the summerhouse.

The police and local doctors were summoned, enquiries set in motion, witnesses collected, an inquest held. Various people who had been in the locality testified to hearing the gunshots which killed Mrs Luard, while those who had observed her husband during the latter part of his walk were able to help police construct a timetable of his movements almost to the minute. The time of the shooting was determined at 3.15 – a time when it was established the General was a considerable distance from the scene and therefore could not have fired the fatal shots.

Professional and amateur sleuths set themselves to solving the mystery. Wild theories about revenge killings and secret assignations at La Casa began to circulate – and in spite of his apparently cast-iron alibi, the General began to receive anonymous letters accusing him of, at the very least, complicity in the crime.

The inquest into Mrs Luard's death was twice adjourned and with rumours mounting that an arrest was imminent, General Luard walked purposefully out of a friend's house on the morning of 18 September and threw himself into the path of a train, which killed him instantly. At the inquest into his death the anonymous letter writers were censured, and it was intimated that the vicious campaign against him had been a factor in the grief-stricken widower's death. The authorities were at pains to point out that the

General had not been a suspect, but in spite of this rumours that the General had had a hand in his wife's death continued to circulate. In the latter half of the twentieth century some local people – including one of those who had originally supplied him with an alibi – still recalled their suspicions of the General.

Suspicions were compounded by the fact that following the General's suicide the Kent police seemingly had no leads to follow. An arrest was made in 1909 but the suspect, an elderly tramp, was released almost immediately. The Fish Ponds Wood murder joined the list of unsolved cases. Many years later, one of the police officers who had been involved in the investigation told his daughter, 'We always knew who did it, but we couldn't prove it.'[3]

Turning the clock forward to Friday 18 March 1910, another victim embarked on a familiar journey which would end in death. The final morning of John Innes Nisbet's life began among scenes very different from the peaceful Kentish countryside where Mrs Luard encountered her killer. Nisbet began his day in the suburb of Heaton where he lived with his wife and two daughters in a terraced house near the railway station; that morning he set out for work in Newcastle upon Tyne just as usual. Nisbet was a colliery cashier based in offices on the Quayside in Newcastle, but part of his job entailed transporting the fortnightly wages to Stobswood Colliery, about 20 miles north of the city.

On 18 March 1910 John Nisbet followed the usual routine: cashing a company cheque at Lloyds bank, stowing the cash – almost £400 – into a large leather bag, then walking to Newcastle Central station to catch the 10.27 Newcastle to Alnmouth train.

The train called at fourteen stations between Newcastle and Alnmouth and the first of these happened to be Heaton, close to where the Nisbets lived. It was Mrs Nisbet's habit to be waiting on the platform when her husband's train passed through, to have a brief conversation with him and possibly – although she always denied this – to secure his pay packet. She was there on 18 March and while the train stood at the platform they exchanged a few words through the compartment window as usual. To Mrs Nisbet everything seemed normal; she did notice another man sitting at the

5

far end of her husband's compartment, but there was nothing remarkable in that.

John Nisbet should have alighted from the train at Widdrington station. The reason he failed to do so became horribly clear when the train eventually arrived in Alnmouth. Here, working his way along the train, checking each compartment in turn, porter Thomas Charlton opened one of the doors in the carriage next to the engine, and discovered a man's body pushed under the seat. John Nisbet had been shot in the head five times and his leather bag, together with its contents, was missing.

The victim's identity was established from his clothing, enabling enquiries to be put in hand immediately. The news hit the evening papers that same day and the police were greatly assisted not only by the accounts of railway staff who had been on duty at the stations where the 10.27 stopped, but also by travellers who read about the murder and came forward to say they had been passengers on that train, or else had seen Nisbet at Newcastle Central station before the train departed. Several of these people claimed to have seen Nisbet with a companion: a man who had apparently got into the train and travelled with him for at least part of the journey. Crucially, one witness immediately put a name to the man he thought he had seen with Nisbet – John Alexander Dickman, a citizen of Newcastle, who would subsequently be charged, tried and executed for the murder.

Dickman consistently denied having had anything to do with Nisbet's murder. He readily confirmed that he knew the murdered man slightly and had travelled on the 10.27 train that morning – but not, he said, in the same compartment as the late colliery cashier. Neither the murder weapon nor the cash was ever traced to John Dickman. The case against him relied on a series of circumstantial events which made it possible for him to have committed the murder, coupled with identifications from people who claimed to have seen him boarding the train with Nisbet.

Although the trial jury and Court of Appeal were satisfied that his conviction was sound, a small but insistent school of thought has always queried the strength of the case against John Dickman. It would be forty years, however, before the emergence of the revelation which has haunted the Luard and Nisbet murders ever since. In 1949 the government set up a Royal Commission to examine the issue of capital punishment: among the many submissions they received was the following memorandum from a Mr C.H. Norman:

This subject has interested me for many years, particularly since the trial of Rex v. Dickman at the Newcastle Summer Assizes in July 1910, who was tried for the murder of a man named *Nesbit* [sic] in a train. Dickman was executed for what was an atrocious crime on 10 August 1910, his appeal at the Court of Criminal Appeal being dismissed on 22 July 1910. The case has always troubled me and converted me into an opponent of capital punishment. I attended the trial as the acting official shorthand-writer under the Criminal Appeal Act. I took a different view to the jury; I thought the case was not conclusively made out against the accused. Singularly enough, in view of the nature of the crime, five of the jurymen signed the petition for reprieve, which could only be based upon the notion that the evidence was not sufficient against the accused.

It may be asked, why raise the question now? I am doing so partly because of Viscount Templewood's evidence, when he was reported as saying there was a possibility of innocent men being executed: partly because of the evidence of Viscount Buckmaster before the Barr Committee on Capital Punishment; but mainly because of the remarkable and disturbing matters concerning the Dickman case which have come to my knowledge over the intervening years, which I will now relate.

The Dickman case is the subject of a book by Sir S. Rowan-Hamilton, which was published in 1914, based on the transcripts of the shorthand notes of the trial and certain other material. I did not read this book till August 1939, when owing to certain passages in the book, I wrote a letter to Sir S. Rowan-Hamilton, who had been Chief Justice of Bermuda, who replied as follows in a letter dated 26 October 1939:

The Cottage
Craijavak
Co. Down

Sir,

Your interesting letter of 24 August only reached me to-day. Of course, I was not present at the incident you referred to in the Judge's Chambers, but (Charles) Lowenthal (junior Crown counsel at Dickman's trial) was a fierce prosecutor. All the same Dickman was justly *[convicted?]*, and it may interest you to know that he was with little doubt the murderer of Mrs Luard [who was shot dead at Ightham, near Sevenoaks, Kent, on 24 August 1908], for he had forged a cheque she had sent him in response to an advertisement in *The Times* (I believe) asking for help; she discovered it and wrote to him and met him outside the General's and her house and her body was found there. He was absent from Newcastle those exact days. Tindal Atkinson knew of this, but not being absolutely certain, refused to cross-examine Dickman on it. I have seen replicas of cheques. They were shown me by the Public Prosecutor. He was, I believe, mixed up in that case, but I have forgotten the details.

Yours very truly
S. Rowan-Hamilton, Kt.

In 1938 there was published a book entitled *Great Unsolved Crimes*, by various authors. In that book there is an article by ex-Superintendent Percy Savage (who was in charge of the investigations), entitled '*The Fish Ponds Wood Mystery*', which deals with the murder of Mrs Luard, wife of Major-General Luard, who committed suicide shortly afterwards by putting himself on the railway line. In that article, the following passage appears: 'It remains an unsolved mystery. All our work was in vain. The murderer was never caught, as not a scrap of evidence was forthcoming on which we could justify an arrest, and, to this day, I frankly admit I have no idea who the criminal was.' This book first came to my notice in February 1949, whereupon I wrote to Sir

8

Rowan-Hamilton, reminding him of the previous letters, and asking for his observations on this statement of the officer who had conducted the inquiries into the Luard case. On 22 February 1949, I received the following reply from Sir S. Rowan-Hamilton:

> Lisieux
> Sandycove Road
> Dunloaghaire
> Co. Dublin

Dear Sir,
Thank you for your letter. Superintendent Savage was certainly not at Counsel's conference and so doubtless knew nothing of what passed between them. I am keeping your note as you are interested in the case and will send you later a note on the Luard case.

> Yours truly
> S. Rowan-Hamilton, Kt.

I replied, pointing out what a disturbing case of facts was revealed, as it was within my knowledge that Lord Coleridge, who tried Dickman, Lord Alverstone, Mr Justice A.T. Lawrence and Mr Justice Phillimore, who constituted the Court of Criminal Appeal, were friends of Major-General and Mrs Luard. (Lord Alverstone made a public statement denouncing in strong language the conduct of certain people who had written anonymous letters to Major-General Luard hinting that he had murdered his wife.) I did not receive any reply to this letter, nor the promised note on the Luard case.

Mr Winston Churchill, who was the Home Secretary who rejected all representations on behalf of Dickman, was also a friend of Major-General Luard.

So one has the astonishing state of things disclosed that Dickman was tried for the murder of *Nesbit [sic]* by judges who already had formed the view that he was guilty of the murder of the wife of a friend of theirs. If Superintendent Savage is to be believed, this was an entirely mistaken view.

I was surprised at the time of the trial at the venom which was displayed towards the prisoner by those in charge of the case. When I was called into Lord Coleridge's room to read my note before the verdict was given, on the point of the non-calling of Mrs Dickman as a witness, I was amazed to find in the judge's room Mr Lowenthal, Junior Counsel for the Crown, the police officers in charge of the case, and the solicitor for the prosecution. When I mentioned this in a subsequent interview with Lord Alverstone, he said I must not refer to the matter in view of my official position.

I did my best at the time within the limits possible. I went to Mr Burns, the only Cabinet Minister I knew well, and told him my views on the case and the incident in the judge's room; which I also told Mr Gardiner, the editor of *The Daily News*, who said he could not refer to that, though he permitted me to write in his room a last-day appeal for a reprieve, which appeared in *The Daily News*. Mr John Burns told me afterwards that he had conveyed my representations to Mr Churchill, but without avail.

C. H. Norman
27 November 1950[4]

This memorandum raises a number of possibilities. Perhaps the most obvious is that the memorandum was a hoax and Mr C.H. Norman never existed: but that is not the case. Mr Norman was a real person, an appeal against Dickman's sentence was indeed published under his name in the *Daily News* on 6 August 1910 and the Home Office files confirm that he was the official shorthand writer at the Dickman trial.[5]

Here then, are some other possibilities. Is it conceivable that John Dickman was guilty of both murders, as the Rowan-Hamilton letters suggest? Some commentators have claimed that such an eventuality is extremely unlikely on geographical grounds alone; but the notion cannot be so easily dismissed. John Dickman's great passion in life was horse racing, an interest which took him all over the country; moreover, a letter used in evidence at his trial threw up the information that he was in London only a few months before the Nisbet murder, amply demonstrating that the distance between Newcastle and Kent did not debar his committing the crime.[6] Somewhat suggestively, both victims were shot in the head with a revolver which fired .320 bullets. Alternatively there is the interpretation favoured by Norman: that John Dickman was framed for the murder of John Nisbet by people labouring under the misapprehension that he was the killer of Caroline Luard.

Was John Dickman an innocent dupe or a double murderer? Who really killed John Nisbet and Caroline Luard?

2

Home in Time for Tea

Seldom can a victim and the man convicted of his murder have had so much in common as did John Innes Nisbet and John Alexander Dickman. Both were born in Newcastle upon Tyne and in March 1910 gave their ages as 44 years. Both were happily married, each to women roughly five years their junior. Both men became fathers in 1893, when their respective wives gave birth to daughters. Their families were each completed by the arrival of second children, born in 1896 and 1897, respectively. These four children, Catherine and Henry Dickman, Cicely and Lily Nisbet would all be fatherless by August 1910, each of them a victim of the train murder in its widest sense.[1]

There were other similarities between the two men. Both belonged to that educated lower middle class who found employment doing clerical work in Newcastle's commercial centre. They knew each other slightly, probably through frequenting the business district of the city. Both sported the handlebar moustache so fashionable at the time and they dressed in a similar style, although they could never have been mistaken for one another – because Nisbet was a slightly built 5 feet 4 inches, and wore gold-rimmed spectacles, whereas Dickman stood 2 inches taller, weighed around 11 stone and was a broad-shouldered man who gave the impression of being taller than he actually was.[2]

John Nisbet seems to have been a steady sort of chap. It is true that his wife may have found it expedient to make sure of his wage packet when the opportunity availed itself on the days when his work took him through Heaton station, and that among his belongings on the day he died the police discovered a flask containing a trace of port wine. This notwithstanding, Nisbet was a trusted employee who had been with the same firm of colliery owners for many years.

John Dickman's career was less straightforward. By the time he was born on 17 May 1864, his parents already had a son and a daughter. In 1867 his 33-year-old mother died while giving birth to a fourth child, and soon afterwards the three surviving children were sent to live with some of their father's relations in Whickham. In the 1860s Whickham was still a village and it was here that John Dickman would live, on and off, for the next twenty years or more: a circumstance which would bring him into contact with Wilson Hepple, a man who would provide fatal evidence when he stood trial for his life.[3]

In his middle teens John Dickman was sent to live with his father and an unmarried uncle, who were by then living in Great Lumley, County Durham, where they ran a successful farming and butchery business. The plan was to train young John as a butcher, but this was not to his taste at all. Determined to take up work in a commercial sphere, the youth returned to Whickham, from whence he sought work in Newcastle, eventually obtaining employment as a clerk with a company called Mason & Barry in Wallsend. Until he could afford to take lodgings in Newcastle, the young Dickman travelled to work and back on foot, a round trip in excess of 10 miles. After several years with Mason & Barry, he took a position with shipowners Dixon, Robson & Co., with whom he remained for about ten years.

He met the future Mrs Dickman while attending a dance in the latter weeks of 1891: here a mutual friend introduced the shipowners' clerk to a young schoolteacher called Annie Bainbridge. Annie was only 21, and on her side at least it seems to have been love at first sight, for later she wrote how on first catching sight of this stranger, a voice in her head seemed to say, 'That man will marry you.'[4] Sure enough, with an acquaintance scarcely stretching beyond a few dances together, John Dickman proposed to Annie Bainbridge in the Grand Assembly Rooms in January 1892. They were married on 5 September of the same year in Newcastle Cathedral.

By this time John Dickman seems to have had little contact with the surviving members of his family and there is no record that any of them came from Durham for the wedding. Although John Dickman was not close to his surviving relatives, he may have idealised his French mother Zelina Royer; certainly, he and Annie named their son Henry Royer Dickman in her honour. He once told Annie that his earliest memory was of creeping into a bedroom and seeing a white figure laid out on the bed – the figure was his dead mother.[5]

When the census was taken in the spring of 1901, John and Annie were living in Rothbury Terrace, Heaton. At this point John Dickman was still employed by Dixon, Robson & Co., but the financial stability of their early married life was about to be shattered. Within a few months of the census Dickman had lost his job. There is no reason to suppose this was due to any malpractice on his part. With no legislation in place, employers could and did dismiss men whenever they pleased. A slump in trade or any kind of reorganisation could precipitate job losses, and suitable replacement work was not always easy to come by. It took John Dickman nearly two years to find a new situation, this time with a syndicate that owned a colliery in Morpeth. This was the first time Dickman had come into direct contact with the mining industry; another unforeseen turn in his affairs, which would eventually provide an element in the evidence that convicted him.

By now John Dickman was in his late thirties, back in secure employment, with a wife and two children. In his leisure hours he often sketched (as a boy he had won prizes for his drawings); he also enjoyed reading and encouraged it in his children, whose education he took seriously. He had fond memories of a particularly influential teacher in Whickham – a man called Tom Burn (who by strange coincidence had later moved to Newcastle where he taught young Annie Bainbridge). Dickman was inordinately fond of animals, and this led to the family's acquisition of a dog. He was also actively interested in horse racing, being inclined to bet – although never, his wife insisted, to a degree which prevented him providing properly for his family.[6]

His new job regularly took him to the Morpeth colliery, so he became a frequent traveller on the Newcastle to Morpeth line, during which journeys he may occasionally have encountered John Nisbet. Certainly, the two men sometimes passed each other on the Quayside, where both their employers had offices. Equally they may have originally run across each other while living in the same neighbourhood – both lived at one time in Heaton. At all events, according to both John Dickman and Cicely Nisbet, by spring of 1910 this slight acquaintance stretched back almost a decade, thereby pre-dating the period when John Dickman became a regular traveller on the Morpeth line.[7]

In 1906 when Dickman had been working as secretary to the Morpeth Colliery Co. for about three years, the company sold their interests to Moore, Brown & Fletcher. The sale was negotiated through a Newcastle coal merchant called Frank Christie, but it was John Dickman who originally introduced the buyer to the sellers, so although the transaction inevitably put him out of a job, he received a generous commission on the sale – an amount in excess of £500, which was then the equivalent of several years' wages. At around the same time his finances were further augmented by a legacy from some distant relatives on his mother's side, from which he received a sum of just over £200.[8]

This dramatic change of fortune enabled him to take a long holiday from work, during which he was able to follow the horses, travelling to race meetings and sometimes placing large bets. Encouraged by his lucrative role in the colliery sale negotiations and some successful wagers, John Dickman seems to have decided to set up in business on his own account. For a time he retained the office in Exchange Buildings, which had previously been rented by the Morpeth Colliery Co. From here he seems to have dabbled on the edge of the mining industry, no doubt hoping to make a lucky connection as he had done with the sale of the Morpeth colliery. He also cultivated the acquaintance of Frank Christie, who shared his interest in horse racing and for whom he sometimes placed bets. In fact, from this time on, Dickman effectively became a professional gambler.

By the time of John Nisbet's murder in March 1910, Dickman had been enjoying this lifestyle for more than three years. By now he had given up his office in the Exchange Buildings, but was still in regular communication with Frank Christie, for whom he was both placing bets and providing information about various mining operations in the area. He was also acting as a bookmaker himself, a necessarily clandestine operation because bookmaking outside race courses was then a criminal offence. This side of his business entailed the use of a newsagents as a forwarding address, and the assumption of a false name for the missives he received there. By way of a further string to his bow, he was attempting to market a roller bearing of his own design, about which he was in touch with a firm in Leeds.

According to his own testimony John Dickman intended to visit the Dovecot Colliery near Stannington on the morning of 18 March. Here he hoped to obtain some information from another of his associates, William Hogg, who was the colliery contractor there. After this he planned to take a look at a new mining operation called the Lansdale Drift, which was not very far away from Dovecot – an errand he was undertaking on behalf of yet another associate, Ernest Houldsworth, a Newcastle coal merchant. This journey entailed taking the 10.27 Newcastle to Alnmouth train.[9]

From his home at 1 Lily Avenue in Jesmond, Dickman took a tram into the city. On arriving at Newcastle Central station, he went straight to the booking hall to buy his ticket and, by his own account, as he approached the ticket window he passed John Nisbet coming the other way. Nisbet wished him 'Good morning' and Dickman returned the courtesy. He always insisted that he never knowingly set eyes on the murdered man again.

According to Dickman it was a completely inconsequential encounter. He could not even remember for sure the previous occasion on which he had exchanged words with Nisbet. When subsequently pressed about it, he said he thought – though he was not absolutely certain – that the last time he had seen Nisbet was when he spotted him at a distance in Northumberland Street among the crowd that had turned out to see Lloyd George at a big political meeting which had taken place some weeks before.

After getting his ticket Dickman bought a newspaper, which he took to read in the third-class refreshment room over a pie and a glass of beer. The newspaper in question was the *Manchester Sporting Chronicle*, the contents of which were particularly interesting to John Dickman that day as it happened to be the morning of the Grand National. After finishing his pie and beer, he made his way to catch the train from Platform 5, making a slight detour en route to pay a call at the urinal on Platform 8. He got into a compartment towards the rear of the Alnmouth train just before it departed, then immersed himself in his newspaper for the entire journey, with the result that although he was not alone, he could subsequently recall nothing about his travelling companions.

As a consequence of this preoccupation, Dickman failed to notice the train stopping at his intended station, Stannington, only realising his mistake when he felt the train negotiating the distinctive curve in the line immediately before Morpeth, which was the next station north. He got out of the train at Morpeth, tendering the excess fare of 2½d as he left the platform. There was another train due to return in the opposite direction almost straight away, but Dickman decided to walk back, reasoning that if he visited the Lansdale Drift before rather than after his visit to the Dovecot Colliery, it would not take him out of his way.

He left Morpeth by the main Newcastle road and had been walking south for about half an hour when he was taken ill. He was later unable to describe precisely where this occurred, but estimated it to be somewhere between the groups of houses at Catchburn and Clifton. As the illness manifested itself in an urgent desire to open his bowels, Dickman climbed over or through a hedge, and attempted to relieve himself in a field. He had the misfortune to suffer from piles and they now occasioned him considerable pain. Eventually he felt so ill that he spread his overcoat on the ground and lay down, getting up every so often to see if he could alleviate the pain. Eventually after some considerable time had passed, he felt able to attempt the walk back to Morpeth, having decided to abort his plans and return home.

He could only manage a slow walk and by the time he got to Morpeth station, the 1.10 Newcastle Express had just left. With half

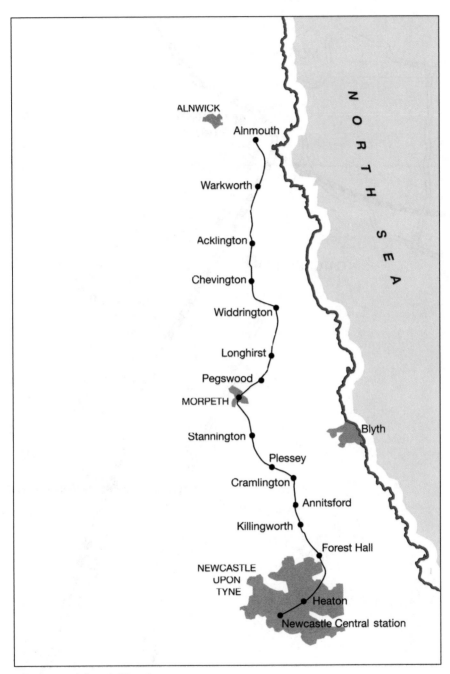

The route of the 10.27 train.

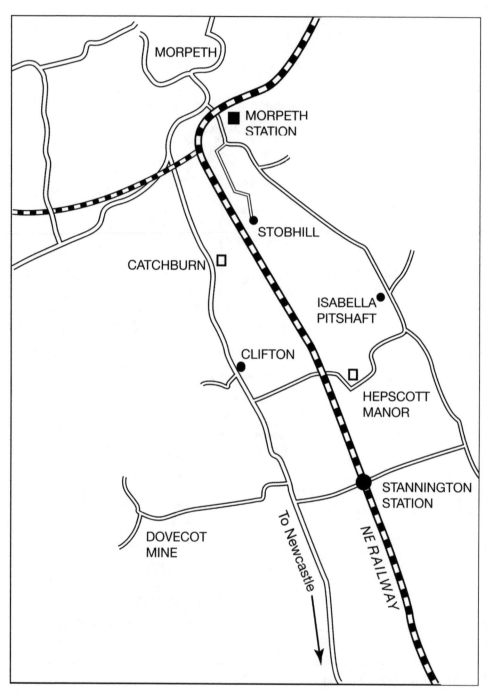

The area around Morpeth.

an hour to kill before the next train south, he decided to visit the coal depot to see how business was there, but saw no one he knew. It then occurred to him to walk into town on the off-chance that Mr Hogg had called in at the Newcastle Arms, but before he got very far from the station he happened to meet an acquaintance called Edwin Elliott. Elliott was accompanied by a man called William Sanderson, who was a stranger to Dickman, and the three of them fell to speculating about the outcome of the Grand National. After this delay Dickman decided he ought to return to the station, which he did, catching the 1.40 train back to Newcastle.

Once back in Newcastle he returned home to Lily Avenue. By the time he got there he was feeling much better; so much so that he was able to go out with his wife and daughter that evening.

Three days later on Monday 21 March at around 5.00 in the afternoon, Dickman answered a knock at his front door and was surprised to find Detective Andrew Tait on his doorstep. Once Tait had identified himself and confirmed that the man before him was John Dickman, one time book-keeper with a city firm of ship brokers, the detective advised Dickman that the police had received information suggesting he had been seen in the company of the murdered man, John Nisbet, on the previous Friday morning. Could Dickman, Tait asked, throw any light on the matter?

Dickman replied that he had known Nisbet for many years, and had seen him in the booking hall the previous Friday morning. Naturally he had read about the murder and realised that he and Nisbet must have travelled by the same train. 'I would have told the police, if I had thought it would do any good', Dickman said.[10]

Tait then asked Dickman if he would mind accompanying him to the police station to make a statement, a suggestion which Dickman apparently fell in with willingly enough, exchanging his carpet slippers for his outdoor boots while Tait looked on. Annie Dickman arrived home at this point, just in time to see her husband donning his outdoor clothes. She had been out shopping and visiting a dressmaker that afternoon and her first intimation of something untoward was the unusual circumstance of arriving home to find her front door standing open, and a smell of cigar smoke in her hall.

'They want me to go to Pilgrim Street, regarding Mr Nisbet', her husband explained.

'Oh', replied Annie. 'And will you be long?'[11]

According to Mrs Dickman, the detective assured her it would not take very long at all and she could expect her husband to return for tea. She prepared their meal accordingly, but John Dickman did not return to eat it. Catherine Dickman, then 16 years old, waited at the front gate with a friend, but when she eventually called out to her mother it was not to say that her father had returned, but rather to announce the arrival of half a dozen police officers, led by Superintendent John Weddell, who proceeded to search the house from top to bottom. This was the first of several visits, which would include such operations as dismantling the family piano and digging up the garden. On this first visit, Weddell informed Annie Dickman that her husband had been detained and would appear before the magistrates at Gosforth the following day.

Thus began a nightmare of prison visits and court appearances, during which the loyal Annie never wavered in her support of her husband and her assertions of his innocence. From the day of his arrest until his execution not quite five months later, Annie campaigned tirelessly for his acquittal and release, but to no avail. John Dickman was not destined to return to Lily Avenue.

John Dickman first appeared in court on Tuesday 22 March and was remanded until the 30th of the month. The funeral of John Nisbet was held the same day. His widow was unable to attend due to illness, but his two young daughters were there. The floral tributes included a white, heart-shaped wreath from 'his sorrowing and heartbroken widow and daughters in memory of a loving husband and father', and a simple posy from the girls who had regularly sold him flowers on the Quayside.[12] Vast crowds turned out, less as a show of respect for the murdered man than to satisfy the morbid curiosity which violent death inevitably arouses among large sections of the public. Nothing sold newspapers half so well as a sensational murder and if it had local connections, so much the better. Every known detail of the case had found its way into the newspapers by the time Dickman stood trial that July, leading many to question whether it was possible to find a jury in Newcastle whose minds were not irredeemably prejudiced against him.

At the inquest into Nisbet's death, it was revealed that no less than five shots had been fired at his head. Strangely, two different calibres of bullet were discovered: of the five bullets, three were .320 revolver cartridges and two were .250 calibre nickel-plated bullets, suitable for firing from a pistol. Throughout the investigation and trial it was assumed that the killer had used two separate guns, but later it came to be accepted that the two smaller bullets had been packed into the chamber of the revolver by padding around them with slips of paper. These bits of paper had been discovered on the floor of the carriage when it was searched on the day of the murder, but their significance had not been immediately understood.[13]

The realisation that only one gun had been involved was never perceived as having great relevance to the verdict against Dickman – if anything somewhat the reverse, because while it was assumed that there had been more than one weapon, it was open to the defence to argue (as they did) that there might have been more than one murderer.

Nisbet's broken spectacles had been discovered beside his body and this led to a theory that he had struggled with his murderer. It seems more likely, however, that the assailant launched himself unexpectedly at Nisbet, firing from close range before the unfortunate man had time to realise what was happening. When the police examined the murder compartment they discovered blood-stains on the upper seat cushions, and blood had run down behind the arm rest and on to the seat, suggesting that Nisbet was shot while in a sitting position. His glasses were probably broken while his body was being manhandled under the seat.

As information about the investigation filtered into the local press, John Dickman continued to protest his innocence. He had accompanied Detective Tait to the police headquarters to make a statement on an entirely voluntary basis, Tait having given him no definite indication that he was a suspect. Only after he had completed his statement was he charged with Nisbet's murder, to which he replied, 'I do not understand the proceedings. It is absurd for me to deny the charge, because it is absurd to make it. I can only say that I absolutely deny it.'[14]

On 30 March when Dickman appeared before the magistrates again, Edward Clark, the solicitor who had now been retained for the accused man, formally requested his client be discharged as there was no evidence against him. The magistrates saw things differently and John Dickman was remanded for a further seven days. As Dickman left the court flanked by two police officers, he stooped to kiss his wife, who was sobbing audibly, and laid a hand on her shoulder.[15]

In the meantime the police had been accumulating evidence. This included reassembling and photographing the vehicles which had been used to make up the 10.27 train on 18 March. This reconstruction took place at Platform 5 in Newcastle Central station and it also afforded the opportunity to carry out tests with respect to the evidence of some of the witnesses, in particular the testimony of Wilson Hepple, the man who had first provided the police with Dickman's name.[16]

After being remanded again on 6 April, Dickman eventually came before the magistrates on 14 and 15 May to hear the case made out against him. During this sitting events took an unexpectedly melodramatic turn, when Cicely Nisbet fainted while giving evidence about the last time she had seen her husband. This occurrence was not in itself so very remarkable. In those days of tight corsets and heavy gowns, fainting fits among ladies were so commonplace that bottles of smelling salts were routinely carried in ladies' handbags. Any startling development in an Edwardian novelette was virtually certain to have some unfortunate female character 'swooning away'; the factor which elevated Mrs Nisbet's fainting to the headlines, however, was what she claimed had caused her to faint – the recognition of her husband's murderer in the dock.

When originally questioned by the police, Mrs Nisbet had not been able to offer any useful information at all about the man she noticed sharing her husband's compartment. She told them that she had been waiting on the platform as usual when the train pulled into Heaton station that morning, but initially failed to spot her husband because she was looking for him towards the rear of the train; this was where he generally travelled, but that day for some reason he never explained, he was occupying a seat in the first carriage. When she eventually saw him leaning out of the window, waving to her, she had to walk some distance up the platform in order to speak to him and, as a consequence, they only had time for a very brief conversation before the train left. Although Mrs Nisbet noticed there was a man sitting at the far end of her husband's compartment, the tunnel just beyond Heaton station was casting a shadow so she could barely see the man at all.[17] It is worth mentioning at this point that the visibility in Heaton station as a whole would not have been particularly good. The platform was below street level, flanked by steep walls to either side, with a frosted glass canopy over the central platform adding to the gloom.[18]

To the newspapers Cicely Nisbet had given the following brief interview in late March:

> When I saw my husband he was laughing and in excellent spirits. I only had time to say, 'You won't be later than six o'clock mind, auntie is coming.' He replied, 'No, I will come straight home after I've been to the office.' The train was then on the move and he pushed the carriage window up and sat down, facing the engine. I saw there was another man in the same compartment, but I can give no description of him whatever, as I only had a momentary glance of him.
>
> My husband was a very affable man, sociable and inclined to be friendly with anyone. He was of a very unsuspicious nature.[19]

All this fits with her original statement to the police: the brevity of their conversation, a domestic reminder and a cheerful acceptance of it, followed as her husband returned to his seat by the merest glimpse of another person in the compartment, a man who was probably obscured from view until her husband resumed his seat and in whom she would not have taken the slightest interest in the normal course of events.

Cicely Nisbet's original statement mentioned that the man wore a hat and had his coat collar up; so quite aside from the compounding factors of the shadow from the tunnel, the moving train and a reasonable certainty that her attention would have been concentrated on her husband rather than this stranger, we learn that most of the man's visage was hidden by his clothing.

After she recovered from her fainting fit, however, Cicely Nisbet made the remarkable claim that as she had turned to leave the witness box at the conclusion of her evidence, she had caught sight of Dickman's profile at exactly the same angle as she had seen it when she saw him sitting in the same compartment as her husband on the day of the murder. From then on Cicely Nisbet would insist that she recognised Dickman as the man she had seen with her husband that morning: a story she would stand by every bit as staunchly as Dickman himself insisted on his innocence.

Although not called as a witness, Annie Dickman also spoke up at the magistrates' hearing, requesting that people be prevented from sketching her husband's likeness in court.[20] This was a forlorn hope. It was entirely usual for likenesses of defendants and witnesses to be used to illustrate newspaper accounts of trials and inquests. Annie's motive for objecting is interesting. It cannot have emanated from a fear that identification evidence would be prejudiced, because by that time the police had already assembled their witnesses. It is noticeable that Annie herself managed to avoid the photographers – by her own account sometimes going to considerable lengths to do so. Already the object of public hostility when she visited her husband, she may have hoped that limiting the number of likenesses published would enable the family to fade more easily into obscurity once her husband was freed.

Her hopes of this outcome must have diminished considerably when the proceedings at the magistrates' court ended with her husband being sent for trial at the next Assizes, which were due to open at the beginning of July.

There was to be one further development before the trial opened. On 9 June, while making a routine inspection in the Isabella Pit, just south of Morpeth, Peter Spooner the colliery manager discovered the leather bag which had been stolen from John Nisbet on the day of his death. It was lying at the bottom of an air shaft, where it had presumably been dropped some time previously. The lock was intact, but the bag had been slit open and most of its contents removed. The Stobswood payslips, together with a few shillings in loose copper, were still in the bag. Peter Spooner also noticed some coppers lying about nearby and a subsequent search of the shaft bottom recovered a total of 19s 3d in copper, which was only 1s 3d short of the total copper coin originally placed in the bag at Lloyds Bank. Of the £370 8s paid out to John Nisbet in gold and silver coin, there was no sign.[21]

The discovery of the stolen bag less than a mile and a half from Morpeth station would form another element in the case against Dickman, as would the fact that Peter Spooner was yet another of Dickman's associates in the mining industry. Not everyone would agree that the discovery of the bag told against the accused man, however. At least one person close to the trial insisted that far from incriminating Dickman, the location and timing of this discovery told very much in his favour. Like so much of the evidence, the leather bag would prove a source of dispute, with each side claiming that it supported their arguments.

The great difficulty facing the police was the lack of hard evidence with which to back up their case against Dickman. This was emphatically not a case where they could rely on a 'smoking gun'. The murder weapon had not been found and in spite of searching Dickman's home several times, the police never managed to locate a gun of any sort – though they did uncover a confusing tangle of evidence relating to guns which Dickman might, or might not, have handled in the years immediately preceding the murder.

Similarly, the spoils of the robbery were never conclusively traced to Dickman. After his arrest the police searched him and found he was carrying £17 9s 5d. This was a tidy sum of money for an ordinary working man to have about his person, and what was more it was being carried in the same type of money bag as the ones Lloyds Bank issued to Nisbet when he cashed the wages cheque on 18 March. This evidence tended to lose its significance, however, when it was recalled that Dickman operated as a bookmaker and therefore tended to carry large amounts in cash. Moreover, many hundreds of identical cash bags were issued to bank customers every year and to cap it all, Dickman had an account with the same branch of Lloyds as did Nisbet's employers. Although the police were convinced the £17 found on Dickman had formed part of the Stobswood Colliery wages, they never managed to trace the vast amount of cash which made up the balance.

To compound the police's difficulties, although Dickman's account of his movements sounded a little implausible, there was evidence to support it. Dickman's story of his chance meeting with Edwin Elliott and William Sanderson in Morpeth was corroborated by both men, neither of whom had observed anything unusual about Dickman's demeanour or appearance. Furthermore, as Sanderson had never met Dickman before encountering him that morning, he had no motive to provide him with an alibi.

The story of Dickman's sudden illness at the roadside could not be dismissed completely out of hand either, because it was ascertained that Dickman did indeed suffer from piles, for which condition he was treated while on remand in prison.[22]

If police hopes rose when they established that William Hogg, the man Dickman claimed he had been intending to see at the Dovecot Colliery on 18 March, had not been expecting Dickman or, as it happened, even been at the colliery on the day in question, they must have fallen again when Hogg confirmed that Dickman was in the habit of turning up without any prior notice, and thus his arriving without an appointment on 18 March would have been nothing out of the ordinary.

In spite of these contradictions, the police still believed they could prove beyond reasonable doubt that John Dickman was the man who killed and robbed John Nisbet. Some of the methods they employed to secure a conviction would subsequently be questioned by the Home Secretary, and have gone down in the annals of murder investigations as being among the worst examples of witness manipulation to have occurred in the early part of the twentieth century.

'I will not swear that was the man'

The trial of John Alexander Dickman opened on 4 July 1910 before Lord Coleridge. Edward Tindal Atkinson and Charles Lowenthal were counsel for the Crown, while Dickman was defended by Edward Mitchell-Innes and Lord William Percy.

Even before proceedings got under way the atmosphere had taken on some aspects of a three-ring circus. A vast crowd of people had packed the area outside the Moot Hall, where the trial was to take place. Entry to the trial was by ticket only, but the hundreds left without a ticket crammed themselves into every possible vantage point simply to get a glimpse of the arrival of the Black Maria with Dickman inside.

In his subsequent book on the case,[1] Sir Sidney Rowan-Hamilton deplored this unhealthy interest in the proceedings and speculated that the trial ought to have been moved elsewhere; somewhat overlooking the fact that the Train Murder, as it was called, had been widely reported all over the country. Nor was the level of public interest displayed in the Dickman case all that exceptional. Murder trials were perceived as a legitimate source of entertainment by the masses, and frequently drew large crowds. The scenes at Dr Crippen's trial later that same year would be even worse. It is impossible to say how much, if at all, the crowds and their partiality influenced juries. In Dickman's case, the degree of bias as the trial opened is uncertain. Rowan-Hamilton claims that as Dickman was taken to court, thousands lined the route booing, while old women hitched up their petticoats and followed the van, 'shouting their execrations'.[2] Contemporary accounts in local newspapers, although depicting vast crowds of spectators straining to catch a glimpse of Dickman when he reached the court, do not reflect anything like such a level of antipathy to the accused man. Annie Dickman's published account of her husband's ordeal (she stood waiting outside the Moot Hall until he arrived) does not record any screams of abuse and although she complained that 'rampant public prejudice' had condemned her husband before he stood trial, only three sentences earlier she had written 'the majority of people thought [before the trial opened] the evidence . . . warranted an acquittal'.[3]

Rowan-Hamilton was not in Newcastle upon Tyne during the trial and Annie Dickman was. There was undoubtedly prejudice against Dickman before the trial opened, but it is questionable whether it had reached the hysterical proportions described by Rowan-Hamilton. What can be construed with some certainty is that if the jurors read the newspapers they would already have had access to most of the evidence which would be presented to them at the trial, because this had been reported without restriction at both the inquest and the hearings before the magistrates.

The trial was a public spectacle in a way which is almost unthinkable today. Many of those who managed to obtain a ticket were women, some of whom had come equipped with needlework and knitting. This was less a reflection of disproportionate feminine interest in the case, than of the fact that married women were more likely than their husbands to be available to devote the whole of an ordinary working day to spectating in court. The high proportion of flat caps which can be seen in the crowds pictured outside the Moot Hall indicates an equal fascination among Tyneside's male population.

Inside the building, newspaper photographers were permitted to use their cameras. Thus even those without a ticket were able to see what the jury looked like and judge for themselves the appearance of John Dickman as he gave evidence on the second day. Various witnesses were also snapped as they entered or left the court. Superintendent Weddell, the prosecution witness Percival Hall and a heavily veiled Cicely Nisbet were among those who formed a double-page spread in the *Illustrated Chronicle*.[4] Only Annie Dickman, assisted out of the building by a kindly solicitor, managed to evade the flashbulbs.

The interior of the Moot Hall is virtually unchanged since 1910 and in spite of its generous proportions and high glass ceiling it retains a strangely claustrophobic air. Witnesses, counsel, judge, jury and the prisoner himself are all within a few feet of one another, while the public gallery seems to rear above them, its six long rows of benches packed with spectators throughout the Dickman trial, while others crammed into two much smaller raised galleries to left and right. The heat generated by this press of humanity was so exceedingly unpleasant that Mr Tindal Atkinson was moved to complain about the lack of ventilation in the packed courtroom. Lord Coleridge assured him that the matter had already been brought to the attention of the appropriate authorities, who had done all they could to improve matters.

Tindal Atkinson continued to grumble, speculating that 'One might have thought some provision would have been made in the roof.' To which Coleridge replied dryly, 'I am not the architect.'[5]

The proceedings opened with appropriate gravity. John Dickman was led into the dock between two warders. He was wearing a suit of light-coloured tweed, which stood out in contrast to the dark clothes of the counsel and the judge. He stated his occupation as 'secretary' and in answer to the indictment, replied 'Not guilty' in a firm clear voice.[6]

Edward Tindal Atkinson opened for the prosecution, candidly admitting from the outset that the case against the prisoner relied entirely on circumstantial evidence. He spoke for an hour while John Dickman listened intently from the dock. Immediately behind the dock, separated from him by an open stairwell, Annie Dickman sat among the witnesses and pressmen, also giving her full attention to proceedings.

The first witness called for the prosecution was Walter Henry Dickinson, a railway engineer. Dickinson provided a plan showing part of Newcastle Central station and gave details of the train itself, explaining where and at what time it had set out. This all went well until Mr Mitchell-Innes's cross-examination, when Dickinson was asked about the position of a urinal on Platform 8. The significance of the urinal would become clear later, but for the time being confusion reigned on the subject. Dickinson had not shown the urinal on his plan and did not in fact know where it was situated. Lord Coleridge became confused by the presence of a lavatory which *was* marked on Dickinson's plan and the urinal which wasn't. Although the existence of a urinal on Platform 8 was never really in serious doubt, this was not an auspicious start for a murder trial.

Dickinson's place in the witness box was taken by Mark Watson Ramsay, who was able to confirm the position of the urinal on Platform 8. However, his real role in the proceedings was to produce the photographs he had taken of the train on the day of the police reconstruction in April, together with other photographs showing general views of the station, in particular the entrance to Platforms 4 and 5 in relation to the third-class refreshment room and a booth which sold cigars.

The third witness, Charles Franklin Murphy, was also there to help with the geography of the case. Murphy was a surveyor at Morpeth and he had prepared a plan of the area between Morpeth station and Stannington showing the positions of the Dovecot Mine and the Isabella Pit.

After this came more scene setting as Thomas Anderson, an ex-colleague of the murdered man, told how on 18 March he had given Nisbet a cheque to cash for the colliery wages. He identified a bag, which the police had brought to show him on 13 June, as the lockable, black leather bag Nisbet had had with him on 18 March. This was the bag which had been recovered from the Isabella Pit. It was still locked, but had been cut along the top and down each side. He also identified the colliery pay bills which were found inside the bag as those issued to Nisbet on 18 March.

John Bradshaw Wilson, a Lloyds Bank clerk, took the story of Nisbet's last journey another step forward. He confirmed that he knew John Nisbet and had cashed the pay cheque for him on 18 March, paying out £231 in sovereigns, £103 in half sovereigns, £35 9s in silver and £1 0s 6d in copper. The gold was placed in three canvas bags, the silver in paper bags and the copper in a brown paper parcel.

Wilson was then shown the canvas money bag which had been found on John Dickman when he was arrested. The witness confirmed that it was a type of bag used by the bank to issue cash to its customers. However he declined to say whether it was exactly the same type and size of bag issued to John Nisbet on 18 March, because Lloyds had recently amalgamated with the North Eastern Bank and Lambton's Bank, each of which had their own named cash bags, all of which were still in regular use and any of which could have been the type given to Nisbet.

Mitchell-Innes for the defence had no difficulty in getting Wilson's agreement that a bag of the type in question could easily find its way into the hands of any Lloyds customer, and therefore demonstrating by logical inference that as Dickman was a Lloyds customer, there was nothing sinister in his having this bag in his possession.

With the next witness the evidence took a far more ominous turn from Dickman's point of view. Charles Raven, a commercial traveller of King John Terrace, Newcastle, testified that he had been walking across Newcastle Central station at about 10.20 on the morning of the murder. When he was about 3 yards away from the entrance to Platform 4 (through which passengers catching a train from Platform 5 needed to pass), he had seen Nisbet and Dickman walk through the gateway together. Once through the gateway the men had turned right towards Platform 5, which took them out of sight behind a booth selling cigars. Raven had not seen them speak to one another, but they had apparently been walking together. He said that he knew Dickman by sight and had been acquainted for several years with John Nisbet, with whom he was on speaking terms. His attention had been drawn to the murder on the day it happened, when he read about it in the papers.

Singularly among the witnesses who would say they saw Nisbet and Dickman together that morning, Charles Raven was the only one who claimed to be able to recognise both men. Even this would not turn out to be as straightforward as it first appeared. As to Raven's knowing John Nisbet to speak to, there is no alternative but to take the matter on trust. He may well have known John Dickman by sight, but Dickman emphatically denied that the cognisance was mutual, stating in his evidence that until Raven appeared against him as a witness, he had never seen the man before in his life.

Considerable play was also made of the fact that Raven had not seen the two men conversing. Defence counsel pointed out that it is possible for two acquaintances to walk almost side by side, each so taken up with their own thoughts as to be completely unaware of the other and thus not in any sense 'walking together' – in spite of outward appearances. Furthermore if, as Dickman claimed, he had visited the urinal on Platform 8 before entering the train, then even if the two men had gone through the Platform 4 gateway together, their paths would have diverged shortly after they disappeared behind the cigar booth, with Dickman heading for the urinal while Nisbet went straight to the train.

If Raven's evidence was tinged with all manner of uncertainties, the testimony of the next witness was less readily open to innocent interpretation. Wilson Hepple was the first of a number of witnesses who had actually travelled on the 10.27 train. Hepple was an artist who lived in Acklington; but he had previously resided for a number of years in Whickham, which was how he came to know John Dickman. He had known Dickman, he said, for about twenty years.

On 18 March, Hepple had first noticed John Dickman when he went to buy his ticket in the station booking hall. Having got his ticket Hepple waited on the station concourse for a while, to find out from which platform the train would depart. Once the departure was posted on the board, he went to Platform 5, found himself a seat in the train and stowed some parcels in the rack. After that he stepped back on to the platform and commenced walking up and down in front of the compartment door, about three paces in either direction. The compartment he had chosen was the last but one in the third coach from the engine. He was sure of this, because he remembered several photographs in the compartment, including one of Brancepeth Castle. (A railway official confirmed that this was the only compartment in the whole train which had a picture of Brancepeth Castle in it.)

While he was walking up and down outside the train, Hepple had noticed Dickman coming along the platform with a male companion, whom he described as being of slight build. He also observed that 'from their demeanour I think they were talking together'. Hepple continued pacing up and down alongside the train, not paying any particular attention to the two men; but as he turned towards the engine he noticed Dickman and his companion were about to board the train together. One of them had his hand on the handle of a compartment in the first coach after the engine. Hepple turned to retrace his steps again, and the next time he turned towards the engine, Dickman and his companion had disappeared.

By then Hepple reckoned he had been walking up and down outside the train for about 7 or 8 minutes, and thought it must be about time to get aboard, which he did. The train departed about a minute later. Under cross-examination he explained that he had not actually heard the men speaking, because they had never been within less than 18 feet of him, but their heads had been turned towards one another as if in conversation.

Hepple also confirmed that on the day when the train was reassembled and photographed, he had taken part in a reconstruction during which he stood outside the compartment he had originally travelled in while two men walked along the train, only stopping when he signalled with his hand that they had reached the point where he believed Dickman and his companion entered the train: a position which corresponded with the door of the compartment in which Nisbet's body was discovered.

After Hepple came one of the witnesses whose evidence would rank among the most controversial of the trial.

Percival Harding Hall, like John Innes Nisbet, was employed as a colliery cashier. Like Nisbet, Hall's duties included transporting wages from a Newcastle bank to a rural colliery, and like Nisbet he travelled regularly on the 10.27 train. He knew Nisbet as the Widdrington colliery cashier he said, and was aware that they were both engaged in the same errand, as they had both been making the same journey by that train for about five years. In spite of knowing the deceased man slightly, Hall had never shared a compartment with him. On the morning of the murder Hall had been travelling with a colleague named John Spink, whose evidence would come later.

Hall told the court that on the morning of 18 March, he and Spink had a compartment to themselves in the coach next to the engine. There were only three passenger compartments in that particular coach and theirs was the central one of the three. After they boarded the train Spink sat down, but Hall stood by the door, looking out of the window. Just before the train was due to leave, Hall saw John Nisbet approaching along the platform, with a man he did not recognise. Nisbet and his companion walked along the train until they were within a few feet of Hall, entering the compartment immediately adjacent to his. The train pulled out soon afterwards.

Hall and Spink left the train at Stannington station. The layout of this station meant that passengers alighting from northbound services could not cross the line to leave the station until the train had continued on its journey, so the two cashiers put their bags down on the platform and waited for the train to depart. As they stood there, Hall could see Nisbet sitting in his compartment, and as the train moved out Nisbet looked in Hall's direction and the two men acknowledged one another. Hall had no doubt that the man he nodded to at Stannington was John Nisbet, but said he could not be sure whether there was anyone else in the compartment with Nisbet at that point. Hall's testimony that Nisbet was alive and well at Stannington was to prove every bit as important as his evidence regarding the man who had got into the train with Nisbet at Newcastle.

Like Raven, Hall heard about the tragedy on the day it occurred and immediately approached the police with a description of the man he had seen boarding the train with John Nisbet – a man about 5 feet 6 inches tall, aged about 35 to 40 years, weighing around 11 stone, of medium build, with a heavy, dark moustache, who wore a knee-length, light-coloured overcoat and a hard felt hat – a man who was well dressed and appeared fairly well to do, and was apparently on friendly terms with Nisbet.

On the evening of 21 March (the night of Dickman's arrest) Hall had been summoned to the police station to attempt an identification. Here, Hall explained, he had been confronted with a line of nine men and was asked to pick out the man he had seen with Nisbet. He had eventually picked out John Dickman, but only with the proviso that 'if I could be assured the murderer was there, I would have no hesitation in pointing the prisoner out'.

Mitchell-Innes subjected Hall to a long and testing cross-examination on the subject of this identification parade. It is clear from the line of questioning he adopted that Mr Mitchell-Innes was aware, presumably from discussions with his client, that there was something very wrong about the whole business of the identification parade which had been organised by Superintendent Weddell that evening; unfortunately the full details and extent of this did not emerge until after the trial's conclusion.

At the trial Mitchell-Innes began by trying to draw Hall on who had been in charge of the identification parade, but Hall claimed he did not know. There were a number of policemen about, he said. Mitchell-Innes then suggested that Hall had walked several times up and down the line of men before picking anyone out. Hall replied that he had only walked down the row once.

'I put it to you that you walked more than once.'

'I think not', replied Hall.

'You think not? Will you swear that you did not walk more than once? Be careful —'

Hall hesitated a long time before hedging that to 'the best of his knowledge' he only walked down the line once before coming straight back to the prisoner. Mitchell-Innes was not letting him off the hook so easily. 'Then you will not swear that you did not walk down the row more than once?'

'No', said Hall. 'I will not swear that.'

Mitchell-Innes had not finished. He now put it to Hall that after walking along the row he had approached one of the officers present and asked him a question.

Hall confirmed that he had approached one of the officers and asked what he was expected to do.

'By that time', Mitchell-Innes pursued the point doggedly, 'you had already walked down the line at least once?'

'At least once', Hall agreed.

Mitchell-Innes then wanted to know whether Hall had not already been made aware of the purpose of the exercise and, if so, why he needed to ask what he was to do. Hall explained that he wanted to know whether by pointing out a particular man, he was swearing that was the man he had seen enter the train with Nisbet.

'How could you come to think that you were swearing anything? You had not been asked to take any oath?'

'Well in my own mind, I understood that that is what identification meant', said Hall, 'but I may have been wrong.'

'You had not in fact been asked to swear anything, or take any oath?'

'I suppose not – no.'

'Was it that you were afraid of binding yourself with the same effect as though you had sworn?'

'That was it, exactly', Hall agreed.

'You were not sure enough to bind yourself absolutely by pointing out anybody?'

'That was just it.'

'When you asked the officer what you were expected to do, what did he answer?'

'He said, "Point him out".'

Mitchell-Innes then had Hall recap how he had only pointed Dickman out after making the proviso that he would not swear the man he was about to point out was the same man he had seen with Nisbet. Having pinned Hall down on this point, Mitchell-Innes then forced him to admit that when he gave evidence before the magistrates, the wording of his deposition had given the impression that he only added the rider that he would not swear Dickman was the man he had seen with Nisbet after picking Dickman out – thereby adding more weight to his identification evidence than might have been attached to it if the court had been aware of his initial reluctance to make any selection from the line-up at all.

Hall's colleague John William Spink followed him into the witness box. He repeated Hall's story of getting into the middle compartment of the first coach, confirming that after he sat down, Hall stood for a time looking out of the window. Being seated Spink had seen nothing of anyone else entering the train, but he did have something to add about the moments he and Hall spent standing on Stannington station. Like Hall he remembered nodding to Nisbet and being acknowledged in return, but he was sure he had seen another passenger sitting facing Nisbet. Although he could not swear that man had been John Dickman, Spink said Dickman did resemble the man.

Cicely Nisbet was next. She explained her custom of meeting her husband's train at Heaton station, 'not for the purpose of getting wages from him, but just to have a little conversation'. She confirmed that he had been travelling in the coach next to the engine rather than in the rear of the train as usual, and that hence she had been waiting on the wrong part of the platform and nearly missed seeing him altogether. She then explained how she had seen another man in the compartment and observed his profile 'quite distinctly'. Mrs Nisbet now placed her husband with his back to the engine and his companion facing it, which was precisely the opposite seating arrangement to the one John Spink had described just a few minutes before.

When it came to Mrs Nisbet's dramatic recognition of Dickman at the magistrates' court, Mr Mitchell-Innes had a field day, asking how it was that she had become more, rather than less certain of what she had seen with the passage of time. Struggling to maintain that she had always been certain about her evidence, Mrs Nisbet found herself continually tripped up as Mitchell-Innes referred her back to statements she had made previously. When she eventually conceded that 'If that is there [in the statement] it must be right, but I scarcely remember', Mitchell-Innes's triumphant, 'I accept that answer Mrs Dickman!' was somewhat crushed by the widow's sharp rejoinder, 'Please will you not call me Mrs Dickman. You have called me Mrs Dickman all through.'

Mitchell-Innes's unfortunate slip aside, it is difficult to imagine the jury taking Mrs Nisbet's identification evidence seriously.

Having dealt with the dead man's journey as far as Stannington, the Crown now began to call the witnesses who would testify to the Morpeth end of the business, the first of whom was John Athey, the ticket collector who had been on duty at Morpeth on the day of the murder.

Athey remembered that a male passenger got off the 10.27 and tendered the outward portion of a third-class ticket to Stannington, together with the 2½d excess fare. Athey said Dickman resembled this man, although he could not state conclusively that it was him. As Dickman did not deny being that man, this did not really matter one way or the other. Dispute did arise over what exactly Dickman had said to Athey when he handed the excess fare over, whether Dickman was wearing his overcoat or carrying it, and whether Dickman had had the ticket and fare ready to hand to Athey. According to Athey, the man already had the coins and ticket in his left hand when he approached the gate. This was significant because the Crown's case relied on Dickman having only one hand available to deal with this transaction, as his other hand must necessarily have been occupied with Nisbet's black leather bag.

After Athey came John Grant, a railway platelayer who was one of the passengers who joined the 10.27 at Morpeth. Grant told the court he had got into one of the compartments in the second coach from the engine. In order to do so he had had to walk past the first coach, in which he had seen only one passenger, a Mr Bruce. He was sure there had been no one else in the first coach.

John Thomas Cosher had been the porter on duty at Longhirst, the next station but one north of Morpeth, and he reinforced the evidence of the empty compartments. It was his job to walk along the length of the train as it pulled into Longhirst, shouting the name of the station. In doing so he had noticed that two compartments in the first coach were empty, although there was someone (Mr Bruce) in the third. He also observed Grant alighting from the second coach.

George Yeoman, the stationmaster at Longhirst, confirmed that he saw Grant leaving the train and that two other passengers, a man and a woman who had travelled from Morpeth, also left the train there. He had not walked to the head of the train and therefore could not confirm whether anyone had been sitting in the first coach.

George Harker, the stationmaster at Pegswood (the station between Morpeth and Longhirst), told the court he saw only two passengers leave the train at his station, a woman and a little girl.

Andrew Bruce, a carriage inspector with the North Eastern Railway, was the last passenger to give evidence. On 18 March he took the 10.27 all the way from Newcastle to Alnmouth, travelling in the coach next to the engine, in the compartment situated between the luggage section and the passenger compartment occupied by Hall and Spink. There had been another man in the compartment with him as far as Chevington.

Bruce testified that he noticed the men he now knew to be Hall and Spink when they left the train at Stannington. He saw them put their bags down on the platform and observed the shorter of the two men (Hall) nod to somebody in the train, just as it was pulling away.

Bruce was followed by Thomas William Charlton, the unfortunate porter who had discovered Nisbet's body when he checked the train at Alnmouth station.

Then Robert Wilkinson, the guard on the 10.27, confirmed the composition of the train and the fact that there had only been one compartment with a photograph of Brancepeth Castle in it.

By this stage the prosecution had already presented a formidable body of evidence. Few of those listening could doubt that the witnesses who claimed to have travelled in the same coach of the train as Nisbet had done so, for each effectively corroborated the testimony of the others. Nor could there be much doubt that John Nisbet was still alive when the train left Stannington station, for Hall had nodded to him and Bruce had seen him do so. Furthermore, it appeared almost certain that Nisbet had been killed as the train travelled between Stannington and Morpeth, because John Grant had observed the compartment where Nisbet had been sitting at Stannington to be 'empty' when he boarded the train at Morpeth, an observation backed up by staff at the next two stations along the route.

George Harker had not looked into the relevant section of the train, but he could confirm that the only passengers to leave the train at Pegswood were a woman and her child. John Cosher had walked the length of the train at Longhirst and he shared Grant's impression that the whole of the first coach was now empty of passengers save for Andrew Bruce. Moreover, George Yeoman confirmed that only three people left the train at Longhirst and all of these had been identified as joining it at Morpeth. This pointed to the killer being the man seen joining the train with John Nisbet at Newcastle, who having shot and robbed his victim between Stannington and Morpeth (which just happened to be the longest distance between any two stations on the line) then left the train at Morpeth, carrying Nisbet's bag.

Whether the prosecution had convincingly shown that man to be John Dickman was another question entirely.

William Hogg took the witness stand next. Hogg was the colliery contractor whom Dickman claimed he had set out to visit on 18 March. Hogg said he had known the prisoner for eight or ten years, meeting him originally when he was secretary of a colliery company at Morpeth. He confirmed that Dickman had been to see him at the Dovecot Colliery on perhaps four or five occasions previously, but had no appointment with him on 18 March, when Hogg was in fact spending the day in Newcastle, having taken an early morning train there from his home at Pegswood. He had last seen the accused man exactly a fortnight earlier, when Dickman turned up at about midday on Friday 4 March, having travelled, Hogg assumed, by the 10.27 train. By Hogg's estimate, it would normally take about 30 minutes to walk from Stannington station to the Dovecot Mine.

Anyone paying close attention to Hogg's evidence might have already spotted two errors in it. If he had only met Dickman during his period of employment with the Morpeth colliery, then he could not have known him much above seven years at the outside, and if Dickman had walked from Stannington station on Friday 4 March, but not arrived at the Dovecot colliery until around noon, then the walk had taken him considerably in excess of 30 minutes, because the 10.27 from Newcastle arrived in Stannington at 11.06. These are not serious discrepancies, but they do suggest a somewhat cavalier approach by Hogg in his evidence, which belied the seriousness one might expect him to attach to testimony bearing on a man standing trial for his life.

Hogg also stated that he had once lent Dickman a sovereign when the latter claimed to be short of money, an incident Hogg thought had taken place in about the previous December.

Under cross-examination by Mr Mitchell-Innes, Hogg agreed that Mr Frank Christie of Newcastle had an interest in the operations at the Dovecot Mine. However, when Mitchell-Innes asked if he had ever discussed this matter with Dickman, Hogg became evasive, only admitting that he 'may' have done. He was also strangely reluctant to concede that he had driven Dickman into Morpeth after the 4 March visit to the Dovecot Mine, adamantly refusing to agree that he actually drove Dickman as far as the railway station.

After this peculiar series of evasions on the subject of a pony and trap ride into Morpeth, Mitchell-Innes again asked Hogg whether Dickman had ever mentioned his arrangements with Mr Christie regarding the sinking operations at the mine.

'He may have done that', Hogg replied.

'You will not say that he did?'

'He may have done that', Hogg repeated.

'You will not say that he did not?'

'I will not say that he did not.'

Mitchell-Innes tried another tack, but Hogg continued to avoid giving any direct indication of what Dickman had or had not discussed with him, saying at one point, 'I am not going to swear to anything.' Even an intervention by Lord Coleridge with the direct question 'Did he [Dickman] not mention Christie at all?' only elicited the response: 'He may have mentioned Christie.'

Hogg proved equally exasperating on even the most trivial details of evidence. 'I think you told us he [Dickman] generally came by the 10.27 train?' said Mitchell-Innes. 'No, I have not told you that', Hogg responded. Cross-examination continued for a while in this vein before Edward Tindal Atkinson had another go at attempting to extract information on behalf of the prosecution; but he fared little better than Mitchell-Innes when it came to any questions touching on conversations which might or might not have taken place between Dickman and Hogg on the subject of Mr Christie.

When Tindal Atkinson abandoned the subject of Mr Christie and questioned the witness about Dickman himself, Hogg suddenly became much more forthcoming. He had no hesitation in confirming that Dickman had left the employment of the Morpeth Colliery Company about six years previously (a gross overestimate), that Dickman had not had a situation since and that the defendant had received a good commission from the sale of the colliery company.

It is not easy to guess what the jury made of William Hogg's evidence. In some ways it should have worked to Dickman's advantage, for Hogg confirmed Dickman's story of visiting without appointments on a number of occasions, and since Dickman had no way of anticipating Hogg's absence in Newcastle on the day of the murder, this would in no way have precluded his setting out for the Dovecot Mine in expectation of Hogg's being there as usual. The prosecution hoped to suggest that Dickman's visit on Friday 4 March had been a trial run for the murder, but it could equally have been another of Dickman's randomly spaced visits to discuss whatever it was he was in the habit of discussing with Hogg.

Over these discussions a veil of mystery well and truly descended. Much as Hogg prevaricated, it was perfectly clear that he and the accused man must have talked about something. On no less than four occasions, when asked whether Dickman had spoken with him about Christie's interest in the Dovecot Mine, Hogg evaded the question by responding that 'He [Dickman] had nothing to do with it.' Yet Hogg was in the habit of receiving Dickman at his place of work, and on his final visit had given Dickman a lift into Morpeth. His refusal to elaborate on the subject of their discussions, issues which on the face of it had nothing whatever to do with the murder, left a very odd impression. If anything the point which William Hogg appeared most at pains to get across was that John Dickman was in no way involved in his business dealings with Mr Christie.

The next witness, Detective Andrew Tait, was a great deal more cooperative. Tait began by explaining how he had gone to

Dickman's house on 21 March and invited him to the police station where, in the presence of Superintendent Weddell, Dickman had voluntarily made a statement, after which Weddell had arrested Dickman on a charge of murder. Tait detailed the items found on the prisoner when he was searched, which included the cash already alluded to, a pair of tan dog-skin gloves and a card case containing, among other items, a moneylender's card noting a loan of £20 made to the prisoner in October 1909.

Mitchell-Innes then cross-examined Tait, who agreed that Dickman had offered him every cooperation; indeed, had volunteered the information that he travelled on the 10.27 train on 18 March, a fact then unknown to Tait, who had merely been advised by the Northumberland police that Dickman had been seen at the station in Newcastle with the murdered man. Tait explained that this original information had come through by telephone on Sunday 20 March, after which he had set about locating John Dickman. 'I made enquiries on Monday, and I was not very sure that I had got the right man, because he was living in a good residential district, living in a £30 house, costing, with rates, £40 per year. All my inquiries amongst people who knew him said that he was very hard up; therefore I was not sure that he was the man.'

Here is an interesting glimpse of a potentially significant side issue. It is easy for us to forget what would have been blindingly obvious to the police in 1910: that John Dickman was quite different from the run-of-the-mill occupants of Newcastle jail. He was intelligent, literate, relatively well spoken, smartly dressed and had a confident air. He lived in a respectable suburb of the city. He was altogether the wrong class of man to be a murder suspect so far as Detective Tait could ascertain. The English class system possessed many subtleties and expectations. In Edwardian England there was an underlying assumption that if robbery, drunkenness and murder was habitual behaviour among the lowest classes, then those a little higher up the social ladder were a different breed altogether, from whom better was expected. The police seem to have conceived an intense dislike of John Dickman and this may not have been entirely due to their opinion that he was guilty of shooting a man in cold

45

blood. Dickman's middle-class manners, the way he failed to fit with their general perception of criminals and criminal behaviour may have led them to believe he really was a different sort of criminal – one possessed of particular wickedness and cunning, as any criminal not belonging to the obviously criminal classes must surely be.

Superintendent John Weddell now gave his evidence. He had first encountered John Dickman when Tait brought him into the police station. He read Dickman's statement to the court, repeating Dickman's comment when arrested, to the effect that he did not understand the charge, and absolutely denied it. Weddell then told of going to 1 Lily Avenue that same evening and searching the premises, in particular the Dickmans' bureau, in which he discovered various bank books. On another visit to the house five days later, he discovered two pawn tickets, both for pairs of field glasses in the name of John Wilkinson of 180 Westmoreland Road, the second one dating from 17 March, the day before the murder, advancing 15s. In addition to the first bank books and pawn tickets, Weddell also produced as evidence some letters and further pass books which he described as belonging 'to accounts the prisoner had at one time at these [Lambtons and National Provincial] banks'.

At this Dickman said, 'Those accounts are not closed. Excuse me interrupting.'

The passbooks were handed to Lord Coleridge who said, 'Apparently the account at the National Bank is closed on 31 December 1909 with a balance of 3s against the prisoner. The other account at Lambton's on 11 August.'

Dickman made no further protest and Weddell's evidence continued, with the superintendent telling the court how various items of clothing had been removed from the Dickman home on 21 March and handed over to Dr Boland.

Weddell went on to describe the experiments at Newcastle Central station, when the 'murder train' was reassembled at Platform 5. He explained how Hepple's compartment had been identified with the aid of the photograph of Brancepeth Castle and how Hepple had then stood outside this compartment, while Weddell and Detective Tait walked slowly along the train until Hepple signalled them to stop where he had last seen Dickman and the man assumed to be Nisbet. Owing to Weddell's somewhat confusing descriptions, the precise result of this experiment was not entirely clear, but there can be no doubt that Hepple claimed to have seen these men on the point of entering one of the compartments in the coach immediately behind the engine.

Under cross-examination Weddell was forced to concur that Dickman had volunteered a great deal of information not previously known to the police, such as his leaving the train at Morpeth, his tendering the excess fare and his meeting with Sanderson and Elliott, who Weddell agreed had readily supported Dickman's account of their conversation, confirming on oath at the magistrates' court that they had discussed the betting on the big race, with Dickman all the while appearing perfectly quiet, rational and normal in every way. Mitchell-Innes then asked Weddell whether it was a fact that he had taken from the prisoner's home every article of clothing owned by the prisoner, both outer and under garments, and yet not found bloodstains on anything, apart from a stain which might be blood on the thumb of one glove and some spots on the inside pocket of a pair of trousers. Weddell confirmed this was the case.

After that Mitchell-Innes went on an all-out attack, forcing the police superintendent to admit that in spite of ransacking the Dickman home, dismantling the piano, taking up carpets, searching the water cistern, removing drawers and digging up the garden, the police had neither located the proceeds of the robbery nor any kind of gun. A police search in the Morpeth area had similarly failed to uncover anything pointing to the prisoner's guilt.

Asked to confirm that Dickman was a betting man, Weddell said his enquiries had indicated that to be the case, and that he understood a subscription had been raised in the Bigg Market to assist with his defence. It was explained for the benefit of Lord Coleridge that the Bigg Market was a street in Newcastle where bookmakers met to do business.

Tindal Atkinson resumed his examination by asking Weddell about four bills in the name of Dickinson, which had been found at Dickman's house. Unlike the pawn tickets, the address on each was

1 Lily Avenue. These bills or receipts were innocuous enough, one being in the name of Mrs Dickinson, for soling and heeling a pair of shoes, another from the Newcastle & Gateshead Water Company and a third from Bainbridge's store. It may have occurred to the jury that if these items proved anything at all, it was the ease with which tradesmen of every kind mis-hear and subsequently misrepresent the names of their customers.

The final witness on the first day was Dr Charles Clarke Burnham, the Alnwick police surgeon who had examined John Nisbet's body at Alnmouth station on the afternoon of the murder. The day had opened with confusion over the siting of a urinal, and as it dragged to a close, Dr Burnham's efforts contrived to engender a level of bewilderment well in excess of anything achieved hitherto.

At the commencement of Burnham's evidence, Lord Coleridge said he felt the best plan would be for the doctor to detail the victim's wounds one by one, explaining where they were and what the effect of each one would have been. He had read the doctor's report, he said, 'and I think, without saying anything derogatory, it is a confused report. I think I should like to have it more clearly described.'

Lord Coleridge's proposal seemed eminently sensible, but this methodical approach was apparently beyond Dr Burnham, who seemed intent on discussing the wounds in an order of his own choosing – which was not the same order he had adopted when preparing his report. The result of this was that the judge assumed him to be talking about the first wound described in the report, when in fact he was describing the third. Junior prosecution counsel Charles Lowenthal tried to alleviate the confusion by helpfully pointing this out.

It had been a long day in court. 'Let us take them one by one', suggested the judge. 'I do not want number three. What is number one? Was there a bullet wound under the left eye, which you described in your report as wound number one?' This brought Burnham back on track, but only temporarily. The doctor launched off again with Lowenthal and Lord Coleridge attempting to clarify matters as they went along, until Coleridge eventually lost the plot completely and asked whether that did not make six wounds rather than five. 'No, five wounds', Burnham responded, leading Coleridge to complain: 'I really do not follow this.'

They stumbled on through the morass of medical evidence with Coleridge commenting, 'It is a great pity you did not keep the wounds in the same order with the same description [as they appeared in your report].'

If anything emerged at all out of this long and muddled peroration of blood and bullets, it was little more than confirmation that John Nisbet died as a result of five bullets being fired into his head at close range. What Dr Burnham's evidence could shed no light on at all was whose hand had fired those bullets.

The first day of the trial was described as 'long and weary' by Annie Dickman. The second, she said, was 'uneventful' until her husband took the stand.[7] This may have been her impression, but the jury, who had already been subjected to a torrent of information, still had a lot to listen to before John Dickman entered the witness box.

The judge opened proceedings on the second morning by recalling ticket collector John Athey. Questioned further about the man who tendered the excess fare, Athey told the court he was sure the man had been wearing a coat, although he could not be certain of the colour. He said the leather bag produced in court was a considerable size and if the man had been carrying it outside his coat, he would have seen it. Therefore if the man had been carrying the bag, then he must have held it under his coat in his right hand, which Athey had not seen.

The first new witness of the day was Miss Henrietta Hymen, manageress of a newsagents in Groat Street, Newcastle. At one time Dickman not only bought his newspapers at her shop, but also had an arrangement whereby letters for him would be posted there, addressed to Fred Black. Miss Hymen said he always collected these letters in person. She had been aware that they were about betting.

'He also had parcels addressed to my shop under the name of Black, one of which contained a gun', said Miss Hymen. She knew about the gun, because Mr Black, as she had then known him, told her he was expecting one. A few weeks after this parcel arrived, a postcard from Bell Brothers of Glasgow came, requesting the return of a revolver sent in error. By then the parcel assumed to contain the gun had been lying uncollected for some time, she thought from the end of October 1909 to around the first week in January 1910. When 'Mr Black' eventually collected the gun and the postcard, he asked Miss Hymen to supply him with a label to send the parcel back.

That was the last time Dickman called at Miss Hymen's shop and on that occasion he told her his real name and address. She recalled that the parcel collected on his last visit was quite small, wrapped in brown paper and tied with string; she could not see what it contained. There had been a previous parcel, however, again done up in brown paper and string, but shaped like a gun, which 'Mr Black' had also collected on an earlier occasion.

It should be explained at this point that guns and ammunition were very readily available at the time. Prospective purchasers did not require a licence and it was perfectly legitimate to buy a gun through the post. The Pistols Act of 1903 specified that a register must be kept of the sale of guns, but since there was no obligation placed on buyers to prove their identity, the measure was effectively useless.

Not surprisingly, shootings and armed robberies formed a significant proportion of reported crime, and the ease with which lethal weaponry could be obtained undoubtedly led to cases of murder which might have been prevented. Possibly the strongest illustration of this was an incident which took place within days of the murder of John Nisbet and only a few miles away. This was the case of Thomas Craig, a recently released convict, who walked into a Newcastle gunsmith at 2.00 on 26 March 1910 and purchased a revolver and fifty cartridges, supplying the cashier with a false name and address. Less than two hours later he had seriously wounded his ex-fiancée and shot her husband dead – having set out with the express purpose of so doing.[8] In an entirely separate incident, only twelve days after the conclusion of Dickman's trial, a youth was arrested in Newcastle for yet another fatal domestic shooting.[9]

Nor was a gunsmith the only outlet for firearms; guns were also sold at some general dealers and hardware stores. In 1913 an 11-year-old boy is recorded as having bought shotgun cartridges at a local cycle shop – a far from exceptional situation.[10] In addition to formal commercial transactions, with so many guns in circulation there were obviously numerous opportunities for guns to change hands privately.

The next witness would also speak of guns. This was Thomas Simpson, an employee of Pape's, a Newcastle gunsmith. Simpson explained which types of gun would normally be used to fire the two different types of bullet which had been used to kill Nisbet, opining (wrongly as it would turn out) that two different guns must have been used.

At the conclusion of Simpson's testimony, there followed an episode which must have appeared confusing to many of those in court. When the next witness was sworn in as Sergeant Peter Halliday of the Newcastle police, Lord Coleridge queried whether there wasn't some further evidence with regard to a pistol, and if so whether it would not be better to take all the evidence relating to guns at the same time. Tindal Atkinson said there was something else, but he did not think it was admissible in evidence. Coleridge seemed to accept this, but before he could move things forward, Tindal Atkinson elaborated further, saying the evidence in question related to a register, but the way in which the register had been kept prevented it being used as evidence in the case. However, he suggested, as there was some 'question about it', perhaps the best plan would be to put the witness in the box. Coleridge decided that as it had been mentioned that was probably the best course to take. Andrew Craig Kirkwood was therefore called to the witness box.

Kirkwood was another Pape's employee. When questioned by Tindal Atkinson, he produced the register of pistols sold and stated, 'There is an entry on the fourth line from the bottom of this page in my handwriting.' He went on to state that he could not confirm, simply by looking at an entry, that he had sold any particular gun to any named individual, because the entries were not always made by the person who actually sold the gun. After Kirkwood had given this explanation, Tindal Atkinson commented, 'That is my difficulty.'

The procedure outlined by Kirkwood was in direct contravention of the regulations, which required the person who made the sale to complete the entry personally in the presence of the buyer – and thus Tindal Atkinson felt Kirkwood's evidence was not admissible.

At this juncture, Mitchell-Innes made a somewhat surprising comment. 'Needless to say, I very much appreciate the absolutely fair spirit in which this is conducted, as one would expect in a case such as this.'

In fact far from being 'absolutely fair', Tindal Atkinson had contrived to introduce Kirkwood into the proceedings, knowing full well that his evidence was inadmissible. This was distinctly detrimental to Mitchell-Innes's client, because although Kirkwood was not allowed to reveal the actual details of the entry on the fourth line from the bottom of the page, it is unlikely to have escaped anyone in the court room that those details must have related to a transaction which had allegedly taken place between Pape & Co. and John Dickman, involving the purchase of some sort of gun.

After this incident, Sergeant Halliday was recalled and told the court that while the prisoner was being held in custody, he had taken the prisoner's clothes and handed them all over to Dr Boland, who was to give evidence next.

Robert Boland was a doctor of medicine and professor at the College of Medicine affiliated to Durham University. Boland's evidence related to alleged bloodstains discovered on various items of Dickman's clothing, the first of which was a pair of suede gloves. One of these gloves had a dark red, smeared stain measuring about ¾ inch by ¼ inch, on the top part of the thumb. As a result of various tests, Boland concluded the substance was blood, though whether human or animal he could not say. He had tested the gloves on 26 March and deduced that the stain was recent and must have been made within the previous fortnight.

Inside the left front pocket of a pair of trousers he had discovered nine small stains, all within an area of about 1 inch by 2 inches. The pocket was 11 inches deep and the stained area was between 4 to 6 inches into the pocket. In the doctor's opinion, it was an area of the pocket where the thumb of a gloved hand was likely to rest when the hand was inserted. The stains varied in size, each being small distinct droplets, the largest no bigger than a pin-head.

Finally he had examined a fawn-coloured Burberry overcoat made of 'what is considered to be rainproof cloth'. Although there was no evidence of blood detectable on the coat, there was a large stain on the front left-hand side, which smelt faintly of paraffin – a substance which Dr Boland said would remove blood from material of the kind in question. The surface appeared frayed, as if it had been vigorously rubbed.

In modern parlance, Dr Boland was the Crown's forensic expert. We have no way of knowing whether the jury were aware of the maxim 'beware of experts', but in Dr Boland's case they certainly should have been. His uncertainty as to whether the blood on the glove originated from a human or an animal raises the question of whether he could be absolutely certain he was dealing with blood at all. He offered no explanation as to how he had arrived at the conclusion that the stain could only have been on the glove for a fortnight; worse still, having told the court it would be possible to remove bloodstains from the material of the coat by using paraffin, when subsequently questioned on precisely this point by Lord Coleridge he completely contradicted himself by assuring the judge that paraffin was not an efficient agent for removing bloodstains.

As if this were not bad enough, Boland's evidence then strayed beyond the 'expertise' he had originally been invited to offer. With the 'forensic evidence' finished, he proceeded to describe how the Burberry coat had large pockets at the front, entered by slits. 'These pockets would very easily hold a revolver of the description which has been produced. The hand could be inserted through the slit and hold it quite easily, and be covered by the coat. Similarly any other article such as a bag, might be held in the same way.'

While the good doctor was keen to explain how Dickman might have sneaked Nisbet's bag past Athey, he did not trouble to address the question of how Dickman could have managed to divert the ticket collector's attention from a supposedly large, recently acquired bloodstain on the left front of his coat.

Peter Spooner, the colliery manager at the Barr Moor East Pit, was called next. He described how he had discovered the bag in the

Isabella Pit while making a routine inspection of an air shaft. He confirmed that he knew John Dickman because at one time they had both worked for the same company. He could recall talking to Dickman about the problem of water collecting in the mine he currently managed; but he didn't know whether Dickman knew the mine's actual location. Describing the iron grid which protected the top of the air shaft, he said he thought the bag could easily have been put down between the bars, and if not, the grid could in any case be lifted by hand.

Under cross-examination Spooner said he was not obliged to inspect the air shaft once a week – in fact once every four to five weeks was adequate. Mitchell-Innes was hoping to suggest that the bag could not have lain undiscovered for almost three months at the bottom of a shaft, which even on Spooner's outside estimate must have been inspected at least once or twice between the murder in March and the discovery of the bag on 9 June. If the bag found its way into the ventilation shaft at any time after 21 March, clearly John Dickman could not have put it there, because he had been in custody since that date.

Alas for Mr Mitchell-Innes's theory, Peter Spooner had given an interview to local reporters the day the bag was found in which he explained that the bag might easily have been overlooked previously because inspections were made by the light of a single safety lamp. In fact, when he initially spotted the dark object in the beam of his lamp, he very nearly ignored it, assuming it to be the remnants of an abandoned navvy's smock or debris of a similar nature which was often left lying around.

In the same interview Spooner described the head of the shaft as lying only a few yards off the Morpeth to Shields road, and accessible through a gate. Although the head of the shaft was hidden from the road by an old pit heap, it did have a hand windlass above it, leading to the conclusion that it would not have been hard to locate the shaft for anyone who specifically set out to do so.[11]

Spooner was followed by Police Superintendent Thomas Marshall of Morpeth, who confirmed the discovery of the bag and of the coins which were recovered later from the bottom of the shaft.

Then came Robert Sweeney, a Morpeth resident who had known Dickman for about six years. According to Sweeney, Dickman had visited him at his office in about October 1909, requesting a loan of £10. He said Dickman had not explained why he wanted the money or given any indication of his financial situation.

The next witness was Samuel Cohen, manager of the Cash Accommodation & Investment Company, Northumberland Street, Newcastle. He said Dickman had first come to his offices on about 15 October 1909, asking about the rate of interest on a loan of £20 for three months. Cohen told him the terms would be £1 per month, with capital repayable on demand. Dickman had returned on 18 October and taken the loan on those terms. The interest was paid promptly each month, but in January 1910 Dickman had requested the loan be extended for a further three months as he could not afford to repay the capital just then. To this Cohen readily agreed. In the meantime, in November 1909 Cohen had received a letter from Dickman enquiring about a loan of £200 for a man named Christie. Cohen had subsequently lent this sum to Christie, the transaction being conducted entirely between himself and Christie, apart from Dickman's initial letter of enquiry. The last payment of interest on the original £20 loan to Dickman had been paid on 17 March; the loan was then repaid in full on 9 May by Mrs Dickman.

This sort of evidence would have made a very bad impression on a 1909 jury. In the twenty-first century credit is the norm and short-term loans are considered a legitimate resource to improve personal cash flow. A century ago, staying out of debt was the aim of every respectable working family, and only the poorest households bought goods by paying for them in instalments, 'on tick' or from 'the tally man'. Raising a loan from a moneylender as Dickman had done would have been perceived as a shameful and desperate measure. Many a family preferred to 'go without' than get into any kind of debt.

Pawning items was another humiliating (if commonplace) method of raising cash. Superintendent Weddell had already given evidence of finding pawn tickets among Dickman's belongings. Now Mr Kettering, a partner of Cush & Co., jewellers of Collingwood Street,

Newcastle, was called as a witness and told how Dickman had come into his shop on 14 February 1910 and borrowed £5, leaving a gold scarf ring set with three brilliants, and a set of gold studs as security. Kettering understood the money was required to finance a trip to Liverpool to see the Waterloo Cup run. He lent Dickman the money, which had never been repaid. He still had the jewellery.

The evidence moved deeper into Dickman's personal finances, when John Dennis Badcock gave evidence on behalf of the National Provincial Bank. Badcock produced Dickman's account for the period from December 1907 to 31 December 1909. On 30 June 1909 the account had dwindled to 7*d*. After that there were very few transactions. On 13 September someone paid in £4 10*s*, but three days later most of this money was withdrawn, leaving a total balance of 3*s* 9*d*. On 18 October 1909 a cheque for £20 drawn by Samuel Cohen was paid into the account, but within three days the balance had been reduced to 2*s* 9*d*. On 24 November another cheque from Samuel Cohen was paid into the account, this time for £200, which had been originally made out in favour of F. Christie. Again, the money did not remain long in the account: Dickman withdrew £160 on 26 November and £40 on 29 November. As the account had incurred 5*s* 9*d* in bank charges, by 31 December the balance stood at a deficit of 3*s*. The witness confirmed that Dickman had held an account at the bank since about 1892.

Robert Sedcole on behalf of Lloyds Bank painted a similar picture. The last payment into Dickman's account with them had been on 13 May 1909. There had followed a series of small withdrawals, the last of which on 16 October 1909 had left a mere 2*s* in the account, and this had been swallowed up by bank charges. Sedcole also confirmed that Dickman had been a longstanding customer.

The next witness should have been Mr James Paisley, of the Co-operative Society where Mrs Dickman had an account, but it was discovered that he had not been told to bring appropriate supporting evidence with him. While Mr Paisley went to fetch the missing documents, the court heard instead from Frank Christie.

The presence of Mr Christie had been hovering uneasily around the evidence for some time. It is possible the jury hoped Mr Christie would be able to illuminate some of the more obscure aspects of the case – if so, they were to be disappointed.

Frank Christie said he was a coal merchant and had known Dickman for about six years. He had occasionally backed horses through Dickman and had obtained a loan of £200 from Cohen, after being introduced to him by Dickman. He had endorsed this cheque in Dickman's favour, although half the money was intended for his 'own private affairs', with Dickman using the other half to place bets on Christie's behalf. It had been understood that Dickman would not get anything out of this transaction unless the betting was successful. It had not been, so all the money was lost.

While Christie had no compunction about discussing his unusual financial transactions and betting arrangements in court, he clammed up considerably once the Dovecot Mine was mentioned, adopting Hogg's tactic of answering ambiguously and reverting to the familiar refrain 'He had nothing to do with it' whenever Dickman was mentioned in connection with the mine. Although he admitted that Dickman frequently visited him at his office and 'might' have talked about the Dovecot Mine and that he 'may' have suggested Dickman go out there with him on one occasion, he flatly denied that Dickman had any authority from him to visit Dovecot or discuss anything connected with it.

After these puzzling submissions, attention reverted to the Dickmans' financial affairs. William Albert Christie of the Post Office Savings Bank gave details of an account Annie Dickman held at the Holly Avenue Post Office. In January 1910 Mrs Dickman had withdrawn £12 out of the £15 0s 9d which had accumulated in the account thanks to deposits made over the previous three years. On 1 February she had withdrawn another £1, another on 16 February and finally a further 10s on 14 March, leaving a balance of just 10s in the account.

Police Inspector James Irving appeared next, for some reason sandwiched in among the financial evidence. Irving had been the officer in charge of John Dickman when he appeared before magistrates on 14 April, on which occasion Irving claimed to have found two pawn tickets on Dickman, both for pairs of field glasses, which he had taken from the prisoner. According to Irving, Dickman told him he pawned the field glasses because, 'When racing, you get mixed up with the Bigg Market boys and after the season is over, they are always asking you for money. . . . If any of the boys asked me for money, I could pull out the pawn tickets and say, "Look here, this is what I am down to", and they think you're hard up.'

James Paisley presumably returned hotfoot from the offices of the Co-operative Society, was the final witness for the prosecution. He showed the society's books which demonstrated that Mrs Annie Dickman's account with the Co-op had steadily increased between 28 May 1904 until 30 October 1907, when the total stood at an all-time high of £73 17*s* 2*d*. Only three deposits had been made since that date, the last of which was £3 on 1 June 1909. Throughout 1909 there had been frequent withdrawals, so that by 17 March 1910, when Mrs Dickman withdrew £2, the balance had been reduced to £4.

This concluded the Crown's evidence, but it was the evidence for the defence which would produce the witness the public gallery really wanted to hear.

4

'I declare to all men that I am innocent'

During the afternoon of the second day, John Dickman entered the witness box to give the evidence upon which his life would depend. He was the only defence witness called at the trial and although he retained his composure, his demeanour and responses failed to convince the jury that they were listening to an innocent man.[1]

In certain respects the decision to call Dickman alone for the defence was a surprising one. Elliot and Sanderson, the two men with whom Dickman had conversed in Morpeth on 18 March, were both in court. Here were two men who could have supported at least part of his story and had appeared at the hearing before the magistrates. Perhaps Mitchell-Innes felt their testimony was not particularly relevant. If this was a curious decision, it was not nearly so damaging as the defence counsel's failure to pursue a variety of points in the evidence of prosecution witnesses, which could and should have been challenged.

For example, the penultimate prosecution witness Inspector James Irving claimed to have found two pawn tickets on Dickman when he appeared at the magistrates' court on 14 April. They were each for a separate pair of field glasses. By this time Dickman had been in custody for several weeks, his belongings had been searched and his clothes confiscated long before, so Irving's story of this discovery and his subsequent conversation with the prisoner does not sound particularly plausible. Moreover, Superintendent Weddell had given evidence on the first day of the trial that *he* had found two pawn tickets, each for a pair of field glasses – not on Dickman's person, but during a search of his home on 26 March. Unless Dickman had actually pawned four pairs of field glasses, which is highly unlikely, then managed to secrete two of the pawn tickets about his person for several weeks, Irving's evidence of finding the pawn tickets and presumably the conversation he claims he had with the prisoner on discovering them were pure fantasy.

Mitchell-Innes also missed a trick with the evidence of both John Grant and John Cosher. The prosecution alleged that by the time the train reached Morpeth, there was no one visible in two out of three of the compartments in the first coach of the train. If correct, this virtually proved the murderer left the train at Morpeth, having killed Nisbet between there and Stannington.

Grant and Cosher both testified to seeing that two of the passenger compartments in the first coach were empty, while Andrew Bruce was seated in the third. This suggested that once the train reached Morpeth, Bruce was the sole occupant visible in the first coach; but according to Bruce's own evidence, he was not alone in the compartment. He said, 'There was another gentleman with me; he got out at Chevington.' Chevington station was two stops north of Longhirst and thus this passenger was sitting in the first coach when it was passed by Grant at Morpeth and Cosher at Longhirst, although neither had mentioned seeing him. If the platelayer and the porter failed to notice one man, might they not equally have failed to notice another? If Grant and Cosher had been challenged on this, the prosecution's contention that Nisbet was dead by Morpeth might have appeared considerably less certain.

These are minor points, but they might have helped undermine a prosecution case which was already shaky in places: unfortunately for John Dickman, Mitchell-Innes failed to make them – and worse was to come.

John Dickman's evidence began with a long statement giving his own account of the events of 18 March and explaining the relationship, or lack of one, between himself and the victim. He freely admitted that he had seen Nisbet at the Central station on the morning of the murder. As he crossed the booking hall to buy a ticket, Nisbet, who had just bought a ticket, was walking the other way and wished him 'Good morning'. He responded in kind, but said he would not have greeted Nisbet if Nisbet had not spoken first. 'I have known Nisbet for several years, but I was never intimate with him. He was no companion of mine, and I never made a point of stopping to speak to him at any time. He was just a casual acquaintance – hardly an acquaintance at all. I knew he was on the Quay, but what he was, or what he was employed in I did not know.' He firmly denied noticing Nisbet again after leaving the booking hall.

At this point it may already have seemed to the jury that Dickman protesteth just a little too much. Here was someone who seemed to know all sorts of people involved in the mining industry, who had himself been employed in a similar capacity to John Nisbet. It had perhaps not escaped their notice that although Hall and Spink only knew John Nisbet slightly, and were not on such friendly terms that they ever shared a compartment with him, notwithstanding that they regularly travelled on the same train, they nevertheless knew that Nisbet was doing the Widdrington Colliery pay run. If in fact Dickman was aware of the nature of Nisbet's employment, or the particular errand on which he was engaged, he might have been wiser candidly to admit this. An open admission might have made a better impression than did his denials.

Dickman explained that after obtaining his ticket he bought a paper, spent some time in the refreshment room, then made his way to the platform. He could not recall which side of the cigar booth he passed *en route*, but did remember visiting the urinal. He got to the train as it was about to start and took a seat somewhere towards the rear – perhaps two compartments away from one which had a 'Reserved' notice on it. There were other passengers in the compartment, but he did not take any particular notice of them, being completely immersed in his paper. Nor was he aware of any of the stations, until he felt the train make a swerve on the bend coming into Morpeth, at which point he realised he had missed his stop.

As to his overcoat, he had not been wearing his Burberry that day. He had a brown overcoat with him (this was produced), which he carried on to the train and stowed in the luggage rack for the duration of the journey. When he got to Morpeth he was still carrying it, either over his arm or over his shoulder. He got the ticket out of his waistcoat pocket, and while the ticket collector was tearing it in half, he took out the change to pay the excess fare, handing it over with the words 'Tuppence ha'penny is the correct fare . . . or something like that'.

Dickman then told his story of setting out along the road, being taken ill, returning to Morpeth, meeting Elliott and Sanderson, returning home and subsequently being arrested late on the Monday afternoon.

When he reached the identification parade, his version differed somewhat from that of Percival Hall. According to Dickman, Hall walked up and down the line of men three or four times, and eventually seemed on the point of walking away, at which 'one of the police officers said sort of jokingly, "You cannot get out of here without choosing someone." The man was very reluctant and if he had not been practically intimidated into it, he would have made none.'

Lord Coleridge became very interested in this and Dickman was encouraged to elaborate further, which he did: 'Hall was walking away, having viewed the rank three or four times, when the policeman got in his way and would not allow him to pass, practically speaking, pushing him back. He sort of joked, or cajoled him into making a selection.'

'That was not put to the witness', Tindal Atkinson interposed. 'Not that he was intimidated or anything approaching it.'

Dickman again explained the way the situation had come about. He also mentioned that for the identification parade he had been wearing his light-coloured Burberry, rather than the outfit he had worn on 18 March. The light-coloured overcoat was a very important element in all the witnesses' descriptions of the man they had seen with Nisbet. Unfortunately, no one saw fit to advise the jury how many of the men in the line-up that night were wearing such overcoats, and whether they were all 5 feet 6 inches tall, 11 stone in weight and had dark moustaches. Whether or not the police had managed to assemble a reasonably uniform group of men, it would subsequently emerge that Hall had a very good reason for being able to pick Dickman out, and this undoubtedly related to the infamous Burberry overcoat.

Moving to other aspects of the prosecution evidence, Dickman readily confirmed that he had used Miss Hymen's shop for his betting communications and also that she had given him the parcel from Bell Brothers, together with the postcard saying it was a revolver sent to him in error. He had returned the parcel unopened, he said, posting it at the same time as he sent off his patent roller bearing to a firm in Leeds.

As for the canvas cash bag, he had been using similar bags to carry money for years, in lieu of a purse. He found it a useful method of carrying the large sums of cash he often needed to pay out bets and so forth.

During cross-examination, Dickman again attempted to emphasise how slight an acquaintance he had with John Nisbet, but in the long run this did him a disservice. When asked initially whether he had known the deceased by name, Dickman said he could not have told it to anyone, if asked offhand. Tindal Atkinson was not having this and pressed the point, while Dickman continued to prevaricate, until eventually forced to admit that he had known Nisbet both by name and by sight: information which would have been better given willingly in the first instance.

Tindal Atkinson then asked whether Dickman had known Nisbet was a colliery book-keeper. Dickman said he did not, pointing out that for all he knew Nisbet might have been employed by one of the firms of shipbrokers or general merchants that had offices on the Quayside. He was equally reluctant to admit knowing that a lot of colliery companies banked in Newcastle and therefore drew the cash for their wages in the city before having it transported out to their collieries by train. He explained that when he dealt with colliery wages it had been via a cheque cashed in Morpeth, and that he was unaware of the specific working arrangements relating to any other mines. Again, Dickman would have done better to freely admit to this knowledge, because evading the issue simply made him appear a slippery witness.

The subject of collieries led into his intended visit to Hogg at the Dovecot Mine. Why had these visits taken place on a Friday, Tindal

Atkinson wanted to know. Dickman said it was because Friday was pay day. At this point the shadowy presence of Mr Frank Christie began to hover over the testimony again. Dickman said he was interested in knowing about the dealings between Hogg and Christie, 'because they were both friends of mine'. Again, there came a sense that something unexplained lay behind all this ticktacking between the three men, but although the prosecuting counsel persuaded Dickman to say that he wanted to know whether Christie was supplying money for Hogg to pay wages, and that this was because he wanted to know whether Christie was being truthful when he claimed to have no money, Dickman clammed up again when challenged as to what that had to do with him, preferring to make no reply.

Tindal Atkinson then took him back through the Central station evidence, asking how, in an uncrowded station, he could have walked alongside Nisbet at the entrance to Platform 4 without noticing him. Dickman said he considered it most unlikely that this had actually happened, stating that he had never set eyes on Raven until the man appeared to give evidence against him. When asked why in his original statement he had not mentioned visiting the urinal *en route* to the train, Dickman, entirely reasonably, said that when making that first voluntary statement, he had not been aware the police had wanted 'such minute details'.

If he had denied knowing Charles Raven, there was no such uncertainty about Wilson Hepple, of whom Dickman said, 'We are very old friends. We lived together at Whickham.'

'He could not make a mistake about your identity?' Tindal Atkinson asked.

'He might now.'

'What do you mean, "He might now"?'

'Well, he is not so young as he used to be.'

'Do you mean to say he is too old?'

'He is very much failed to what I used to know him – very much failed.'

There followed a long exchange throughout which Dickman firmly insisted that the only possible explanation was that Hepple had made a mistake.

Tindal Atkinson then attempted to pin down precisely which compartment of the train Dickman claimed to have travelled in. When it became evident that this compartment must have been in the same coach as the one outside which Hepple claimed he was walking up and down, Dickman again said he had not seen Hepple at all that day, adding that if he had seen him he would have travelled with him.

Next, Tindal Atkinson asked Dickman about his coat. Dickman repeated that he had his brown overcoat with him that day, although he had worn his light-coloured Burberry in the evening, because it had rained after tea. If he was very sure of this, he was far less certain about the passengers with whom he shared a compartment that morning. He thought that several people had got in and out during the course of the journey, and that they had all left the train by the time it reached Morpeth. He could not even recall whether they were male or female. His whole attention, it seemed, had been devoted to his newspaper.

Then came an exchange the significance of which was apparently lost on everyone.

Tindal Atkinson asked, 'Did you know Mrs Nisbet?'

'Just by sight', replied the accused man.

'Did you see her on the journey?'

'I did not.'

Here the defence team failed to pick up yet another item of crucial importance to their client's case: for if John Dickman knew Mrs Nisbet by sight (a fact which the prosecution was evidently aware of at that point), was it not reasonable to assume that she might also know him – and if so, what bearing did that have on her identification evidence?

The cross-examination then dwelt on the subject of Dickman's alleged stop at the side of the road, forcing him to explain his 'infirmities' in rather greater detail than would have been tasteful under normal circumstances. The more squeamish observers in court were probably relieved when Dickman's haemorrhoids were left behind and the story reached his return walk to Morpeth. He denied knowing where the Isabella Pit was, or even having heard of it. He knew Peter Spooner because Spooner had been manager at the Morpeth Colliery when Dickman himself had been secretary there. He was aware that Spooner now managed another colliery which was somewhere east of Morpeth station: he knew it as the Hepscott Mine but did not know exactly where it was.

As to the suede gloves on which Dr Boland had identified blood, Dickman said he had not worn them since before Christmas. He bought them thinking they would stretch and discarded them when they failed to do so; they were too small for him, and had been left in the hall-stand drawer at home. He could not account for the blood on them, unless it was from a nosebleed or something of the sort, nor could he see how they would have acquired any recent stains.

The blood in the pocket of the trousers which he had worn on 18 March might likewise have been from a nosebleed, which was something he frequently suffered in the mornings. (Although his defence did not point this out, tiny specks of blood from a crumpled handkerchief would just as easily have transferred blood into a pocket as would the thumb of a glove.)

As for the stain on his Burberry, that had originated when he accidentally squirted bicycle oil on his coat while attempting to lubricate one of the patent roller-bearing devices he was working on. This had occurred round about Christmastime and his wife had attempted to get the stain out using a patent cleaner, which might account for the traces of paraffin. The patent cleaner was one he had bought in London a few months before.

He claimed his bank accounts were misleading, because he was in the habit of keeping a large reserve fund of cash. At the end of November 1909 he had about £120 cash in hand, £50 of which he had given to his wife before Christmas. By the time of his arrest he had about £17 left – an ample sum with which to start the flat season.

If this was so, he was asked, why had he gone to Mr Cohen for a loan? In order to see if the advertised rate of interest was correct, Dickman replied. He had no recollection of telling Cohen he could not afford to pay the money back in January, saying he could have paid it back at any time, but did not choose to as the payment terms were so favourable. To a modern audience this does not sound so very incredible, but in 1910 when the avoidance of any sort of debt was a paramount aim, the notion of paying a monthly sum in order to keep twenty times that amount as available capital was unheard of for private citizens. In any case, Dickman's reason for securing the loan sounded totally implausible: once Cohen had verbally confirmed his terms, there was surely no need to discover them by actual experiment.

Of Swinney's claim that he had attempted to borrow £10 the preceding October, Dickman said he thought that had been well over a year ago. He agreed that he had borrowed £1 from Hogg one afternoon, but this had only been to save him having to return home for some money.

The jewellery had been left at Cush & Co. for safe-keeping because there had been a spate of burglaries in his neighbourhood. The field glasses had not been pawned because he needed cash. One set had been given to him in lieu of a debt. He had decided to sell both pairs and buy new ones for the forthcoming season, but having failed to find a buyer he pawned them instead.

And why, Tindal Atkinson wanted to know, had he used a false name and address to do so?

'I don't know', said Dickman. 'Just on the spur of the moment.'

He denied that he had ever been in difficulty over paying his rates. He might have allowed his wife to think he was short of money at times, but that was only to encourage her to keep her expenses down.

Unfortunately, Mr Mitchell-Innes then elected to ask his client directly whether his wife had ever complained of needing money, to which Dickman replied in the negative. This gave Tindal Atkinson the opportunity to introduce a letter from Annie Dickman to her husband in which she did appear to be anxious about money with which to settle bills. The letter had been written on 25 January 1910 when Dickman was temporarily away from home, and the following extract was read out in court:

Dear Jack,
I received your card and am very sorry that you have no money to send. I am needing some very badly. The weather here is past

description. I had to get in a load of coals which consumed the greater part of a sovereign. The final notice for the rates has come in – in fact came in last week, which means they must be paid before next Thursday. Also Harry's school account. With my dividend due this week and what is in the post office, I dare say I can pay the most pressing things, but it is going to make the question of living a poser, unless you can give me some advice as to what to do.

Dickman responded to this by saying that an outsider would put a very different construction on the letter than that which was intended between husband and wife. He said there was sometimes a little bickering between himself and his wife as to which of them should settle which bills. Mitchell-Innes then assisted his client by reminding the court that at the time of that letter Annie Dickman's accounts had been shown to contain a total in excess of £30 – an amount which would have been ample to cover all the items she mentioned. All the same, the letter must have made a damaging impression on the jury, and with hindsight it seems foolish of Mitchell-Innes to have presented his opponents with an opportunity of using the letter in evidence by introducing that particular line of questioning in the first place.

On this somewhat unfortunate note the evidence for the defence concluded.

Tindal Atkinson now made his closing address on behalf of the prosecution. He spoke for an hour, opening as he had originally by repeating that the evidence against the prisoner was circumstantial. It was for the jury to link together the facts, he said, and see if they formed a complete chain. He revisited the prosecution's case step by step, exposing what he claimed to be falsehood after falsehood told by the prisoner.

It was a clever speech, but during the course of it the prosecuting counsel made a serious error. In 1898 the law had been altered to allow the spouse of an accused person to appear in their defence, if they chose to do so. If however a spouse elected not to appear as a witness, the prosecution was strictly forbidden to draw the jury's attention to this omission. This had been the legal position for more than a decade by the time John Dickman stood trial, so there was absolutely no excuse for Tindal Atkinson to be unaware of it: yet, quite incredibly, he remarked during the course of his address that Dickman's wife had failed to offer corroboration to the elements of his story where she might have done so.

In the introduction to his book on the trial, Rowan-Hamilton says, 'Mr Tindal Atkinson inadvertently commented on the fact that Mrs Dickman had not been called to give evidence.'[2] It is not easy to see how such a remark could 'inadvertently' slip out, and having observed the way Tindal Atkinson seized his opportunity to introduce Mrs Dickman's letter, to say nothing of his managing to get the gunsmiths' salesman into the witness box in spite of knowing full well that his evidence would be inadmissible, it is not difficult to suspect Tindal Atkinson of some sharp practice here.

This 'inadvertent slip' placed Mitchell-Innes in a quandary: ought he to object immediately, thereby perhaps drawing even more attention to the issue – or keep completely silent on the point, then offer it as a reason for a re-trial if the prisoner was found guilty? Whichever course he took, it would not alter the fact that the remark had been made and could not be erased from the jury's memory, however much they might be advised to disregard it – a similar situation to the 'evidence' of the gun sales register, which probably made a bad impression on the jury, in spite of the fact that they did not actually 'hear' it.

In the event, Mitchell-Innes opted for the worst possible course. As with the gun register episode, so with the 'inadvertent' mention of Mrs Dickman's not giving evidence, Mr Mitchell-Innes seemed more interested in playing mutual admiration games with opposing counsel than with fighting his client's corner. Mitchell-Innes did not immediately raise an objection to Tindal Atkinson's comments, but during the course of his final address he embarked on a convoluted, wordy speech about exercising judgement for the prisoner's best interest; explaining how in the event that the prisoner's spouse is not called to give evidence, he is 'protected from any strictures being passed by the prosecution on the conduct of the defence in not doing so'.[3] Mitchell-Innes made such a meal of this, it is unlikely that the jury had the slightest idea what he was getting at.

Tindal Atkinson, of course, knew exactly to what Mitchell-Innes was referring and leapt into the fray, saying 'May I say . . . as my friend has mentioned the matter, I made the comment with regard to the absence of the wife by inadvertence, having forgotten for the moment the extent of the terms of that statute which my friend has referred to. If my attention had been called to it, I would not have said a word with regard to it . . .'

It is difficult to see how anyone could have anticipated Tindal Atkinson's gaffe in advance and 'called his attention to it' until after the words were out of his mouth and the damage done. In his enthusiasm to agree that he ought not to have made the observation, Tindal Atkinson took the opportunity to speak a while longer, managing to work in the words 'absence of the wife' again, thereby further compounding the damage.

Mitchell-Innes replied, 'I accept that absolutely from my learned friend, and he will believe me when I say that my reference was not made in the spirit of sharp criticism on his conduct of the case, which, if I may say so without impertinence, he has so fairly and ably presented to the court.'

Faced with this saccharine nonsense, it is hardly surprising that the official shorthand writer could later come to believe there was a conspiracy operating to see John Dickman hang.

Mitchell-Innes's address to the jury took even longer than Tindal Atkinson's. He reminded them of the refusal of several witnesses to swear that Dickman was the man they had seen with Nisbet, and of the way Mrs Nisbet's evidence had radically altered from the original vague description of the man she had seen that morning to become a positive identification of the prisoner in the dock. He was kind to Cicely Nisbet, reminding the jury of what she had suffered and how very much she must desire to see justice done for her husband, concluding all the same that they should be wary of 'accepting her evidence as anything like conclusive or reasonable'. He pointed out that Raven never said he had seen the two men speaking to one another. It was quite possible, he suggested, that

John Dickman had been walking close to John Nisbet at one point without realising it; as for Wilson Hepple, did the jury not consider it possible he might have been mistaken?

With regard to the murder being committed between Stannington and Morpeth, even assuming that were the case, did the jury seriously believe the murderer would still have been on the train at Morpeth? It was a relatively slow-moving train and surely the killer would not have risked remaining in a compartment with the blood-stained cushions, streams of blood running across the floor and the body of the victim barely concealed under a seat, until the train pulled into Morpeth, one of the busiest stations on the line? 'Of course, there was nobody on the seats at Morpeth or Pegswood', said Mitchell-Innes. 'Nor did the murderer get out at any of the stations. . . . He would have escaped from that carriage as soon as he could.'

Another of Mitchell-Innes's theories inevitably centred on the discovery of Nisbet's bag. It had not been found during previous inspections because surely it had only arrived in the bottom of the shaft long after the prisoner was already in custody, when the real murderer had leisure to place it there. He ridiculed the blood evidence, asking why none had been found on the prisoner's boots when there had clearly been blood on the carriage floor. Neither the proceeds of the robbery nor the weapons used in the crime had been traced to the prisoner, he said, and not a shred of evidence had been produced connecting the accused man with the second type of gun used, a pistol.

Mitchell-Innes had very little to say on the question of Dickman's possession of a revolver. On this matter it was, for once, the prosecution who seem to have made a glaring omission. During Henrietta Hymen's evidence, she stated quite clearly that she had received two parcels on Dickman's behalf, the first of which had been shaped like a gun. The second parcel had been followed up by a postcard requesting its return, and stating that it contained a revolver which had been despatched in error. For some reason both the prosecuting and defending counsel focused exclusively on the second parcel, questioning the prisoner about if and when the parcel had been returned, and whether or not Miss Hymen had supplied a label to assist the process. No one bothered to ask Dickman what the first parcel had actually contained, or what had become of the contents. On this particular issue it is Tindal Atkinson who seems to have missed a trick.

At the conclusion of Mitchell-Innes's speech the court was adjourned for the day. The jury were taken to a city-centre hotel, but Lord Coleridge consented to them being taken for a drive in Gosforth Park – which must have provided a welcome breath of fresh air after having been closeted for two days in the stuffy intensity of the Moot Hall.[4]

The third morning of the trial, Wednesday 6 July, was cool and damp. When the court resumed Annie Dickman was noticeably absent from her customary position behind the dock. Owing to the rain, the crowd that lingered outside waiting to be among the first to hear the verdict was much smaller than usual.[5]

Lord Coleridge spent the morning summing up. At the outset he stated that if the facts were clear then motive was irrelevant, but since the prosecution had sought to demonstrate a motive, he revisited it in detail – the bank accounts, pawn tickets and loan from Cohen – before looking to the facts of the crime itself. There could be little doubt, he said, that Nisbet was murdered in the train by a companion who travelled with him, but the question was, had the prosecution proved to the jury's satisfaction that Dickman had been that travelling companion? Although Coleridge took them through all the evidence which had been presented, he rightly identified the central issue: if Dickman got into the train with Nisbet that morning, there could be no reasonable doubt that he was the killer.

The jury retired at 12.55 and did not return to the courtroom until just after 3.30. Instead of asking them for their verdict straight away, Lord Coleridge addressed them as follows: 'Gentlemen, before you give your verdict, there is an incident in yesterday's proceedings which I forgot to allude to. Learned counsel for the prosecution commented upon the absence of the wife as a witness for the defence, in connection with the allegation made by the prisoner that the wife had cleaned his coat. Such a comment is forbidden by law

. . . . I ought to have said so . . . therefore the comment ought to be banished from your minds and not influence your verdict. If you allowed that comment to affect your minds . . . I must ask you to reconsider your verdict, dismissing such comment from your minds. If you have not allowed it to affect your minds in any way, then you can deliver your verdict.'

'It has not', said the foreman.

'You have not allowed it to affect you?' Coleridge asked again.

'We have not', the foreman repeated, without consulting any of his fellow jurors. 'It has not been mentioned.'

Then came the moment of truth. Were they all agreed on their verdict? They were.

'We find him guilty.'

The clerk addressed the man in the dock, using the customary form of words: 'John Alexander Dickman, you have been convicted of wilful murder. What have you to say why the court should not give you sentence of death, according to the law?'

Dickman responded: 'I can only repeat that I am entirely innocent of this cruel deed. I have no complicity in this crime, and I have spoken the truth in my evidence, and in everything I have said.'

Coleridge made a brief speech before passing sentence: 'In your hungry lust for gold, you had no pity upon the victim whom you slew, and it is only just that the Nemesis of the law should overtake the author of the crime.'

It was John Dickman, however, who would have the last word that day. When Coleridge had finished reciting the terrible formula and the chaplain had pronounced his Amen, Dickman, half turning to face the public gallery, said, 'I declare to all men that I am innocent.'

5

Your Ever Affectionate Jack

Annie Dickman's support for her husband never faltered; but knowing it was likely that the verdict would be given on the third day, she stayed at home in order to be with her children when the news came. It was an interminable wait; 'no one', she wrote afterwards, could ever know 'the agony experienced by me, the fearfulness of all who knew us intimately'.[1]

There is no doubt that some friends stuck by the Dickmans in their darkest hour. The subscription raised for John Dickman's defence has already been mentioned, and several of his letters from prison expressed his gratitude that Annie was being supported by certain of their friends.[2]

Annie and his other supporters did not give up hope in the face of the guilty verdict. An appeal was set in motion immediately, based on claims that Lord Coleridge had misdirected the jury, that evidence had been withdrawn from the jury, and that the prosecution had commented on the omission of the accused man's wife to give evidence. In addition to all this, two issues had finally been uncovered by Dickman's defence which threw further doubt upon the verdict. Both related to the controversial identification evidence which had been presented in court.

It is no longer clear how Dickman's legal team finally became aware of one absolutely crucial issue relating to Cicely Nisbet's identification evidence. With hindsight this should have been guessed from something that was said during the trial, but there is a distinct possibility that it finally came to light as a result of a private letter of protest which someone wrote to the Home Office. However it came about, the truth emerged that Cicely Nisbet had known John

Dickman by sight for several years, a fact which made an absolute nonsense of the occasion on which she dramatically recognised him as the man she had seen with her husband.

Between the trial and the appeal Mrs Nisbet was questioned about this by the Newcastle police. She made a statement which was presented at Dickman's appeal, in which she explained that although she had never actually been introduced to John Dickman, she had known him by sight for about eighteen years. She continued to stand by her claim that although she had not initially recognised the man in the train as anyone she knew, his profile so exactly matched Dickman's that once she saw him at precisely the same angle in court as she had seen him in the railway carriage, she knew she was looking at the same man.[3]

If this were not bad enough, Percival Hall had also been asked to elaborate further on the circumstances of his picking out Dickman at the identity parade, and this had revealed a level of chicanery considerably worse than the 'coercion' described by John Dickman in court.

According to Hall, when he and Spink arrived at the police station to take part in the identification procedure, they were kept waiting in a passage for about 10 minutes. There were various policemen standing around and after a while one of them invited Hall and Spink to look through an internal window, which they did, but were unable to see anything. Hall and Spink were then positioned alongside a door, through which police officers were periodically coming and going, and on the next occasion the door was opened, the two men were invited to look inside. They saw a man sitting with his back to the door, wearing a light overcoat; his hat was off, which enabled them to see the colour of his hair. Hall and Spink then seem to have gone off for a cup of tea, and having discussed matters between themselves, almost concluded that the man in the room was not the man they had seen at the railway station or on the train with Nisbet, because he seemed much bigger. When they were taken up to the identity parade, Hall recognised the man in the light-coloured overcoat as the man he had seen through the open door earlier.[4]

When this evidence was presented at the Court of Appeal, although commenting that 'they deprecated' what had taken place at the police station, the judges felt that Hall's identification evidence was not as important 'as it might have been if Dickman had claimed never to have been on the train'.[5] In this the trio of Alverstone, Lawrence and Phillimore demonstrated a disturbing lack of familiarity with the salient facts of the case. Hall's identification did not merely place Dickman on the train, which was never in dispute, but in a position which made him Nisbet's travelling companion and thus by inference almost certainly Nisbet's killer. It was one of the vital links in that chain of evidence about which Tindal Atkinson had spoken.

Their lordships were no clearer regarding Mr Mitchell-Innes's argument that the murder might have been committed further north than Morpeth. 'But the appellant does not suggest . . . he changed carriages', Phillimore remarked, obscurely. Nor were they impressed by suggestions that during his summing up Coleridge had mis-directed the jury by failing to mention Dickman's alleged visit to the infamous urinal on Platform 8.

At times it seemed that even Mitchell-Innes hardly understood what he was suggesting: at one point presenting a hypothesis that Nisbet could have been killed at any time after Heaton station because that was the last place he was seen alive. This was sheer nonsense because Spink and Hall had confirmed that Nisbet was still alive at Stannington. The feeling that Mitchell-Innes had lost the plot is reinforced by his claim that the judge had misled the jury into thinking Stannington station came immediately after Heaton, when in fact there were five stations in between.

Mitchell-Innes attempted to cast doubt on Hepple's evidence by describing him as 'an old, deaf man' – not perhaps the best line of attack when faced by a panel of judges with a collective age pushing 200 – but the appeal judges could not see how the infirmities described made Hepple's evidence unreliable. (Oddly enough, it does not seem to have occurred to anyone to establish how old Hepple actually was.)

Mitchell-Innes's argument, that the bag was put down the mine-shaft long after Dickman's arrest, Lord Alverstone described as 'a desperate one'. (Aside from anything else, the presence of the copper coins argues strongly that the bag was dumped on the day of the murder. If the bag had been taken elsewhere, before being dumped at a later date, the thief would surely have taken the trouble to remove all the money – £1 6d was a large sum to throw away, but a nuisance to someone in a hurry.)

In some respects Mitchell-Innes's strongest card ought to have been Tindal Atkinson's reference to Annie Dickman's absence from the witness box. A point of law had been contravened in a way which might have adversely influenced the jury. Moreover, Coleridge had failed to direct them to ignore Tindal Atkinson's remarks before they retired to consider their verdict, which was a serious omission. Mitchell-Innes pointed out that when Coleridge eventually raised the matter, the foreman did not bother to confer with his colleagues before stating they had not been influenced by the incident, although he was surely not in a position to know what might or might not have been in his fellow jurors' minds.

The appeal judges took the view that the comment about Mrs Dickman had been withdrawn from the jury by Mitchell-Innes's own remarks on the matter, and that the jury had been given the opportunity to say whether it had affected their judgement, which it had not. 'In law', Alverstone said, 'the foreman speaks for the whole of the jury.' This sounds a little as if their lordships wished to apply the law to the letter only when it suited them. They also noted that Tindal Atkinson's comment was 'an accidental slip' – though how its being accidental in any way altered the effect it may have had on the jury's perception of the evidence, they did not explain. The most charitable thing which can be said here is that the subtleties of the episode were lost on them. At any event, thanks to the foreman saying the jury 'had not spoken about it', they did not consider a mistrial had taken place.

With the appeal turned down, the date of John Dickman's execution was set for 9 August. The only recourse now was an appeal direct to the Home Secretary.

The Dickman case had continued to occupy the headlines in the northern newspapers. (In the London papers 'The Train Murder' had been somewhat eclipsed by the unfolding drama of 'The Cellar Murder', as the Crippen case was generally known.) It was not merely the question of John Dickman's guilt which exercised the pens of the journalists, but also the treatment of this prisoner and his wife. It was revealed that Annie Dickman and her children had been refused permission to visit her husband on one occasion because the appropriate paperwork had not been procured, and that when they did visit they were separated by a wire grille and never allowed to touch.

Annie also alleged that her husband had been forced to give evidence after a long fast, when he was both hungry and thirsty and that during the lunch intervals at the Moot Hall he was kept locked in solitary confinement and not even allowed a newspaper or book with which to occupy himself.[6]

Her own treatment at the hands of the mob made uncomfortable reading. There had never been any suggestion that Annie, still less her children, had been complicit in the crime, but she received a series of letters and postcards of an exceedingly unpleasant nature, and when she visited her husband in prison it was often in the face of 'morbid crowds', who booed her and peered into the face of her weeping daughter. On one occasion an old woman attempted to strike her with a key, on another a piece of coal was thrown at the window of her departing taxi.[7]

There is no doubt that publication of these details appalled many people. Letters of sympathy arrived from all over the country, with many wishing to add their names to the petition for a reprieve. One newspaper set up a fund for Mrs Dickman: there were even offers to adopt young Harry.[8]

Not everyone was sympathetic, however. A fierce debate raged on the letters pages of the local papers. One correspondent hoped that when assessing the numbers who had petitioned against Dickman suffering the death penalty, the Home Secretary would bear in mind the views of the even greater numbers who had not signed. For every one who thought the evidence too flimsy a thread on which to hang a man, another considered Dickman's guilt so absolutely apparent a child might see it. Most of these correspondents were oddly reluctant to be identified, signing themselves, 'Wickhamite', 'Humanitus', 'Citizen' or 'Not a Bookie'.[9]

One individual who had no objection to associating himself publicly with his opinions was John Dickman's older brother. Writing a few days after the verdict, he made it very clear that he was no upholder of his brother's innocence – in fact when the *Newcastle Daily Chronicle* published William Dickman's letter on 11 July, they mentioned that 'from consideration of fairness to the convict we have deleted a number of serious statements from Mr Dickman's letter'.

William Dickman said he was writing to the newspaper because it had annoyed him to read 'the numerous letters from fanatics'. In his opinion the prosecution had been fair, the judge's summing up impartial and the jury 'had the courage to give a verdict on the evidence placed before them'. He said he was sorry for his brother's position, and grieved to think he had committed such a terrible crime, but 'I cannot allow my grief to outweigh my conscience as to right and wrong'. His motive for writing was to stop the foolish letters and remove doubt about the verdict from people's minds. He had been visited by detectives himself and was very relieved when he learned that he would not be called to give evidence. The police had sympathised with his family, William Dickman wrote, having found them to be 'respectable'. As for his brother, 'His own punishment will soon be over, but he has put a blot on the name of his family and all relatives will have to bear the disgrace, not for years, but for generations.'

William Dickman was certainly correct about the problems of shame by association. Only a couple of days later a firm of Newcastle caterers operating as J.R. Dickman requested the local press to publish a disclaimer, pointing out that they were no relation whatever to the condemned man.[10] Meanwhile, William Dickman's letter predictably failed to stem the correspondence on the subject of his brother's case. If anything his intervention merely fuelled the debate, as 'Pro Bono' wondered how a brother could write such a letter about another who was under sentence of death and 'An Interested Reader' questioned what William Dickman could possibly know about the murder and suggested he would be better employed in trying to lift the stain from his family name 'by gathering all the evidence he could for the defence'.[11]

As the date of execution was announced the campaign to save John Dickman gathered pace. A small advertisement was placed in a London newspaper at the end of July: 'EXECUTION of DICKMAN on purely circumstantial evidence. PROTEST by POSTCARD to the Home Secretary, London. Sympathisers please repeat in local papers.'[12]

The Newcastle papers ran an interview with a woman who claimed to have overheard a conversation between 'the real murderers' in Leazes Park. Although it was a transparently ridiculous story, it was picked up by others outside the area and became the source of yet more 'evidence' of Dickman's innocence.

Even though the case had now largely disappeared from the national papers, the socialist *Daily News* continued to include letters from all over the country expressing dissatisfaction with the verdict or the sentence on a variety of grounds. On 3 August the *Daily News* printed a letter from an Ealing correspondent, pointing out that in the opinion of three of the jurymen Dickman was innocent. Quite how this squared with the unanimous guilty verdict the writer did not explain. On 6 August, C.H. Norman's article 'Ought Dickman be Hanged?' appeared and on 8 August one J.C. Arnold's piece 'On Circumstantial Evidence' opposed capital punishment, alluding among others to the Dickman case. On the same day the editor wrote that the paper had received a mass of letters on the subject, the vast majority of them in Dickman's favour, then put in a plug for the Society for Abolition of Capital Punishment and the separate Penal Reform League.

In the meantime the *Newcastle Illustrated Chronicle* was running a well-publicised series of articles written by Annie Dickman, which began on 2 August and appeared daily until her husband's execution.

Even when the Home Secretary's decision had been known for several days, it did not prevent a group of women handing out handbills in London with the plea 'MUST DICKMAN BE HANGED ON TUESDAY? NO NO NO. Write to the Home Secretary at once and wash your hands of complicity in a legal crime.'[13]

In the meantime John Dickman awaited his fate in Newcastle Gaol. According to the prison authorities he ate and slept well, exercised regularly, attended chapel and read a great deal.[14] He continued to protest his innocence. Throughout his imprisonment he maintained a correspondence with Annie, between her much longed-for visits. In these letters he often referred to his faith that justice would somehow prevail, invariably ending with expressions of love for herself, Kitty and Harry, and signing off 'Your ever affectionate Jack'.[15]

On the day before her husband's execution, Annie took the children for a last visit. John Dickman talked to them quietly and deliberately about the future for herself and the children, Annie said later. He particularly advised Harry never to mix in bad company and counselled clean living in body and mind. With regard to the charges against him, he said his conviction was 'the greatest outrage ever perpetrated' and he was convinced that one day his innocence would somehow be proved.[16]

At the end of the permitted half hour the prisoner asked permission to kiss his wife and children. This was denied, so the little party stood and waved him goodbye as he was led from their sight for the very last time.[17]

On the morning of his execution, John Dickman dressed in the suit he had worn for his trial, took a breakfast of bread and butter and porridge, then awaited his final moments. That night the *Newcastle Evening Chronicle* contained a brief report, presumably leaked by someone who had shared the condemned man's last moments. When the chaplain invited the prisoner to speak the truth about the crime, John Dickman did not reply. This notwithstanding, the anonymous observer said, John Dickman appeared to be the calmest man in the cell. He 'marched to his execution as erect as a soldier, never flinching, even when the rope came into view'.[18]

For most murderers, a brief account of how they met their death marks the end of newspaper interest, but it was not to be so with John Dickman. Not only did his case continue to excite controversy, but within five days of his execution, allegations would emerge claiming he was guilty of another murder.

6

Well Rid of a Scoundrel

By a curious irony, another robbery at gunpoint took place on a train on the very day John Dickman was executed. The assault was committed between Baker Street and Swiss Cottage and in spite of sustaining bullet wounds, the victim survived. The assailant was apprehended not far from the scene of the crime while attempting to hide in a tunnel. As if to underline the opportunities afforded by railway travel for robbery with violence, a second serious incident occurred on the same day in a third-class carriage travelling between Nottingham and Trent Junction, when a Miss Grace Clark was attacked and robbed by a fellow passenger.[1]

In this case the assailant was unarmed and although injured Miss Clark escaped with her life. The man had initially lunged at Miss Clark, punching her in the head and face and grabbing her satchel, but getting rather more than he bargained for when his victim, who was on her way to compete in a tennis match, recovered sufficiently to reach the communication cord, to say nothing of her tennis racquet, which she took down from the luggage rack and used to defend herself. Alas, the thief wrenched it from her and struck her about the head with it before leaping from the train as it slowed in response to her raising the alarm. By the time help arrived, Grace Clark lay bleeding on the floor of the compartment, her attacker having effected his escape.

There is no known connection between these episodes and the incident on the Newcastle to Alnmouth line nearly six months earlier, but they inevitably sparked comparison with the Nisbet case. One reader speculated that there might be some connection between the shooting near Swiss Cottage and the previous 'Train

Murder', deploring the fact that the authorities had probably hanged an innocent man; others with more thought for their own skins questioned why 'something' was not done about the dangers of train travel.[2]

Meanwhile on the Sunday of that same week, the *People* published an article intimating that one of their reporters had received some inside information about the recently executed murderer – information which blackened his reputation still further.[3] According to this piece, when the police took Dickman's house apart following the 'Train Murder', although they found little to link Dickman to that crime, they did discover a lot of evidence which implicated him in another, until then, unsolved murder. This was not the case of Caroline Luard, which was never mentioned, but that of a Sunderland moneylender called Herman Cohen.

One of the peculiarities of this report was the implication that the police had discovered more evidence to link Dickman to the Cohen murder than they had to link him to Nisbet's. This has a curious echo of the claim that those involved in trying Dickman for the Nisbet murder, 'knew' him to be guilty of the murder of Caroline Luard. Apparently although there was substantial proof that Dickman was guilty of two other murders, it was deemed wisest to put him on trial for the murder where very little hard evidence was available to link him to the crime.

'Was Dickman a Double Murderer?', the *People* asked. According to this story, the police had discovered among his belongings 'evidence that he had had some transactions with Cohen' and 'some jewellery'. The jewellery was significant because of the circumstances of Cohen's murder, which were briefly included in the report.

Cohen had been murdered on 8 March 1909. It was an attack of particular ferocity, the *People* explained, during which Cohen had been slashed about the head and had his little finger cut off, so that his killer could make off with the ring he habitually wore on it, as well as with the contents of his cash box. The last person seen talking to Cohen had been a tall man, who was wearing a light-coloured overcoat. Apparently the paper's reporter had 'good grounds for stating that had he been acquitted of the murder of

Nisbet, he [Dickman] would have been asked to account for his movements on the night of March 8 1909'.

The newspaper's unnamed source also explained that people in the neighbourhood of Lily Avenue considered themselves 'well rid of a scoundrel'. Apparently a mystery assailant had been knocking people down and relieving them of their cash, snatching ladies' handbags and even entering and robbing local houses, but Dickman's arrest had signalled the end of this mini crime wave. (Logic suggests that if these incidents had bedevilled the district, the constant presence of policemen at 1 Lily Avenue following the arrest of the householder might have acted as a disincentive to criminal operations in the vicinity whoever the culprit – if indeed there was a culprit at all.) These allegations take on a somewhat farcical note when one reads that some of the victims had now belatedly 'recognised' that Dickman had been their attacker.

The entire story smacks of a few beers with an inventive member of the Newcastle constabulary, and it was not generally taken up by the rest of the press. In fact it is obvious that whoever fed the *People* this line, it was not someone who had been closely involved with the investigation into Herman Cohen's murder.

Although described in some papers as a 'German Jew', Herman Cohen had lived all his life in Sunderland. He was aged about 40, a bachelor and a well-respected member of the local Jewish community who had at one time been president of the Villiers Street Synagogue. He lived at 24 Harold Street, Hendon, with Mr and Mrs Yamkelowitz (she was one of Cohen's cousins); the household also included Mr Yamkelowitz's brother and the couple's children.[4]

By the account of those who knew him, Herman Cohen had been an amiable man. Mr Yamkelowitz told reporters that he was easy-going in business and inclined to let others take advantage of him.[5] Cohen ran a combined drapers and moneylending business from 24 Harold Street, where he used the front room as an office. While this may appear a somewhat unusual arrangement, in the days when large stores did not extend credit to any but the gentry, someone like Herman Cohen offered a valuable service to customers from the poorer classes, who might need to replace their husbands' work shirts or their children's bedding, but did not have the ready cash to do so. In spite of the fear of getting into debt, many households had a permanent arrangement with traders like Mr Cohen, obtaining more goods as soon as the previous items were paid off. Small loans for other purposes were a natural extension of the credit side of his business – and by keeping stock at home and operating out of the front room, overheads were kept as low as possible.

Payments fell due every Monday, so the normal pattern of Monday evenings was for Herman Cohen to spend the early part of the night at his desk in the front room, admitting a succession of customers and receiving their payments; sometimes popping upstairs to fetch items from the stock of shirts, blankets and other necessaries he always had available.

While Cohen dealt with his business, the rest of the family went about their normal domestic routine, which centred on the kitchen. Callers on Monday night were invariably coming to see Cohen, so Mr and Mrs Yamkelowitz left it to him to answer the door bell. However, at around 7.15 on the night of the murder, when Cohen failed to answer the bell, Mr Yamkelowitz went to admit the caller himself. It was one of Cohen's customers, so he let her into the hall, then opened the door of the front room, where they discovered Herman Cohen on the floor, bleeding from a number of terrible head wounds.

A doctor was summoned immediately, but although Cohen was still alive when the doctor reached him, he died shortly afterwards having been unable to say anything. His little finger had been severed in the attack and it was initially reported that his killer had done this in order to make off with the ring Cohen usually wore on that finger. In fact, Cohen had not been wearing his ring that night: his family later discovered it upstairs among his things.[6] The finger was probably severed as Cohen instinctively raised his hands to protect himself from the onslaught. This was certainly the theory of the doctor who reported to the inquest. He detailed eight wounds to Cohen's head, any one of which, he said, was sufficient to be fatal. He thought they had been inflicted with a large sharp implement, such as a hatchet, or possibly a butcher's knife or cleaver.[7]

The Sunderland police seem to have done a creditable job in putting together, as far as possible, the jigsaw of Cohen's final half hour. Several customers who had called during this crucial period gave evidence at the inquest, as did the driver of a laundry van, who had been delivering in Harold Street at about 7.00 that night, and members of the household who had passed through the hall at various times during the early evening. The last witness thought to have seen the victim alive was a customer who timed her departure at 7.05. As she left the house, she noticed the catch had been left up on the front door, presumably to save Herman Cohen from constantly getting up and down to answer it, but also leaving open access to anyone who wished to come and go without being observed.

One witness had noticed a tall man in a light-coloured overcoat, who stood in the hall waiting for Cohen while the latter fetched some stock from upstairs; but it was far from clear whether the tall man was actually Cohen's final visitor. This man failed to come forward, but that does not necessarily make him the guilty party, and save for the fact that he happened to be among the hundreds of men in the north-east of England who possessed a light-coloured overcoat, there was no reason to suspect he was John Dickman – and several good reasons for thinking he was not.

Although it may have been possible for the killer of John Nisbet to emerge from a railway carriage without being covered in gore, the method used to despatch Herman Cohen was altogether messier. There cannot be the slightest doubt that Cohen's murderer would have been covered in blood. He left 24 Harold Street via the front door, having had no opportunity to wash his hands or clean his clothing, and carrying about his person a large blood-stained weapon, which was never discovered in spite of an extensive search of the streets, yards and gardens in the locality. Can it seriously be suggested that John Dickman, or indeed anyone, would have risked going very far in such a condition? No one in their right mind would have risked travelling 10 miles back to Newcastle, along gaslit streets, via tramcar or train in such a state. Cohen's killer was surely a local man, who melted into a convenient dark alley before making his way swiftly home.

Apart from anything else, the spoils were not worth the risk. Cohen was a small-time draper and moneylender, whose life was taken in exchange for a paltry £27. The notion that someone would attempt a murder as risky as this, unless absolutely down to their last few pennies, was frankly preposterous. At the time of Cohen's murder, John and Annie Dickman's combined resources in various bank accounts amounted to rather more than the total in Cohen's cash box.[8]

What then of the evidence which had allegedly been discovered at the Dickman home? Any jewellery the police did find cannot have been connected with the crime in Sunderland because although the popular press continued to peddle the story of the severed finger and the missing ring, the police investigating the case knew perfectly well that stolen jewellery was not a factor. Jewellery had been mentioned at Dickman's trial, but it was jewellery belonging to Dickman himself, which had been left as security for a loan with Cush & Co.

Similarly, evidence of Dickman's dealings with a moneylender called Cohen had emerged at his trial: but this was an entirely different Cohen – Mr Samuel Cohen, proprietor of the Cash Accommodation Company, whose loan to Dickman had been thoroughly chewed over in court; as had all the various financial transactions involving John Dickman which could be used to demonstrate how progressively hard up he had become during the final eighteen months of his life. Given that the prosecution produced supporting evidence down to pawn tickets and a request for Hogg to lend him a couple of pounds, is it likely that they would have omitted to mention whatever they could muster about Dickman's dealings with another moneylender, had such evidence existed?

It is clear that the whole story of Dickman's implication in the murder of Herman Cohen is fantasy from start to finish. It is impossible to say whether it emanated from the fertile imagination of a *People* reporter, or whether it began as some off-the-record speculation on the part of a member of the Newcastle police force. There is some reason to suspect the latter, because by August 1910 the Newcastle force had no reason to love John Dickman.

7

The Chain, the Mug and Other Revelations

If John Dickman can confidently be declared innocent of the Herman Cohen murder, is it possible that he was equally innocent of John Nisbet's?

Throughout the summer of 1910, letters debating whether Dickman should be hanged appeared in various local and national newspapers. In reality this was not a single question, but three separate ones. The first related to the whole issue of hanging itself. By 1910 there was already a steadily growing body of opposition to capital punishment, and even some who favoured the death penalty for convicted murderers felt that hanging was barbaric and ought to be replaced by more humane methods.

Although the rights and wrongs of capital punishment are not strictly relevant to a modern exploration of the Dickman case, it is vital to recognise that this issue was of central importance to the growing abolitionist lobby, and that some of those who campaigned against Dickman's execution undoubtedly added their signatures to petitions and their voices to the outcry because they were opposed to hanging on principle. This necessarily meant that not all such petitioners were wholly convinced of his innocence. It is noticeable that many of the letters which appeared in the press and cast doubt on Dickman's guilt also contained an unmistakable subtext of opposition to capital punishment *per se*.[1]

Moreover, from the point of view of those campaigning overtly or covertly for the abolition of the death penalty, any case where the slightest doubt could be raised about a suspect's guilt was a propaganda tool, drawing attention to the awful possibility of mistakes being made, and thereby whipping up public feeling and the profile of the issue generally.

The second question relates to the phrase 'reasonable doubt'. For Dickman to hang, a jury had to be convinced not only that he was guilty of the deed, but that his guilt had been demonstrated beyond reasonable doubt. The public were aware that all sorts of doubts had been raised about what was essentially the purely circumstantial evidence that had convicted John Dickman. A number of entirely neutral observers have commented that, while on balance it would appear that Dickman murdered Nisbet, they could not say this was demonstrated 'beyond reasonable doubt' at his trial.

The jury clearly thought otherwise – but 'reasonable doubt' can be a difficult commodity to pin down; a doubt which may appear eminently reasonable to one man could seem unrealistically far-fetched to another. Given the circumstances of this particular crime, some might question whether it would ever be possible to prove the case against Dickman to universal satisfaction.

The final question and central issue is not about proof, doubt or methods of punishment but is, quite simply, whether John Dickman actually murdered John Nisbet. John Dickman consistently denied this, but as he continued to hope for a reprieve that is not entirely surprising. The account he gave of his activities on 18 March 1910 could have been a truthful one. It is possible to travel for the best part of 40 minutes so engrossed in a newspaper that you lose track of your whereabouts and miss your station. Indeed, the nature of the line between Newcastle and Morpeth would facilitate this, because once out of Newcastle there are very few distinguishing features to be seen from the windows of the train. There *is* a steep bend on the approach to Morpeth station which forces the train to slow down, and the distinctive sound made by the train wheels as they negotiate it could be enough to jolt a passenger into the realisation that they have missed their stop. John Dickman did suffer from piles and was treated for this longstanding complaint while on remand.[2] On a lonely stretch of road, a man might have little recourse other than to nip behind a hedge and it is possible, if stretching credulity slightly, that the situation might have been such that he lingered in a field alongside the road for the best part of an hour, waiting to recover.

A great deal of the evidence ranged against Dickman was essentially irrelevant. His dealings with Hogg and Christie may have been peculiar or even dishonest, but they had nothing whatever to do with the death of John Nisbet. John Dickman's finances may have been in a parlous state: on 18 March 1910 there were any number of people in Newcastle who were equally short of cash – some of them may even have travelled on the 10.27 train to Alnmouth; but that did not prove that they killed a colliery clerk and made off with his cash bag.

The real kernel of the matter lies in the evidence of three witnesses. That chain of witnesses who placed Nisbet and Dickman together at Newcastle Central station, starting with Charles Raven, who knew Nisbet and saw him apparently in company with another man he recognised as John Dickman. Dickman claimed not to know Raven, but it is feasible that Raven knew who Dickman was without Dickman having known Raven.

This aside, Raven's view of the two men as they went through the Platform 4 gateway is not in itself all that compelling. The men he saw might have been only coincidentally walking near one another – the fact that they were apparently together at the Platform 4 gate was no guarantee that they would ultimately travel in the same compartment. As anyone familiar with the layout of Newcastle Central station knew, in order to reach Platforms 5, 6, 7 and 8, travellers had to cross the footbridge from Platform 4. Platforms 5 and 6 were the east and west ends of a single platform. Platforms 7 and 8 were two halves of a single platform which ran back to back with 5 and 6. This meant that in spite of their numbering, Platforms 5 and 8 were actually in close proximity to one another, so Dickman's story of diverting to visit the urinal on Platform 8, when catching a train from Platform 5, was perfectly reasonable. Had Raven been the only witness there would have been no case.

However, the trail of evidence was then picked up by Wilson Hepple. Hepple recognised Dickman because he had known him over a period going back twenty years. He saw Dickman with a man who fitted Nisbet's description and he observed these two men walking along the platform, and then on the point of entering a compartment together, in the section of the train where John Nisbet was murdered. Two things stand out about this in relation to Dickman's own account of his journey. Hepple travelled in the third vehicle of the train and he was walking up and down outside the door of his compartment until about a minute before the train departed. Dickman claims to have travelled in the same coach as Hepple, presumably in a virtually adjacent compartment. To do so he must necessarily have entered the train quite close to where Hepple was walking – yet Hepple did not see him do so. It might be argued that Dickman left it to the very last minute to board the train, but while it is possible to present a version of events in which Dickman and Hepple travel in the same section of the train without seeing one another, on balance the evidence supports Hepple's story of seeing Dickman about to get into the front carriage with Nisbet.

The prosecution drove home the point that not one of the people who supposedly travelled in the same compartment as John Dickman came forward to confirm his story. Again, it is possible to conjecture that they did not bother, had forgotten him, or were somehow unaware of the significance of their being on the 10.27 that day – but again we are trying to invent explanations for a complete absence of corroborative evidence for Dickman's story.

Hepple's evidence is crucial – Hepple knew Dickman and recognised him. Even so, Hepple's evidence could have sounded a little peculiar to anyone unfamiliar with the geography of the station: in fact, Lord Coleridge enquired whether Platform 5 was exceptionally wide and was answered in the affirmative.[3] Not only was it a wide platform but the footbridge brought passengers to the side furthest from the rails and because Platform 5 was only one half of the platform (the western end was designated Platform 6), trains departing from it were drawn up at the extreme eastern end. Thus, when passengers for the 10.27 descended the footbridge, they had a distance of around 60 feet to cover before they even got level with the rear of the train, and it was therefore perfectly natural for them to continue walking well away from the platform edge until they cut across to board the train. At this distance, it is hardly surprising that Hepple, although able to recognise John Dickman walking a mere 20 feet or so away in broad daylight, would not have been able to distinguish the men's voices in the hubbub of the station where sounds are swallowed up by the echoing arches of the roof. This oddity in the layout of Platform 5 also helps explain why John Dickman, whose attention was probably focused partly on his companion and partly on the furthest end of the platform, failed to notice Wilson Hepple.

Dickman's defence claimed that the Raven sighting was no more than of two men coincidentally walking in the same direction at the same time, while the Hall evidence proved nothing other than that a man of very similar appearance to John Dickman boarded the train with John Nisbet. With Hepple's evidence, however, Dickman's supporters had to resort to another tactic altogether. Hepple became 'an old man' – his faculties no doubt dimmed by his great age. For anyone who had not observed Wilson Hepple at the trial, his apparent inability to hear Dickman and Nisbet talking could even turn him into 'an old, *deaf* man' – which was how Mitchell-Innes described him to the appeal judges.[4] There is something of a problem with this, in that anyone who troubles to find out a little more about Wilson Hepple will quickly discover that he was far from an old man in 1910; furthermore, by his very nature Hepple was likely to be a particularly sound witness.

Wilson Hepple was born in 1853. At the time of Dickman's trial he was only in his late fifties – and would live for another twenty-seven years. Hepple was, moreover, a person trained to observe – an artist, whose work is collected to the present day. During the Edwardian period, Hepple produced some of his best-known work and at the time of John Dickman's trial was very far from the diminished and doddering elderly gentleman Mitchell-Innes sought to portray. Although Hepple had lived at Acklington for some time by 1910, he regularly travelled into Newcastle, where he maintained a studio. He undoubtedly knew John Dickman because for a long period both men lived in Whickham. This is not to say he was a close friend – Dickman's query as to why, if Hepple had seen him, he did not speak, may have been a rather desperate throw of the dice. It seems unlikely that Hepple, the man commissioned to paint the King's visit to the city, and Dickman, a man who operated as a bookmaker in the Bigg Market, were likely to be bosom pals. It is possible that more than the mere width of the platform deterred Hepple from hailing his 'old friend' that morning.[5]

Having attempted to suggest to a possibly bemused court that Hepple's faculties were 'much failed', Dickman could only fall back on the claim that Hepple's evidence was entirely mistaken. Yet insofar as it could be tested, Hepple proved to have an accurate recall – he remembered the picture of Brancepeth Castle in his compartment, just as he remembered seeing John Dickman on the point of entering the train with John Nisbet.

The only real way out of this for Dickman would have been to claim that he walked up the platform with Nisbet but then returned to a different compartment: a story even Dickman was not willing to attempt. Not only was there no plausible reason to justify these actions, but Hall's evidence was that the man who walked along the platform with Nisbet got into the compartment with him. Unlike Hepple, Hall had not inconveniently looked the other way at the crucial moment – and Hall's evidence is therefore the final link in the chain which places Nisbet and Dickman together in the compartment.

In this context Percival Hall's evidence is absolutely crucial. Hall testified that he saw a man getting into the compartment next to his with John Nisbet. He was not prepared to swear that the man he saw was Dickman, only that Dickman resembled the man. Thus, had Hall's been the only evidence, Dickman must surely have walked free. However, there can be no doubt that what Hall and Hepple describe are two halves of the same whole – each from a different angle witnessed the progress of a pair of men and one of them (Hall) saw the men actually enter the murder compartment together. Both Hall and Hepple could identify one of the two men. The only way in which these two men might not have been part of the same pair would be if either of them, Dickman or Nisbet, had been one half of a different pair of men entering the first vehicle of the train.

Here the layout of the train becomes an important part of the evidence. Neither Hall nor Hepple had the slightest doubt that the two men were entering a compartment in the first carriage of the train. There were only three passenger compartments in that vehicle. One of these was occupied by Hall and Spink, one was occupied by Andrew Bruce, whose travelling companion (the man who travelled from Newcastle to Chevington) was neither Nisbet nor Dickman. The unavoidable conclusion is that Dickman and Nisbet got into the remaining compartment together.

Hall and Spink were also able to testify to John Nisbet's still being alive as the train pulled out of Stannington station. Hall acknowledged him and received a nod in return. His gesture towards Nisbet was observed by Andrew Bruce. Stannington station was a tiny rural halt – no more than a level crossing, a station-master's house and narrow platforms to either side of the track. Hall and Spink had to wait for the train to move off and the crossing gates to be opened before they could set off up the lane to Netherton colliery, and while they did so they must perforce have stood within a few feet of the compartment in which John Nisbet sat. There is not the slightest possibility of them mistaking whom they saw. The fact that John Nisbet was still alive at Stannington is another crucial point in the case against Dickman. For it is self-evident that the man who killed John Nisbet could not have left the train before Stannington but had left it before the train arrived at Widdrington, the station at which John Nisbet failed to get off.

Mr Mitchell-Innes hoped to convince the jury that the killer did not necessarily get off at a station at all, but like several of his arguments, this one fails to stand up. The one thing anyone leaping from a moving train cannot manage to do is close the door behind them. At least one victim in a train murder was discovered almost immediately because the door of their compartment was swinging open when the train arrived at the next station. In the event that the door of Nisbet's compartment had been open when the train halted anywhere on its route, it is inconceivable that whoever went to close it would not have seen the trails of blood running across the floor, if not the body itself.

Thus we know that the murderer left the train at one of the stations between Stannington and Widdrington. There are only three possibilities: Morpeth, Pegswood or Longhirst. Only two passengers alighted at Pegswood, a woman and her small child. (The woman was subsequently identified as a Mrs Dawson.[6]) Only three got down from the train at Longhirst – all of whom got on at Morpeth, which inevitably turns attention back to the relatively small number of passengers who left the train at Morpeth.

Morpeth was a much busier station than most of the others on the line, so it presented the best opportunity on the journey for Nisbet's killer to blend in with a crowd. The question of precisely how many people left the train at Morpeth was not asked of ticket collector John Athey at the trial; but after the appeal judges pronounced against John Dickman, investigations into the safety of his conviction continued. Two substantial files of Home Office papers survive, testifying to the diligence with which Home Office officials conducted their own behind-the-scenes investigations on Churchill's behalf, to see whether it was appropriate for the Home Secretary to intervene. Among these papers are not only John Athey's answers regarding exactly how many passengers did alight from the Newcastle to Alnmouth train that day,[7] but a great deal of other evidence which, for various reasons, was never made public at the time.

The Norman memorandum implied that Dickman's appeal to the Home Secretary was doomed from the outset: because, according to Norman, Churchill believed Dickman guilty of the murder of Caroline Luard. In fact, the copious files on the Dickman case, far from betraying prejudice against the convicted man, give every impression that the case generated a healthy degree of concern at the highest levels. It is clear that the civil servants involved took every possible step to satisfy themselves that justice had been done.

Even before the appeal was heard, the Home Office were already investigating claims that the identification parade involving Hall and Spink had been rigged. Enquiries were made of these two gentlemen, and it became perfectly obvious that they had been encouraged to get a good look at the prisoner through an internal window, then an open door, before the identity parade began: and that in Hall's case he was intimidated into making an identification, when he had already expressed himself uncertain that the man he had seen with Nisbet was in the room.[8]

The Home Office began to press the Northumberland Chief Constable Captain Fullarton James for an explanation of these events, which led to a lengthy exchange of correspondence. On 19 July the Chief Constable wrote a long letter, explaining that statements about the alleged incident had now been taken from Hall, Spink and Hall's father, who had also been present at the police station that evening. Statements had also been taken from the police officers on duty that night, and Fullarton James drew attention to the 'remarkable corroboration of police statements in disproof of those of Hall and Spink'. He went on to say that in his opinion 'Hall and Spink did try to look in through the windows . . . these incidents have been greatly magnified by Hall and Spink . . . who were no doubt very much excited at the time'.[9]

As a piece of bare-faced cheek, the suggestion that Hall and Spink had initiated these shenanigans takes some beating (how they could have known the accused man was behind the windows in question, the Chief Constable does not attempt to explain). Fullarton James went on to say that it would be impossible to determine precisely which policemen had been in the corridor at the same time as Hall and Spink because there had been twenty-eight officers in the building at the time.

The Home Office refused to stand for this nonsense and instructed Fullarton James to muster all twenty-eight men for an identity parade, which he did.[10] Hall and Spink attended, but four months had elapsed since the original incident so, not surprisingly, they were unable to pick out any of the officers involved. The Home Office refused to let the matter drop and were still in correspondence with Fullarton James on the subject in October 1910. Fullarton James stuck to his assertion that no officer had deliberately allowed the witnesses to get a look at Dickman, and as the attempt to identify the culprits had failed, the matter eventually fizzled out, with the Home Office able to do no more than circulate a firmly worded memo, reminding all police forces of the correct procedures to be observed when conducting an identity parade.[11]

After all this it is small wonder that the Newcastle force was not particularly fond of John Dickman.

Nor was the Chief Constable of Northumberland the only official to find himself in the line of fire over his staff's handling of John Dickman. Criticism had appeared in the newspapers following allegations by Annie Dickman that her husband had been forced to give evidence on an empty stomach. The Home Office wrote to the prison governor at Newcastle asking if this had been the case. They learned that although Annie had exaggerated the problem inasmuch as her husband had received a decent lunch in his cell below the court, it was true that he had gone to court that morning having consumed only tea and bread and butter, that being the standard prison breakfast. The Home Office considered this inadequate for a man about to face the ordeal of examination on a capital charge, and the governor was instructed not to allow this to happen again.[12]

There had also been adverse publicity concerning the way Dickman's wife and children had been denied a last embrace and the Home Office required an explanation of this, too. The prison governor replied that 'the cunning and daring of the prisoner and his wife' made any relaxation of the rules impossible. Apparently they had conceived the notion that John Dickman's nearest and dearest might attempt to pass him poison, thereby cheating the hangman. According to the prison governor, he had been warned about the 'cunning and daring' of John and Annie Dickman by the police superintendent in charge of the case.[13] Here is further evidence of the level of police antipathy towards not only John Dickman, but also his wife – a woman never formally accused of anything.

The Home Office initially became involved in the Dickman case because of their responsibilities with regard to the treatment of prisoners and the conduct of identification parades. By the time the prisoner's appeal had failed, they were also in receipt of letters questioning the verdict, and petitions appealing for clemency.[14]

A number of correspondents had their own theories about the case. Several drew attention to the story of the lady who claimed she had overheard the murderers discussing their crime in a Newcastle park. Others had read a story about a train guard who came across a traveller claiming to have shot another man: which, if it happened at all, had no relevance whatever to the murder of John Nisbet. One writer even went to the trouble of drawing little diagrams of the train in order to illustrate how witnesses had contradicted themselves about whether Nisbet had been seated facing the engine or not.

Several letters repeated the claim that two or sometimes three jurymen had signed the petition for reprieve, thereby casting doubt on the unanimity of the verdict. A careful check by Home Office staff established this to be untrue[15] – but once started, such a rumour is impossible to quash, and by the time C.H. Norman submitted his memorandum in 1950, the number of jurors allegedly signing the petition had leapt to five.

The case had clearly touched the hearts of many. Letters from smart London addresses sit alongside a petition signed by twenty-one residents of Eugenia Road, Rotherhithe, most of whose handwriting suggests little familiarity with a pen. Letters also arrived from Annie Dickman, who was by then living at 54 Glenthorn Road, Jesmond. Annie wrote in a clear, confident hand and used sophisticated language. She complained, among other things, that her personal letters had been used extremely selectively in court in order to place a particular construction on them. The family had not been hard up, she said, in fact 'we were quite affluent'. The last letter on file from Annie was written a month after her husband's execution, requesting the Home Office to instruct the police to return all the personal papers and letters they had removed from Lily Avenue. She pointed out that with all manner of bills and receipts missing, it was extremely difficult for her to sort out the family's affairs. The Home Office replied that this was not part of their jurisdiction. There is no record of whether or not these items were ever returned.[16]

As well as fielding all this correspondence, the Home Office conducted a detailed investigation of their own. This included requesting Chief Constable Fullarton James to initiate further enquiries with the ticket collector John Athey in order to establish who else got off the 10.27 at Morpeth that day, apart from John Dickman. Athey had originally estimated the number at twelve. Of these passengers, only one had tendered an excess fare and this man was known to be John Dickman. Of the other eleven, four had been miners from Cramlington, one was Mr Rutherford, a Morpeth draper, and another was a man not known to Athey but understood to have been a Morpeth market gardener, who had come forward to confirm he was on the train, as had a Mr Pringle, a bootmaker from Morpeth and his sister, both of whom Athey knew but had failed to recall. Of the remaining three passengers, two had been season ticket holders and one was a man with a return ticket from either Newcastle or Corbridge. As this left at least three passengers who had never been identified, the ticket collector's evidence was inconclusive, inasmuch as it only made Dickman one of a very small number of men who might have been the murderer.[17]

Churchill himself expressed doubts about the 'blood' evidence given by Dr Boland. He was so perturbed by this that he asked his civil servants to seek the opinion of another expert, specifically querying how Boland could be so certain that the stains found on the glove were of such recent origin when he could not actually determine what they were. Churchill also wanted to know about the compartment in the train marked 'Reserved' to which Dickman had referred in his evidence – had there been such a compartment, where had it been situated and for whom was it reserved?[18]

Then there was the evidence of identification. Cicely Nisbet's identification evidence was dismissed as 'not at all credible'. A hand-written note on the file states: 'I think Mrs Nisbet's evidence should be disregarded. The strong evidence is that of Raven, Hepple, Hall.'[19]

From Hall's statement about the identity parade, it had become apparent that several men in the line-up had been clean-shaven and their heights had varied, so unlike John Dickman they did not resemble the witness's original description of the suspect. This notwithstanding, and in spite of the deplorable circumstances which surrounded the conduct of the identity parade, the Home Office felt there was a ring of truth about the rest of Hall and Spink's evidence; which, if anything, was underlined by their refusal to swear more than that Dickman was 'very like' the man they had seen. Their original descriptions of the suspect were of a man exactly like John Dickman, right down to his newspaper (even their estimate of his weight was accurate).

In one sense the Home Secretary had an advantage over the jury at Dickman's trial because he had copies of all the original witness depositions at his disposal to peruse at length. These included the testimony of shopkeeper Henrietta Hymen, who quite clearly stated that John Dickman had told her that he was expecting a parcel containing a revolver, which he collected from her shop *before* the arrival of the second parcel from the Glasgow gunsmiths, which was returned.[20]

There was also the statement of Andrew Kirkwood, the assistant at Pape & Co.[21] Tindal Atkinson had managed to insinuate what Kirkwood's evidence might have been before it was deemed to be inadmissible because the firearm sale register had been improperly kept. This technicality prevented the jury from discovering the exact nature of the entry made in Kirkwood's hand, but the Home Office knew that it recorded the sale of a .25 automatic pistol to J.A. Dickinson of 1 Lily Avenue, Jesmond. Irrespective of whether it was Kirkwood or one of his colleagues who conducted this transaction, the fact remains that someone calling himself J.A. Dickinson bought a pistol from Pape & Co. on 8 November 1907, giving his address as 1 Lily Avenue. As the purchase of firearms was completely legitimate, it is not easy to see why anyone should use this particular name and address if they were not their own – nor why this person would know the middle initial and give it correctly and yet make a mistake over the actual surname.

The police had checked with the Dickmans' landlady, who confirmed that no Dickinson had ever lived at 1 Lily Avenue, and they also checked that no other Dickinsons lived at any other house in Lily Avenue.[22] These enquiries turned up an H.E. Dickinson of 17 Lily Avenue, but his initials did not match the entry in the register and he assured the police he had never owned a gun. At this point the prosecution's introduction of various other bills discovered among the Dickmans' papers, made out in the name of Dickinson, falls into place.

The most startling revelations, however, came from none other than William Dickman, the condemned man's elder brother. William Dickman had been visited by the police at an early stage in their enquiries and had given them a long statement.[23] As will have been adduced from the tone of William Dickman's letter to the newspaper, the brothers were not close. By the beginning of the twentieth century, William Dickman reckoned they had not been in touch with one another for perhaps nine years. When they came together again it was because John visited William, who was then living with his wife and family at Chester-le-Street. This was during the period when John Dickman had lost his job with Dixon, Robson & Co. According to William, his brother told him that he was in such desperate financial straits that he had taken an axe on to Newcastle Moor, intending to knock someone down, but no one had come by.

Not long after this, John had obtained the job with the Morpeth Moor Colliery at a salary of £2 per week and it was several years before William saw him again. They were next brought together by the receipt of a legacy following the death of one of their mother's relatives. After this they had run into each other occasionally in Newcastle on market days, and John had lent William some money when he was 'short'.

Unfortunately, John then ran short again himself and turned up at William's house, wanting the money back. When William, who was out of work at the time, was unable to oblige, things had become quite heated. John had then speculated about premises where money might be kept and whether they could jointly break in. His brother had no inclination towards this sort of enterprise and told him 'not to talk rot'. At this John laughed and said he could do such things and not be found out, mentioning that twice when stranded at race meetings he had stolen bags out of racks in corridor trains to facilitate his journey home. William replied that this was nothing to boast of. During this conversation, John also mentioned that colliery pay clerks presented a possibility for robbery. Relations between the brothers soured further when John continued to press for the return of his money, upsetting William's wife in the process.

The last time William saw his brother was during the summer of 1908. On this occasion John mentioned that he was still short of money, commenting that he didn't know what he would have done, if he hadn't fallen in with 'a mug' – a Mr Christie who used to give him £20 or £30 at a time to put on the horses, much of which William suspected was not going on the horses at all.

The only doubt which arises on reading this account is whether William Dickman was so consumed with hatred of his younger brother that he would concoct a story in order to portray him in such a terrible light. This is demonstrably not the case, because the police had separately obtained a statement from Frank Christie – who was not personally known to William Dickman – which corroborated at least part of William's story. The Home Office copy of Frank Christie's statement has two words pencilled in the margin 'the mug'.[24]

Christie's statement began by outlining the history of his business relationship with John Dickman, which emanated from the Morpeth Moor Colliery buyout. Christie was a keen follower of the turf, a member of both Stockton and Gosforth Race Courses, and although he claimed not to have been aware that Dickman was a bookmaker, he 'had occasionally backed horses through Dickman'. Dickman claimed to have a successful betting system of his own, which Christie had agreed to try out: borrowing £200 from Cohen to finance the experiment. Dickman had worked his system, but unfortunately the money had all been lost. He then approached Christie with a view to financing the ball-bearing patent he was hoping to introduce, but Christie declined.

There is no suggestion in the tone of Christie's statement that he ever worked out that Dickman was fleecing him. However, it seems likely that once Christie refused to back the patent ball-bearing, Dickman realised he could not count on 'the mug' for further cash advances.

Winston Churchill's final deliberations regarding Dickman's conviction run to six typewritten pages, in which the evidence is given measured consideration, but concludes: '[the evidence]leads directly to the conclusion of his guilt. . . . I have been unable, though I have searched for it, to find any ground for differing from the conclusions which Judge, Jury, Court of Appeal and Home Office experts have, from such differing points of view, successively and independently arrived.'[25]

Faced with the weight of evidence on file, it is impossible not to share Churchill's view. John Dickman planned and executed the robbery and murder of John Nisbet and what is more, he very nearly got away with it. But for the presence of Wilson Hepple on the 10.27 that morning, it is unlikely that he could have been definitively placed in the same compartment as Nisbet. It was a double misfortune for Dickman that he happened to travel right next door to Hall and Spink – had they been at the other end of the train, the conclusive evidence that Nisbet met his death after Stannington would also have been lacking.

It seems probable that Dickman made a trial run a fortnight before the murder, much as the police conjectured. On the day after Dickman's arrest, long before the trial-run theory became public, a commercial traveller called Mr Brocklehurst told a reporter from the *Newcastle Daily Chronicle* that when travelling on the 9.30 Express from Newcastle to Morpeth about a fortnight previously, he and his travelling companions had been startled by what sounded like gun shots at a point on the line somewhere between Annitsford and Stannington. On lowering the window they saw the framework of their compartment window was splintered, which they thought had been caused by someone in the adjacent compartment firing a revolver.[26]

The police assumed that Dickman travelled by the 10.27 when he visited Hogg at the Dovecot Mine on 4 March, but it is equally likely that he had taken a much earlier train to Morpeth and walked back, working out the details of the scheme he was planning to effect a fortnight later. Hogg thought Dickman turned up at Dovecot 'about noon' that day – which did not fit with the time he ought to have arrived if he got off the 10.27 at Stannington, but fitted perfectly with a journey to Morpeth on the

9.30 Express, followed by a morning exploring various options in the vicinity.

On the morning of the murder Dickman could have fallen in with the readily sociable John Nisbet easily enough, guiding him to a compartment towards the head of the train where the noise from the engine would help cover the sound of the shots he intended to fire. It can be safely assumed that Dickman no longer had the automatic pistol he bought from Papes in 1907, just a couple of left-over bullets which he packed with paper so that he could use them in his more recently acquired revolver.

At the outset of the journey he may have removed his coat precisely to avoid getting any tell-tale stains on it; either folding it in the rack or on the seat beside him (the stain Boland found on it probably *was* a combination of bicycle oil and patent cleaner). After shooting Nisbet and pushing his body under the seats, he wiped his hands on a handkerchief, which he then placed in his trouser pocket where it left the pin-head blood stains which were discovered later. Finally, he donned his coat in readiness to disembark from the train.

Getting out of the train at Morpeth was essentially the riskiest part of the operation. There was always the possibility that a passenger joining the train might open the door of the compartment he had just vacated, discover the recently deceased colliery clerk and raise the alarm. Dickman might try to bluff it out and claim to have travelled in a different compartment, but his possession of Nisbet's bag would have been a complete giveaway.

It is therefore a strong possibility that Dickman threw the money bag out of the train window before reaching Morpeth, perhaps noting some distinctive tree or trackside feature as a marker by which to locate it later. At all events, either concealing the bag under his coat or more likely unencumbered by it, John Dickman tendered his excess fare and set out along the main Newcastle Road towards the Dovecot Colliery. It would have been extremely risky for him to turn the other way out of the station and make straight for the Isabella Pit shaft. Dickman was reasonably well known in Morpeth and witnesses might have seen him leaving the station. In fact, he may have hoped that witnesses would come forward to confirm that he set off down the Newcastle Road, but if so he was out of luck, because although he must have passed people on the road, no one did recall seeing him.

At some point he left the main road. In his account of the morning this was for a prolonged sojourn on the western side of the road, but in reality John Dickman entered the fields which lay to the east. Once past the farm at Catchburn there were no dwellings at all, just a broad expanse of hedged fields between the road and the railway line. In March there is very little chance of meeting anyone working in the fields, and with no buildings in sight the risk of encountering any inconvenient witnesses was not particularly great. Cutting across these fields along a predetermined route, John Dickman recovered the bag he had thrown from the train, crossed the railway line and made for the Isabella shaft. Here, too, there was an almost complete absence of human occupation. Once he had cut open the bag and disposed of it down the shaft, he could return the way he had come, emerging back on to the Newcastle Road and so back to Morpeth. This cross-country addition to his walk would have occupied the 'missing hour', when he was allegedly recovering from an attack of piles at the roadside. A direct walk along the Shields Road from Morpeth station to the Isabella Pit shaft would not. Again, he may have hoped to encounter someone who would confirm seeing him come back into Morpeth that way – but again he was unlucky. He probably planned to catch the 1.10 Express back to Newcastle, but he missed it by minutes and had to wait for the slower train.

Thus far, John Dickman had got away with murder: but he knew the hue and cry would be up as soon as anyone opened the compartment door and discovered Nisbet's body. He could not count on the train getting all the way to Alnmouth before that happened and was smart enough to realise that by the time he got back to Morpeth the hunt would already be on: anyone might be considered a suspect, merely by virtue of having travelled on the same train. Having carefully worked out an alibi, he was surely not going to risk the police discovering the murder weapon, or proceeds of the robbery, if they came calling at his house.

This opens up two possibilities. One is that John Dickman had an accomplice in Newcastle, a confederate with whom he could safely leave a very large sum of money and a revolver. This seems unlikely. The second possibility is that John Dickman had allowed for the eventuality of being stopped and searched when he returned to Morpeth to catch the train home. He had not constructed his plans so carefully only to be caught red handed, his pockets weighed down with stolen gold. (There is, in any case, some doubt that he could have unobtrusively stowed such a large amount of cash about his person.)

It is highly probable that after he recovered the bag from the trackside and extracted a few pounds for immediate needs, John Dickman stashed the rest of the money in a hidey hole somewhere in the fields between the Newcastle and Shields roads. Having previously located a suitable hollow tree trunk or something of the sort, Dickman assumed that he would be in a position to recover the rest of the cash at a later date. The likelihood of a police search uncovering the money, or anyone stumbling across it in the ordinary course of events (in the short term at least), was extremely slim. What John Dickman had not anticipated was being arrested within three days of committing the crime.

If Dickman concealed the money and was unable to return to it himself, did he manage to convey the vital information of its whereabouts to Annie? This seems an unlikely scenario. Once under arrest, he was never again allowed to be alone with his wife. It is in any case doubtful that he ever shared the terrible secret of the murder with her. So the gold sovereigns and half sovereigns may yet be lying where he left them; or perhaps someone found them years ago and, guessing how they got there, decided there was no need to report this treasure trove to the relevant authorities – a case of finders keepers, losers silenced forever.

8

The Shorthand Writer's Story

C.H. Norman's enduring faith in John Dickman's innocence appears to have been misplaced, but this does not automatically mean the implications of his 1950 memorandum can be dismissed out of hand. According to Norman's memorandum, evidence existed which implicated John Dickman in Caroline Luard's murder. Norman doubted the reliability of this evidence, but then he also queried the evidence in respect of the Nisbet murder. Since the mid-twentieth century, Norman's memorandum has been reproduced in various accounts of the Luard and Nisbet murders, but Norman himself, the court shorthand writer who was apparently no more than the accidental conduit for these surprising revelations, has remained a shadowy figure.

It is now time to direct the spotlight on Clarence Henry Norman, and to reveal the true nature of his role in the story of the Nisbet/Luard murders.

Clarence Henry Norman was born on 30 August 1886. His father, Clarence Charles Norman, was also a shorthand writer, who came originally from the Channel Islands but had a somewhat peripatetic early married life – his elder son Richard was born in Belfast, the younger son Clarence in Kingston upon Hull. By the turn of the century, however, the Norman family had settled permanently in the south-east of England, where they enjoyed a comfortable suburban life in Teddington. Not only was Clarence Norman Sr a shorthand writer: his wife and both sons followed this profession too.[1] Clarence Norman Jr specialised in court reporting, but although this took him all over the country as he followed the Assizes from city to city, he chose to base himself in the heart of

London, where he lived in a succession of rented rooms and flats until his death in 1974.[2]

Although only 24 years old when he took notes at the Dickman trial in 1910, Clarence Norman already had considerable experience of trial work. In addition, he was a seasoned political campaigner,[3] and engaged in part-time journalism, regularly contributing to the *New Age*, a socialist magazine then edited by A.R. Orage. In common with most of the publications linked to the Labour movement at the time, *New Age* was constantly short of funds, so less well-known contributors were unlikely to be paid. Nor were the sentiments or subject matter of C.H. Norman's writing likely to find an outlet in anything other than the left-wing press.[4]

The *New Age* published contributions from such luminaries as G.K. Chesterton, Victor Grayson MP, Hilaire Belloc and Walter Sickert, and included articles across a wide range of subjects in fulfilment of its threefold promise of being 'a weekly review of politics, literature and art'. The latter two categories were not covered by young Mr Norman, who writing both under his own name and the pen name Stanhope of Chester (not infrequently employing the plural 'we' as if to convey a mighty body of opinion behind his words), directed his fire on all manner of evils, from alleged Colonial Office malpractice in the Gilbert and Ellis Islands, to abuses of civil liberties in India. Issues closer to home were of equal concern. In 1909 he warned British workmen against 'the machinations of secret diplomacy' and 'the evil results of the King's dabbling in finance'.[5] No monarchist, he referred to Edward VII as 'an interfering individual from the House of Hanover', while Lord Rothschild, another *bête noire*, was 'a Jew financier', part of an 'unholy alliance' that included Jews, American and Irish journalists, and peers.[6] Aside from embarrassingly anti-Semitic ranting and a mistrust of the Establishment generally, Norman also took an interest in such questions as the amount of sexual disease suffered in the British army and sexual allegations against government officers in East Africa.

Nor was this angry young man just at odds with those he perceived to be his political enemies. In the summer of 1911 he wrote a highly critical letter to Ramsay MacDonald on the subject of Labour Party policy in the House of Commons. When MacDonald replied at length, justifying the issues raised, Norman wrote again refusing to back down. This elicited a further reply from the party leader, who pointed out, 'You seem to change the ground of your attack in your second letter . . . in order to give yourself a case . . .'.[7]

Unabashed, Norman wrote again and MacDonald responded, complaining that 'it is a pity those who criticise do not take the trouble to keep in touch with everything . . . [but] charge religiously their memory with points with which they disagree and apparently forget everything else'.[8] If MacDonald hoped the young man would be deterred by this obvious rebuff, he was to be disappointed. Norman wrote once more, this time focusing on the subject of National Insurance, to which he appears to have objected. MacDonald responded yet again: only to be confronted with yet another Norman missive complaining about the recent settlement of the railway strike. MacDonald had clearly lost patience: 'With reference to the terms of the Railway Strike, do you really know what you are talking about? The comment you make seems to show you do not.'[9]

Clarence Norman was a staunch opponent of the First World War and in August 1915 he put a resolution before the Independent Labour Party Conference to condemn Labour Party MPs who had assisted with army recruiting: the motion was carried by 121 votes to 120.[10] Before very long this opposition to the war would bring him into direct conflict with the law.

On 19 August 1915 the police raided the headquarters of the Independent Labour Party in London, seizing hundreds of anti-war pamphlets. The pamphlets in question had been published by various Independent Labour Party members, one of whom was Clarence Henry Norman. Although Norman's part in the affair was so minimal that he was originally described in the charges under the collective heading 'and others', singularly among those whose publications had been seized and destroyed, Clarence Norman decided to take on officialdom; commencing a lawsuit in which he claimed, among other things, that the Act under which the papers had been seized (the Defence of the Realm Act) had not been validly passed through Parliament.[11]

Norman appeared as a litigant in person, thereby avoiding the expense of qualified legal representation. When his action was dismissed as 'frivolous and vexatious' he appealed. When his appeal was dismissed in the same terms, he appealed to the House of Lords; but before this matter reached any conclusion, the long arm of the law caught up with Norman again, in respect of a not entirely unrelated transgression.

As a single man under the age of 41, Norman was liable for conscription. Conscientious objectors were permitted to appeal to a local tribunal who could, subject to their being satisfied of the objector's convictions against military service, allocate such men to other kinds of war work. Norman had not registered with a tribunal, electing instead to ignore the arrival of his call-up papers. Nemesis arrived in the form of a police sergeant, who stopped Norman outside the divorce courts where he was working as a court reporter, and questioned him about his liability for military service. Norman refused to give any information and was arrested.[12]

Brought before the magistrates, he initially declined to state whether he was a British subject or unmarried, but when the magistrates ordered him to be remanded in custody, Norman swiftly changed his mind and replied in the affirmative to both questions. He was allowed bail on two sureties of £25 each and ordered to appear again in seven days.

At this second court appearance Norman described himself as an 'author and treasurer of the Stop the War Committee', and claimed to have believed himself exempt from the conditions of the Military Service Act because he had an appeal going through the House of Lords in respect of the seizure of his pamphlets. He also claimed to have appealed direct to the King for exemption (surely not to that son of 'an interfering individual from the House of Hanover'?). Unimpressed, the magistrates fined him 40s and committed him into the custody of a military escort.[13]

Four weeks later Norman was back in court again. As a member of the National Committee of No-Conscription Fellowship he had refused all military orders and was therefore sentenced to two years' imprisonment.[14]

Any interpretation of the events which followed has a tendency to be coloured by the political perspective of the observer. Throughout the summer of 1916 horrendous casualty lists were published on a daily basis, while telegrams containing news of sons and brothers who would never come home brought grief to castle and cottage alike. Against this backdrop of duty and sacrifice, feelings against 'conshies' ran high among all sections of society. In spite of this, there was a considerable degree of respect for men whose religious or political convictions were such that they volunteered to serve at the Front as non-combatants. Conscientious objectors who refused to cooperate with authority in any shape or form were a different matter. These individuals may have seen themselves as serving the common good – perhaps even as heroes and martyrs for a cause; but apart from a minority who shared their political convictions, this was emphatically not the general perception of this acute form of civil disobedience.

There is no doubt that conscientious objectors were treated harshly during their detention. They were sent to military barracks where they were guarded by army personnel, some of whom were men who had sustained injury in the course of their duties, rendering them unfit for active service: this was a potentially explosive situation, fraught with ugly possibilities.

It is clear that some of the military went out of their way to inflict unpleasantness on their 'political' prisoners; but it is equally clear that a small number of conscientious objectors were in league to disobey orders, refusing to bathe, clean out their quarters or adhere to any instructions issued by the men placed in charge of them, sometimes going to considerable lengths to provoke their jailers. Clarence Norman elected to follow this particular path and managed to do so in a well-publicised manner.

On 26 June 1916, Mr Whitehouse MP took advantage of Prime Minister's Questions to ask whether Clarence Norman had been confined to a straitjacket which was too small for him, thus causing him great agony and whether, following a hospital admission, he had been returned to the military barracks and subjected to further brutality by its commandant. Mr Tennant MP replied that although Norman had been placed in a straitjacket because he threatened suicide, he had not been subjected to brutality or unnecessary discomfort.[15]

After gaining some publicity for the conscientious objectors' cause, Norman seems to have done a deal with the authorities because a few weeks later he was allowed to transfer to a detention centre on Dartmoor on the basis that he would carry out work of national importance.[16] Cooperation with the authorities was relatively short-lived. Early the following year Norman was before the courts again, because on 8 February 1917 a number of the conscientious objectors detained at Dartmoor had refused to carry out their work, and investigations persuaded the authorities that this 'strike' had been organised by Norman. Norman denied that this was the case, claiming that the men had taken this course after a ballot. Ballots do not organise themselves, however, and the court decided that Norman had breached his undertaking to carry out war work, and thus forfeited his right to exemption from military service. He was sentenced to a year with hard labour.[17]

Norman's litigation in respect of his confiscated pamphlets had failed, and the costs he had been ordered to pay at the conclusion of the case were still outstanding; but this did not deter him from returning to the courts again as soon as he possibly could. This time he commenced an action in respect of an alleged assault committed against him by Lieutenant Colonel Brooke during his incarceration at Wandsworth Detention Barracks. In addition, he instigated proceedings against William Brace MP, chairman of the Committee on Employment of Conscientious Objectors, seeking a declaration that certain regulations issued by that committee were void, as well as damages in respect of the detention of certain papers under those regulations. He also started an action against Major Reade, the manager of the Princetown Work Centre, alleging illegal arrest. As if this were not enough, he commenced an action against the Director of Public Prosecutions relating to the seizure of his pamphlets, and another against the MP Herbert Samuel in which he claimed that an agreement signed by conscientious objectors was void; finally he instigated a separate action against the officer commanding the Exeter Detention Barracks, seeking a rule nisi for habeas corpus.[18]

Several of these actions were struck out almost immediately, but others proceeded to trial. The case against Brooke came to court in 1917 and lasted for several days, during which it received the newspaper coverage which Norman no doubt desired.[19] The defence did not deny that Norman had been confined in a straitjacket, which they explained was due to Norman having threatened to commit suicide; nor that he had been force-fed through a nasal tube, that being the normal medical action taken when prisoners went on hunger strike. Norman's allegations that Brooke had spat at him, that the straitjacket was too small for him, and that he had been left lying unconscious on the floor for over an hour, were emphatically denied. (Ironically, Mr Tindal Atkinson appeared for Lieutenant Colonel Brooke.) Norman denied that he had ever threatened suicide, but when his diary was produced it contained an entry which was open to that interpretation. Mr Justice Darling – no fan of conscientious objectors – found in Brooke's favour and awarded costs against Norman, who naturally lodged an appeal.

In March 1918 another of Norman's actions was before Darling: this time relating to allegations of illegal arrest at the Exeter Barracks following the refusal of a group of conscientious objectors to carry out their work. Norman fared no better here, with Darling not only finding against him, but also observing that the affidavit sworn by Norman to get the case into court contained a statement which was a deliberate and incontrovertible lie.[20]

By April 1920 Norman's unpaid legal costs exceeded £350. Although incurring few expenses himself as a litigant in person, the other side invariably applied for and were granted a costs order against him, and since the defendants had all been acting in an official capacity, their representation had all been funded by the government. As Norman was a shorthand writer with very little work, living in rented rooms in Chancery Lane, the Treasury solicitors concluded that they had virtually no chance of recovering these costs. In the meantime it was obvious that Norman intended to pursue these various doomed appeals to the bitter end, thereby wasting further time and public money, to say nothing of generating adverse publicity for the Establishment with his continual allegations of false arrest, ill treatment and other unlawful behaviour by government officials. At this point, with the possibility that his personal possessions might be seized in lieu of cash, Norman offered to withdraw all his ongoing litigation, including the appeal against Brooke, if the Treasury would agree to waive all the outstanding costs.[21]

When confronted with this proposal, the first reaction of officials at the Treasury was to be astonished by its bare-faced cheek. The debt was an enormous amount to simply write off and there was no precedent for doing so. They thought it improper that taxpayers would effectively subsidise Norman's 'appetite for litigation'. Aggrieved confidential memos passed between the civil servants and their solicitors.

'[Norman] is evidently a litigious objector of the most obstinate type and should suffer the full consequences of his obstinacy . . . he seems to have deliberately entered upon his various actions fortified by quasi legal knowledge . . . with intent to embarrass public officials.'[22]

The civil servants even discussed the slight possibility that if the Brooke appeal was heard before a more sympathetic judge, Norman might actually win his action, because placing him in a straitjacket could be deemed to constitute actual assault. Very creditably, these officials did not consider that the potential embarrassment of losing the case was any reason for 'buying Norman off' by forgoing their costs, as the Treasury should not 'be party to an arrangement for impeding the course of justice'.[23]

Memoranda went to and fro until September, when it was reluctantly agreed that the costs would be waived providing Norman stopped all the outstanding litigation. The decision was eventually settled by the Treasury Solicitor G.L. Barstow, who considered that pursuing Norman for the outstanding costs 'gives

1. The Sevenoaks Murder postcard.

2. Parts of Ightham Mote by C.E. Luard. *(National Trust)*

3. An artist's impression of the Train Murder which appeared in the *Illustrated Police Budget*.

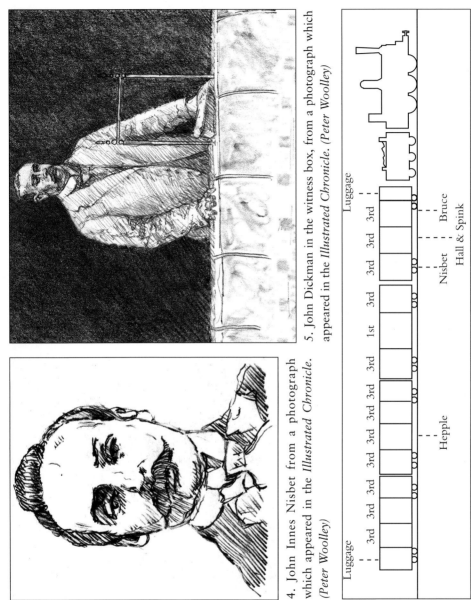

4. John Innes Nisbet from a photograph which appeared in the *Illustrated Chronicle*. *(Peter Woolley)*

5. John Dickman in the witness box, from a photograph which appeared in the *Illustrated Chronicle*. *(Peter Woolley)*

6. The layout of the 10.27. *(Peter Woolley)*

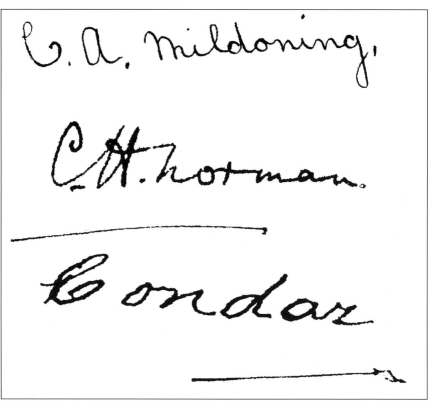

7. The signatures of C.A. Mildoning, C.H. Norman and Condor. *(National Archives)*

8. A view of La Casa. *(Getty Images)*

9. The summerhouse as it would have appeared to anyone approaching from the wicket gate. Caroline Luard's body was discovered at the nearest end of the veranda. (*Peter Woolley*)

10. *Above:* Major General Charles Luard. *(Peter Woolley)*

11. *Above right:* Caroline Luard. The *Kent Messenger* was one of the few newspapers to obtain a copy of an up-to-date photograph.

12. *Right:* Chief Constable Lieutenant Colonel Henry Warde. *(Kent Police Museum)*

13. The inquest at Ightham Knoll – General Luard takes the oath before Coroner Buss. An artist's impression which appeared in the *Daily Graphic*.

14. General Luard at his wife's graveside. *(EMPICS)*

15. Witnesses at the George & Dragon. The artist's impression which appeared in the *Daily Graphic*.

16. Captain Charles Luard and Colonel Charles Warde arrive for the inquest at Teston. *(EMPICS)*

him an advertisement and he will only take up the time of a lot of people who would be better occupied'.[24]

This curtailed Norman's appearances in court for the time being, but not his taste for fighting battles against officialdom. He became a supporter of ex-Inspector John Syme, whose dismissal from the Metropolitan Police in 1910 resulted in a twenty-year campaign for his reinstatement and recompense. Syme's more extreme activities led to various spells of imprisonment, culminating in his being certified and transferred to Broadmoor. In 1931 the Home Office reached a settlement with Syme whereby he received financial compensation and his supporters were able to claim that 'his good reputation had been restored' – although the more sceptical might interpret this formula as a means to quell a nuisance who had provided a focus for political agitation and whose activities had wasted a great deal of public time and money.[25]

Clarence Norman continued to submit letters to the press on a variety of other controversial topics. The ultra-conservative *Times* published one of these in 1929, in which Norman protested at the perceived injustices inherent in the British electoral system. By the 1960s the subject matter of Norman's correspondence had turned away from political topics to discussions of the disposal of stolen goods and the use of the word gimmick.[26] Yet the leopard had not really changed his spots: in the same year that Norman was helpfully explaining the usage of the word gimmick, he was also to be found in court, appealing against a judgment made against him two years earlier.[27]

This particular case found its way into the papers, as markedly eccentric legal actions inevitably do. It appears that in 1960 Clarence Norman had issued a writ – against the Inland Revenue Commissioners no less – claiming that his old age pension, derived from payment of voluntary contributions under the 1946 National Insurance Act, should not be subject to income tax. At the appeal in 1962, the Master of the Rolls commented that 76-year-old Norman had presented his appeal 'with the clarity and courtesy that those who had known him so long would naturally expect', thereby signalling that although Norman's activities had not generally rated a mention in the newspapers, he had continued his one-man crusade in the law courts. In spite of Norman's clarity and courtesy, his Lordship failed to be impressed by the litigant's arguments, and dismissed the appeal. Naturally Norman sought leave to appeal to the House of Lords, but Lord Reid 'did not see how the applicant could get over the position that the Income Tax Act of 1952 made pensions under the National Insurance Act taxable under Schedule E'.[28]

All this may seem a long way from Norman's innocent expression of interest in the Dickman case and the resultant revelations from Sir Sidney Rowan-Hamilton, but a pattern is emerging and it crystallises still further on examination of the papers in the Home Office files on John Dickman.

In Clarence Norman's 1950 submission on capital punishment, he comments that the Dickman case has troubled him for many years. The word 'troubled' suggests a moderate level of concern, in keeping with a signature on a petition, the appeal published in the *Daily News*, and the request that his cabinet minister acquaintance Mr Burns make a personal appeal to Churchill. There is no reason why Norman should have mentioned the various other letters he had written directly to the Home Office regarding the case, but had he done so, his memorandum might have been read as emanating from a somewhat less neutral, disinterested party.

Norman first wrote direct to Winston Churchill from the Commercial Hotel in Leeds, where he was staying while covering the Assizes there. This letter was dated 24 July 1910 and must have been penned as soon as Norman heard that Dickman's court appeal had failed. The letter was respectful in tone and congratulated Churchill on some recent reforms he had effected concerning the treatment of prisoners. It went on to list a whole series of concerns about the trial, including the great hostility which Norman felt had been directed towards Dickman by both judge and counsel.

Norman mentioned that from his position in court, he had been able to observe Cicely Nisbet closely and 'she impressed me most unfavourably'. He was equally unhappy about Hogg and Christie and considered it perfectly obvious that these men had been concealing something about their relations with Dickman. He also mentioned the unsatisfactory nature of the blood evidence, and various other points besides. In conclusion, Norman urged that the sentence be commuted.[29] By the time this letter arrived, the Home Office had already instigated their own investigations into some of these issues, so they took Norman's letter seriously and cross-checked his various comments.

In the meantime the Home Office was also in receipt of a whole series of communications from people and organisations with whom it is now possible to divine both direct and indirect links to Norman, including a petition from readers of *New Age* and a letter from A.R. Orage its editor, who happened to be a personal friend of Norman.[30]

By 6 August Norman knew the final appeal for clemency had failed. He now sent a letter to the Home Secretary couched in much less complimentary terms: 'I deplore the decision [which] has only confirmed my view that so long as matters of life and death are placed in the hands of irresponsible officials, who cannot be punished adequately . . . when a mistake is committed, there is no ground for maintaining the punishment of death . . .'. (This does not altogether square with Norman's subsequent claim that the case 'converted' him into an opponent of capital punishment.) Norman went on to say 'Should Dickman be innocent . . . it would not disturb the digestion or appetite of the gentlemen responsible . . . to execute a man on suspicion . . . is a principle so immoral and horrible that it could only emanate from the minds of the Home Office staff'. A pencil note on the file comments 'Abuse of Home Office staff. Lay by.'[31]

Nor was this Norman's final contribution to the Dickman file. On 11 August he wrote a further letter, requesting the return of a memorandum he had submitted about the case, because 'I have received certain very grave statements confirming my view that John Dickman was wrongly executed [and] it may be necessary for me to take grave action in this matter. I am satisfied that the bag discovered in the Isabella Pit was placed there after the arrest of John Dickman.'[32]

By now Norman was back at home in Hyde Park Mansions, so quite how this 'grave' information confirming John Dickman's innocence had reached him, or where it had come from, is difficult to say.

This missive from Norman was among the last items the Home Office would receive on the subject of John Dickman for fifteen years. Then, in 1925, a remarkable document arrived, courtesy of the editor of *Truth*, to whom it had originally been sent. It was a confession signed by someone calling themselves 'Condor', who claimed to have murdered John Nisbet on 18 March 1910. The Home Office was accustomed to receiving confessions – there had already been one in respect of the Nisbet murder back in 1910 – but several things singled this confession out as particularly unusual, not least the extraordinary length of the document, which ran to approximately 40,000 hand-written words, spread over 205 pages.[33]

It was also unusual to receive a confession so long after a crime, without any fresh developments having occurred to prompt public interest. Furthermore 'Condor' knew a great deal about the murder, including the fact that the smaller set of bullets had been wrapped in paper to make them fit the chamber of a revolver (information probably gleaned from Rowan-Hamilton's book which was published in 1914). 'Condor' claimed to be writing the confession because he had only a short time to live – in which case one might have expected him to be a little less long-winded, as the preparation of these 205 pages must have been the work of many weeks. Perhaps the most curious factor was the peculiar underlying thrust of the confession, which stressed repeatedly the injustice of Dickman's trial, and spent inordinate amounts of time explaining away every single piece of evidence which had convicted him.

As the present writer sat reading this confession, she was struck by the sudden conviction that it had been written by C.H. Norman. Norman had extremely distinctive, showy handwriting, so if he was the author of the 'Condor' confession he would have had to disguise this. Although on the face of it the Condor writing is unlike Norman's, on closer examination there does appear a slight similarity in the formation of some letters. At several points during the confession the handwriting alters, suggesting the writer was not using his accustomed style.

Truth magazine had analysed the confession themselves before passing it on to the Home Office, listing fifteen points which they considered to be likely characteristics of the author:

1. He was probably present at the trial.
2. Must have kept notes and reports.
3. Has an apt mind for this sort of work.
4. A man of abnormal mentality.
5. Has a personal interest in the case.
6. Has a profound belief in Dickman's evidence.
7. For some reason this matter is of permanent concern to him.
8. He has concocted this story to throw doubt on the court's decision.
9. He has a strong antipathy to the local police.
10. He hopes to stimulate reform of police procedure.
11. He suffers from violent malice and is quite unscrupulous.
12. He has no sympathy for the victim, or the victim's relatives.
13. Over elaborates detail.
14. Has a cold blooded style.
15. Has acted for personal ends of his own.[34]

There is no need to point out which of these observations relate directly to what is known about C.H. Norman. Nor was the present writer alone in her suspicions, for on turning to the Home Office staff's observations, one discovers that they too had strong suspicions that the Condor confession was the work of C.H. Norman, noting that 'He is just the person to concoct such a story.'[35]

The Home Office staff had also picked up the similarities in the formation of certain letters, and the way the confession concentrated on the innocence of Dickman, rather than the guilt of Condor. They too had observed how Condor occasionally used the exact phrases which appeared in Norman's original letters regarding the hanging of innocent men on circumstantial evidence; then there was the fact that Norman always insisted the bag had been placed down the Isabella air shaft long after Dickman was in custody, which just happened to be the way Condor described events too. They noted that Norman had always exhibited a marked dislike of Cicely Nisbet and, more significantly, that he had been involved in 'police agitations', specifically citing his active part in the Syme Testimonial Committee.

Describing Norman as 'a most artful dodger', a civil servant who was clearly familiar with his various political activities noted that Norman 'seeks to discredit the administration of justice, and alleges prejudice on the part of the bench and the Home Office'. He went on to speculate that Norman may have had a hand in a great deal of the agitation at the time of the Dickman appeal, although there was nothing tangible to connect him to it.[36]

Finally the Home Office memo pointed out that there were some similarities between the Condor confession and the only other confession ever received in respect of Nisbet's murder. This was a much shorter document, sent to the governor of Newcastle Gaol on 27 July 1910 and signed by a C.A. Mildoning.

C.A. Mildoning claimed to have travelled with Nisbet in the train from Newcastle, shot him, then jumped out of the moving train in advance of Morpeth station. It ended on the unlikely note: 'One murder is quite enough for me to do without being the cause of an innocent man being hung. I hope that J.A. Dickman will forgive me for all he has suffered.'[37]

The Home Office memo further noted 'a very small point . . . the names C.H. Norman, Condor and C.A. Mildoning each have three letters in common – C O N. . .'.

In the light of this emerging picture of C.H. Norman, it is time to revisit his submission to the Royal Commission in 1950.

The first paragraph contains an error of fact, when Norman states that five jurors signed the petition for Dickman's reprieve. This story had been promulgated in 1910, but the Home Office had established that the statement was false. Norman's source for this may have been some half-remembered gossip, but since the story about jurymen signing the petition seems to have originated in the London press, it is legitimate to wonder whether this rumour owed its origins to Norman himself.

The second paragraph of Norman's memorandum opens with the rhetorical query, 'Why raise the question now?' This is an important point and one to which we will return shortly. Norman's answer is that some remarkable and disturbing evidence has come to his attention comparatively recently, a statement with strange echoes of his threatening letter to the Home Office back in 1910.

Norman sets out a story which, taken at face value, sounds eminently reasonable. He explains that although Rowan-Hamilton's book on the Dickman case was published in 1914, he himself did not read it until 1939.[38] Given Norman's considerable personal interest in the case, this long delay seems unlikely. According to Norman, he wrote a letter to Rowan-Hamilton about the book in 1939 and received a reply which made some very startling claims. Apparently Rowan-Hamilton not only believed John Dickman had murdered Mrs Luard, but claimed he had seen definite proof to that effect.

On receipt of these amazing revelations, Norman apparently did nothing. He made no attempt to publicise them and did not even bother to reply to Rowan-Hamilton, questioning some of the obvious peculiarities in the story. Not only is this completely out of character for Norman, it is all the more remarkable because Percy Savage's book had been published only a few years before.[39] The publication of the Savage book had been widely advertised, and here was Norman sitting on some sensational revelations about one of the most famous cases which appeared in it, with alleged links to another case in which he had a particular personal interest – and yet he did not get round to reading the Savage book until 1949. One might think it a singularly unfortunate coincidence that it took twenty-five years for Rowan-Hamilton's book to come to Norman's notice, then more than a decade for him to register the existence of Savage's book.

Once he had read Savage's book, Norman wrote at once to Rowan-Hamilton (whose letter he had fortuitously retained for nearly ten years) reminding him of their previous correspondence and asking him for his observations. Rowan-Hamilton replied on 22 February 1949, offering to write to Norman more fully in due course. Norman replied with thinly veiled hints at the conspiracy between all the major figures involved, which he believed had led to Dickman's receiving an unfair trial. He did not hear from Rowan-Hamilton again.

Norman leaves this absence of reply hanging suggestively in the air, but the reason Rowan-Hamilton failed to respond was probably straightforward – he died in November 1949. From the point of view of sending further information to Norman, this was of course most inconvenient – but it also meant that Rowan-Hamilton was not in a position to confirm or deny that he had written to Norman in the terms quoted.

By 1950 not just Rowan-Hamilton but also Alverstone, Coleridge, Lawrence and Phillimore were all dead – as was Major General Luard. (All this information was available to Norman in 1949, just as it is available to us now, through the pages of *Who's Who* and *Who Was Who*.) As a consequence, there was no living person who could confirm or deny the existence of friendships between these men. Norman's political activities had given him access to many members of the Labour Party, but in spite of name-dropping a cabinet minister and his alleged conversation with Lord Alverstone, Norman simply did not move in the same social circles as General Luard and his supposed friends, and thus it is difficult to see how he would have known of the existence of these friendships.

By 1950 the only living person cited by Norman as a friend of the Luards was Winston Churchill. The late Stephen Knight, a writer on true crime, wrote to Churchill's widow in the 1970s and she replied stating that she had never heard of anyone called Luard.[40] In fairness to Norman's theory, Clementine Hozier did not marry Winston Churchill until the month of General Luard's suicide. It is, therefore, entirely possible that Churchill had run across General Luard before he began to court Miss Hozier. Both men enjoyed social contacts within the same stratum of society. Both moved in political circles (the Luards numbered several Members of

Parliament among their close acquaintance) and in the world of house parties and dinners, it was entirely possible to become briefly acquainted with literally dozens of people. Such slight acquaintance would not necessarily mean that Churchill would have sent a wreath to the Luard funeral, still less that he would have attended it. So although there is no direct evidence of this mutual acquaintance, we cannot entirely rule the possibility out.

Throwing in Churchill's name, however, may have been a long shot on Norman's part. By 1950 the Churchills had been established for many years at Chartwell, which is barely 10 miles from Ightham. Norman may not have appreciated that the Churchills did not move to Kent until the Luards had been dead for more than a decade – had they lived there contemporaneously, it is virtually certain that the two couples would have met socially at some point.

Setting aside the alleged links between the Luards and the lawyers involved with the Dickman trial, two major points stand out in Norman's account of this correspondence. The first is the carefully constructed chronology by which Norman accounts for the way this information only surfaced in 1950 – just a few months too late for Rowan-Hamilton to contradict anything in it. The second is the alleged contents of Rowan-Hamilton's 1939 letter. Forget for a moment the highly unlikely contention that, having become a victim of Dickman's fraud, Mrs Luard would have arranged to meet him secretly at an isolated summerhouse in the middle of the woods. Consider, rather, how the forged cheque or a replica of it could ever have found its way into the hands of Sir Sidney Rowan-Hamilton.

In 1908 cheques were returned to the bank on which they were drawn. When Mrs Luard received her statement she would have noticed something was wrong and initiated a correspondence with her bankers about what appeared to be an error. (If she did not, the matter would never have been flagged up and a replica cheque could never have found its way to Rowan-Hamilton.) Only when the bank responded to her enquiry, perhaps enclosing the original cheque, would the fraud have been confirmed. Assuming she kept either the cheque or the correspondence, it would have been discovered among her papers at Ightham Knoll after her death.

After the General's suicide, the house was searched by the Kent police; assuming they entertained no suspicions about the cheque or correspondence, the discovery would have been left to Mrs Luard's son or her brother Thomas Hartley when they sorted out her estate – something which took place in 1908. If these close family members had entertained the least suspicions about a possible fraud, the evidence would have been handed over to the police and Percy Savage at Scotland Yard would surely have heard about it. The police would have traced the payment back to Dickman, who would have been arrested and charged – almost two years before he was charged with murdering Nisbet.

There are no possible circumstances in which this cheque, to say nothing of the information about it, could have come to the attention of any of those involved in trying the Dickman case, unless it came via the Luard family or the Kent police. Nor is there the remotest likelihood that Dickman, an ex-company secretary who understood the workings of cheques and bank accounts and therefore the inevitability of detection, would have embarked on such a clumsy, pointless fraud in the first place.

Moreover, Rowan-Hamilton's statement that Tindal Atkinson only refrained from questioning Dickman about this because he 'wasn't absolutely certain' is a preposterous one to make – and the retired judge Sir Sidney Rowan-Hamilton would never have made it, knowing perfectly well that Dickman could not be questioned on this entirely unrelated matter when he was standing trial solely for the murder of John Nisbet. Given Norman's own experience of the courts, it would be a remarkably stupid contention even from him.

Subsequent writers, while questioning the peculiarities of Rowan-Hamilton's letter, have generally assumed that he was the author of it. In the light of Clarence Norman's track record and his particular obsession with the Dickman case, it seems virtually certain that Norman himself was the author and originator of the entire correspondence. The careful chronology of events and the highly contrived story of the suspected fraud bear all the hallmarks of the Condor and Mildoning confessions. The language and structure of Rowan-Hamilton's letter read remarkably like Norman's own, while the notion that Dickman's conviction was the subject of a conspiracy, in which the judiciary and Home Office were in cahoots against an innocent man, is entirely in keeping with his tendency towards conspiracy theories, mistrust of officialdom, and what a Home Office official once described as his determination to 'discredit the administration of justice'.

Though there is no hard evidence to prove Norman wrote the whole text with the motive of discrediting the British judicial system, possible malicious intent can be detected in the various falsehoods it contains. His contention that the jurors signed the petition for Dickman's reprieve is incorrect. It may be argued that he was merely repeating something he assumed to be true – but in making so serious an allegation, surely he had a responsibility to get his facts right? He also states that Lord Alverstone made a public statement denouncing the anonymous letter writers who had attacked General Luard. Several public statements were made deploring the letters, but Lord Alverstone made no public pronouncements on the case at all – this is another invention, but again one which Norman thought he could get away with because few people were likely to check back among forty-year-old newspapers to find out the truth.

It is also pertinent to ask how Norman's memorandum ever came into the public domain. When the Royal Commission on Capital Punishment opened in 1949, it invited written submissions from anyone who wished to express a view.[41] Literally hundreds of bodies and individuals responded. In common with all those other submissions, Norman's memorandum would have been read, considered, then filed somewhere within the fourteen boxes of submissions which have been retained in the National Archives. Its contents were thus unlikely ever again to see the light of day – and yet C.H. Norman's memorandum has been quoted in one true crime article after another. How has this come about?

The answer lies in Wilson and Pitman's *Encyclopaedia of Murder*, first published in 1961.[42] In a Prefatory Note the authors thanked various people who had given assistance during the preparation of the book, including 'the correspondent' who sent them a copy of C.H. Norman's memorandum, to whom they apologise for having inexplicably lost track of his identity. Had Colin Wilson and Patricia Pitman uncharacteristically mislaid the covering letter they originally received with the memorandum? Or had there never been a covering letter, identifying the mystery correspondent? For who, apart from Norman himself, would have been likely to have access to a copy of this document? The Royal Commission had presented its report years before, so by 1960 Norman's submission was presumably boxed up with the rest of the Commission's papers and subject to the usual closure rules.

Sending a copy of this memorandum to the compilers of *The Encyclopaedia of Murder* virtually guaranteed it a place in the annals of true crime in perpetuity: but Norman could not risk the authors tracing the memorandum back to him, lest this generate a request to examine the non-existent original letters from Rowan-Hamilton. He probably reasoned that an anonymous submission would be accepted at face value and no attempt made to track down the author – who, if he had been present at a trial in 1910, must necessarily have been quite old when he wrote the memorandum in 1950, and might possibly be surmised to have died by the time Colin Wilson and Patricia Pitman were putting together their book in 1960.

This theory gains unexpected circumstantial support from a subsequent investigation into the Dickman case undertaken by a researcher working on a BBC television series called *Second Verdict*, in which fictional detectives Barlow and Watt attempted to solve real-life murder cases.[43] In this well-researched programme, the characters quoted at length from Norman's memorandum and went a step further than anyone had gone before, by managing to track down Norman's last known address and trace the whereabouts of his papers.

The character of Inspector Watt, taking on the role which in real life had been carried out by the programme's researcher June Leech,[44] claims to have trawled through C.H. Norman's papers, saying that Norman was 'a squirrel' – a man who had saved all manner of ephemera including even tickets and bills, stretching back over three-quarters of a century – and yet among those papers, there was a notable absence of anything connected to the Dickman case.

This was all the more remarkable for the fact that Norman had maintained an interest in the case that outlasted almost every other cause he espoused throughout his long life. In the BBC drama a suggestive silence surrounds the missing Dickman papers, allowing conspiracy theorists to assume that someone had been through Norman's archives and extracted all the relevant material – perhaps in an attempt to cover up the alleged chicanery which marred Dickman's trial. This is a tempting theory – but almost certainly the wrong one. C.H. Norman had blown open the 'conspiracy' back in 1961 with the publication of his memorandum. Any attempted cover-up would be pointless – the matter had been out in the open for years and moreover not one of those involved was left alive.

There is another explanation for the missing papers which, although it can never be proved, is the most likely explanation of all. At some point after compiling his memorandum on capital punishment, C.H. Norman himself removed and destroyed all his papers relating to the Dickman trial. Norman guessed that some future researcher would see his papers as the Holy Grail as far as the Dickman–Luard connection was concerned, and would trawl through those papers in search of further clues.

He knew that his alleged correspondence with Rowan-Hamilton had already been preserved for posterity and that his role in the affair had been accepted at face value. With luck, no one would ever question the authenticity of Rowan-Hamilton's letters. It might be assumed that others apart from Norman had seen the originals – that the originals even existed in some dusty file or other. Providing all the Dickman papers were missing, the logical assumption would be that Rowan-Hamilton's original letters were missing along with the rest of the file. If, however, the Dickman papers were left intact, *apart* from the originals of the letters from Rowan-Hamilton, someone might start to wonder why those letters alone were missing, then begin to question whether the originals had ever existed in the first place. It is just the kind of attention to detail which Norman practised – and if this is the true explanation for the missing papers, then Norman very nearly had the last laugh – managing successfully to hoodwink researchers for more than half a century.

It appears that the alleged link between the murders of Caroline Luard and John Nisbet was no more than a red herring – a cynical ploy by a seasoned campaigner, another manoeuvre in his long battle against authority, essentially motivated by a desire to discredit the British justice system. Clarence Norman probably was convinced of John Dickman's innocence. In spite of being a man of formidable intelligence, he appears to have been capable of convincing himself of the rightness of just about any lost cause which attracted him. It is also possible that his sympathies might have been aroused if he read the local papers at the time of the trial and became aware of Annie Dickman's public espousal of socialism.[45]

Norman may not have been the originator of the alleged connection between John Dickman and Caroline Luard. Crime writer H.L. Adam first set out a version of the story of the forged cheque in his book *CID: Behind the Scenes at Scotland Yard*, which was published in 1931.[46] Here Adam claimed that when Dickman was arrested the police discovered a letter from Mrs Luard in his pocket, from which the whole tale of fraudulent cheques and deception was apparently deduced. The story is such patent nonsense that it does not deserve reproduction. In the absence of a confession from Dickman, the alleged chain of events could only have emerged after a detailed investigation had uncovered other correspondence and documentation: furthermore the list of items discovered on Dickman's person after his arrest did not include a letter from Caroline Luard.[47] The story is clearly a speculative invention on the part of Adam or some third party, which Norman's later version improves upon slightly by omitting some of the least credible details.

Adam claimed that he could not reveal his 'perfectly reliable' source, who was 'a well known Colonial Judge'.[48] It has been inferred from this that Adam's source was none other than Rowan-Hamilton, someone with assumed insider knowledge thanks to his editing the book covering Dickman's trial; and this is no doubt precisely what Adam intended his readers to infer – while at the same time not actually leaving himself open to libel by the mention of a specific name. H.L. Adam was the author of a whole series of books on crime and police work, including *The Story of Crime, Woman and Crime* and *The Police Encyclopaedia*. The Luard murder seems to have been one of his favourites. He described it in *Murder by Persons Unknown*, also published in 1931,[49] when he implied that Mrs Luard had been the victim of an escaped lunatic, again hinting that he had inside information – this time about the carelessness of those charged with the detention of dangerous lunatics.[50]

Adam's 1931 account of the Luard murder is littered with errors and inaccuracies, some of which apparently stem from his own imagination. His sensational accusation against Dickman in his CID volume encompasses the old chestnut that Dickman was also 'known' to be the murderer of Herman Cohen, and here Adam trots out all the errors originally published in the *People* and adds one or two of his own.[51]

The year 1936 saw the publication of *The Fifty Most Amazing Crimes of the Last 100 Years*,[52] a compendium whose contributors included H.L. Adam, who provided the chapter on the Luard murder. He reproduced his original account from *Murder by Persons Unknown*, not bothering to incorporate the allegations about John Dickman, which had provided such a sensational conclusion to his otherwise fairly dull Scotland Yard book. It would appear that Mr Adam was more interested in royalty cheques than accuracy.

The Adam and Norman accounts have too many similarities to be coincidental. Norman was evidently a fan of crime books, so it can be inferred that he read Adam's book on Scotland Yard. He would have instantly appreciated the reference to a 'Colonial Judge' and perceived how, with very little embellishment, he had the necessary elements with which to weave a conspiracy. It is even possible that Norman himself was responsible for planting the idea with H.L. Adam – another anonymous submission to an author perhaps? We will never know.

Clarence Henry Norman died in a Westminster Council nursing home in 1974. His death was registered by a member of the staff and he apparently had no surviving close relatives. In such cases, the deceased's papers are usually kept for a few years against the possibility of any claimants coming forward, and fortunately it appears that a BBC researcher managed to see them while they were still in storage in 1975: they have since been routinely destroyed.[53]

With the Dickman connection finally demolished, it is clear that even had they survived, Clarence Norman's papers would not have yielded up any clues as to the identity of Caroline Luard's killer – the answer to that mystery must be sought elsewhere.

Shocking Tragedy at Seal Chart

Although they came from very different backgrounds, John Alexander Dickman and Charles Edward Luard had one thing at least in common. Each was a younger sibling who had lost his mother in childhood.

Charles Edward Luard came from a respectable upper-class family whose seat was Blyborough Hall in Lincolnshire.[1] The Luards had a strong family tradition of making their careers in the army or the Church, and when Charles was born in Leith on 13 October 1839 his father Robert Luard was serving as a captain in the Royal Artillery. Robert Luard was the youngest son of Peter John Luard, who had inherited Blyborough Hall at the end of the eighteenth century. Robert's wife Mary Elmhirst came from an identical background: her father achieved the rank of colonel and she too came from Lincolnshire. When Charles was born in 1839 the couple already had an elder son Robert – both boys were destined for the army, but Mary, alas, did not live to see either of them reach manhood.

When Charles was 11 years old, his father remarried. It was rather a grand match, to an heiress, Lewis Marianne Bigge, neé Selby, a widow several years his junior, who brought two children to the marriage, her son Charles, then aged 15, and a daughter Sybil, who was 4. To the four children they already had, Robert and Marianne, as she was usually known, added two more, Bertram born in 1853 and Beatrice born in 1855.

It was entirely due to his stepmother that Charles Luard's life became inextricably linked to Ightham. Marianne was the daughter of Prideaux Selby, the famous artist and ornithologist, whose family estate was at Twizell in Northumberland. He inherited Ightham

Mote in 1845, on the death of his cousin's widow Elizabeth Selby, and on Prideaux Selby's death in March 1867 the house passed to his daughter Marianne.

Ightham Mote is a uniquely beautiful moated manor house, parts of which date back to the fourteenth century. Frequently described as the loveliest medieval manor house in Britain, it casts a spell over all who see it and the young Charles Luard was clearly no exception. Although the Mote did not technically become Marianne's until 1867, she and her husband spent a good deal of time there before that date. They were married in Ightham church, and Robert Luard was listed as a resident there in the 1850s, so it is possible to conjecture that the young Charles spent some of his school holidays and army leaves in this most romantic of settings.

There had been Selbys at Ightham Mote for nearly three hundred years so when Marianne inherited the house from her father she and her husband formally changed their name to Luard-Selby (sometimes rendered Selby-Luard) to maintain the tradition. Their family life seems to have been a happy one – theirs had certainly not been a match made for financial expediency because Robert Luard, although unmistakably a gentleman, had retired from the army on half pay in 1845 at the recommendation of the medical board and, being the eighth son in a large family, had few financial expectations.

Nor does there seem to have been friction between their various children and stepchildren. When Charles and Caroline Luard died in 1908, all of Charles's surviving stepbrothers and sisters were still in close touch and attended their funerals.

During their thirty years at the Mote, the Luard-Selbys fulfilled their duties as members of the local gentry: Robert became a Justice of the Peace and on a lighter note, some of the extended family occasionally turned out to play cricket for the village team, as occurred in July 1875, when Plaxtol took on Seal in a local derby. Captain Charles Luard was out lbw for 17, but none the less Plaxtol won the day.[2]

That same month, the family celebrated two weddings. Marianne's daughter Sybil married Dr William Church at Ightham, while the airier church at nearby Plaxtol was the scene of Captain

Charles Luard and Miss Caroline Hartley's nuptials. The latter ceremony was performed by one of the plentiful supply of Luards in holy orders, who traditionally turned out to marry their various relations in every generation.

It was somewhat unusual for the wedding to take place from the groom's home, but this may have been partly due to the fact that Caroline's father had been dead for many years, coupled with the expediency of the bridegroom's being able to travel more easily to Kent from his London posting.

Charles's bride Caroline Hartley was the youngest daughter of Thomas and Georgiana Hartley, of Gillfoot in Cumberland. The Hartleys were landed gentry and marriage to an army captain could have been seen as a step down in the world for 'Daisy', as Caroline was frequently known. All sources agreed, however, that Charlie and Carrie were very much in love and that their married life was 'one long honeymoon'.[3]

Two sons were born to the marriage, Charles Elmhirst Luard on 5 August 1876 (Charles Luard, like John Dickman, honouring his deceased mother in the name of his eldest son) and Eric Dalbiac Luard, born on 6 April 1878. (Dalbiac was another family name, which had belonged to Charles Luard's grandmother). Both boys would follow their father and grandfather into the British army.

As an army officer's wife, Caroline could expect a peripatetic lifestyle. In one respect they were particularly fortunate because Charles's thirty-year career coincided with a period of relative peace throughout the Empire. His overseas postings were to Corfu, Gibraltar, Bermuda and Natal, and as a Royal Engineer his work was not infrequently concerned with interesting building projects at home, where he was responsible for laying out the United Services Recreation Ground at Portsmouth and the reconstruction of the Household Cavalry Barracks at Windsor. The closest Charles Luard seems to have come to active military service in the usual sense was when he happened to be stationed in London during the Fenian disturbances in 1867. There is no reason to believe that he was not a competent and resourceful officer when the need arose. In 1864 Luard was the lieutenant in command of a company at Woolwich, when an exploding powder magazine at Erith blew a 100-yard breach in the Thames wall. Under Luard's instructions, the men closed the breach in the course of a single tide, thereby averting the flooding of towns and countryside for several miles around.[4]

On 21 October 1887 Charles Luard retired with the honorary rank of Major General. Strictly speaking, neither he nor Caroline had any surviving connections with Ightham. His father had died at the Mote almost seven years before and after her husband's death Marianne went to live with her eldest son in Wales. The Mote had been let to tenants for several years and would be sold in 1889, the family fortunes not having kept pace with the running costs of such an expensive house. (In 1880 Major Robert Luard's personal estate was valued at less than £100 and a decade later his widow left less than £7,000.)

Nonetheless, Charles and Caroline's love affair with the district was undiminished and they took temporary lodgings in Tonbridge while looking for a house. They found what they wanted in the shape of Ightham Knoll, a house situated just outside the village of Ightham, surrounded by 8 acres of garden and available on a long lease. They took up residence on 21 February 1888.[5]

Major General Luard was already a respected figure in the neighbourhood thanks to his longstanding connections there. He was appointed a Justice of the Peace and elected to serve on Kent County Council. He became a member of his parish council and served as a church warden at Ightham, took an active interest in local education and supported military charities. Caroline was also active in the community and well known for her charity work. After her death, one local resident would describe her as a 'Lady Bountiful', but intending none of the sarcastic connotations which such a phrase might imply today.[6]

The Luards had many friends in the area and enjoyed a particularly close friendship with the Wilkinson family who owned the nearby Frankfield estate. Both families shared a sense of duty and obligation to the less fortunate and together with one of the Wilkinson daughters Mrs Luard sponsored a convalescent home for poor children from London. It was a tiny affair, set up in a cottage on the Wilkinson family estate, but it offered a lifeline to a handful of children suffering from conditions such as rickets and psoriasis and it was said that Mrs Luard 'would do anything for those children.'[7]

In addition to their civic and charitable work, the Luards led an active social life, but although they mixed with the cream of county society they were not enormously wealthy. Their two maids, cook and gardener were a far cry from the small regiment of staff Caroline had been accustomed to in childhood and Ightham Knoll, although boasting half a dozen bedrooms, including a servants' wing, was a modest dwelling in comparison with the homes of many of their friends and relatives. Caroline's brother Tom, for example, lived in the palatial Armathwaite Hall on the shores of Bassenthwaite, which he had bought and modernised at huge expense in 1880. Such things are relative, however – Charles Luard left an estate worth in excess of £7,000 when he died. He and his wife lived comfortably and there was no question of money problems.

Their life at Ightham was not untouched by sadness. In March 1890 Charles's stepmother Marianne was laid to rest alongside her husband in Ightham churchyard. Then, at the end of 1903, the couple suffered a much greater personal loss when their younger son Eric died from a fever contracted while serving in the Somaliland campaign. He was only 25 years old and his death echoed an earlier tragedy, inasmuch as Charles's elder brother Robert had died aged only 20 when a powder magazine accidentally exploded while he was serving as an ensign with the 9th Foot.

Lieutenant Eric Luard's body was conveyed home for burial on the SS *Avoca* – unbeknown to his grieving parents, his coffin was concealed by a plain outer packing case labelled EDL and appeared on the ship's manifest under the heading 'Natural History Specimens' in order not to upset the ship's crew.[8] This outer disguise had all disappeared by the time the coffin was loaded on to the train bound for Wrotham station, where Major General Luard was waiting to escort his son's body on its final journey. Eric Dalbiac Luard was buried in the churchyard at Ightham with a simple stone to mark the place; the inscription reads:

Eric Dalbiac Luard – Lieutenant in the Queens Own (Royal West Kent) Regiment & in the Kings African Rifles – died in the Somaliland Campaign on 13 November 1903 age 25 – brought home to Ightham on 12 July 1906.

His parents also erected a brass plaque in his memory on the north side of the altar in Ightham church. After a period of mourning, Charles and Caroline Luard's lives continued much as before.

In *Who's Who* Charles Luard listed his recreations as fishing, shooting and golf, but there was much more to him than that. His surviving drawings of Ightham Mote reveal a gifted artist with a sensitive touch. He also produced treatises on various subjects, including one on the Mote, published in 1893.[9] By then the house belonged to Sir Thomas Colyer-Ferguson, but the Luards were regular guests there and aware of the various improvements and alterations the new owner had made.

Charles Luard's *Ightham Mote – Description & Plan* first appeared in a publication called the *Builder*, but owing to the considerable interest in the house it was subsequently reproduced as a stand-alone volume. Several things stand out about this little book. The first is that it is intelligently written and not merely a retired country gentleman waffling in print. The second is that when the Luard-Selbys inherited Ightham Mote in the 1860s, they clearly instigated what was effectively the first serious historical and archaeological research into the house: again suggesting a family whose interests ranged rather wider than mere 'huntin', shootin' and fishin''. The third and strongest impression is of Charles Luard's evident love for the Mote. His descriptions of the lawn's 'velvet slope', the 'noble cedars', the careful reassurance that the flow of water from the moat into the lower pond ensures the house is free of damp, all betray a deep affection for the place.

Nothing in any of this suggests that Major General Charles Edward Luard was the kind of man who would coldly execute his wife on an August day in the thirty-third year of their marriage – and yet within days of her murder local people and strangers alike would begin to suspect him of doing exactly that. There would be rumours of infidelity and jealousy and intimations that in taking his own life, the General had 'fallen on his sword': taken the honourable way out, rather than face trial and conviction.

The first senior police officer to reach the scene of Caroline Luard's murder on 24 August 1908 was Superintendent Albert Taylor of Sevenoaks, who arrived there at 7.50 that evening.[10] By the time he reached the little summerhouse in the woods, dusk was falling and the victim had been dead for about four hours. Television drama has ensured that most people today are aware of the need to leave a crime scene untouched until the police arrive, but such requirements were not necessarily part of the Edwardian psyche.

Before Taylor's arrival, the victim's husband had touched her body, as had a local doctor, and any evidence in the vicinity of the summerhouse had been potentially contaminated by the arrival of the owner's butler, the local constable and the vicar from the nearby church. The summerhouse itself had been unlocked and candles obtained from within to illuminate the scene, and very shortly after the arrival of Superintendent Taylor, a local newspaper reporter responding to a hot tip would also arrive. The reporter walked unimpeded along the path which led directly on to the summerhouse veranda where Caroline Luard's body had been found and, before being ushered aside, had even managed to get close enough to observe Dr Mansfield making his preliminary examination of the dead woman.[11]

This was not a propitious start to a murder investigation and although Superintendent Taylor has subsequently been criticised for allowing Mrs Luard's body to be removed and for failing to seal off the scene of the crime, the truth is that the area had already been infiltrated and contaminated long before he gained control of it.

Taylor made notes of the scene and did his best in the failing light. The ground around the veranda where Mrs Luard's body had fallen was hard and yielded no footprints, but he did find one set of tracks leading away from the side of the building, through a gate which led to some stables, about 40 yards away. A few yards on from the stables, he could see where the bracken had been trodden down alongside a hedge which headed north towards the fish ponds from which the woods derived their name.

Once Dr Mansfield had made a brief examination, Taylor gave permission for the body to be moved. It was lifted on to a mattress borrowed from one of the camp beds inside the bungalow, then carried inside the building. The Revd Scott, vicar of nearby St Lawrence's, had persuaded Major General Luard to leave the scene for a while, but the General soon returned and requested permission to take his wife's body home. Taylor acceded to the request and the mattress bearing Caroline Luard's body was carried out on to a horse-drawn fruit van, the only conveyance which could be procured at short notice, and carried back to Ightham Knoll under cover of darkness, with the General walking at the head of the melancholy procession for most of the way.[12]

Taylor had already sent word to the Chief Constable of Kent, together with an urgent request for more manpower. Leaving a solitary constable to stand guard at the Casa (an unenviable task in the lonely woods), together with Sergeant Paramour and a couple of other constables Taylor did what he could to make a limited search of the darkened woods and nearby fields in the vague hope of flushing out the perpetrator of the deed.

Beyond this damp, almost deserted stretch of woodland the murder was an immediate sensation. Although the first news of the crime cannot have reached the outside world before the early evening of 24 August, by the following morning the London dailies were full of it. In spite of getting some details muddled – the Luards were gifted a third son they did not have by one newspaper, and Mrs Luard's age was wildly inaccurate in another – a huge amount of information pertaining to the crime managed to find its way into the press within the space of the first twelve hours. Some editors managed to obtain photographs of the General, his late wife and even of the summerhouse itself for their morning editions.

Readers learned that the General and his wife had set out on a walk to the golf club, parting at the wicket gate a short distance from La Casa. Details of Mrs Luard's fatal injuries were revealed: she had been shot twice, one bullet entering just below her left eye, leading to a widespread assumption that she had been facing her attacker when the fatal shots were fired.

Perhaps more surprising was the way reporters were already aware of two witnesses who had heard the shots. One of these was a 'woman in her garden' and the other 'a farm hand', and according to virtually every account published on the day following the murder both these individuals placed the time of the shots at around 3.30. These witnesses also stated that no cries for help had been heard before the shots were fired.

Robbery was suggested as a motive by several papers. Mrs Luard's rings were missing, as was her purse – although it was not thought she would have been carrying very much cash in it. Tramps and hop-pickers were suspected and there was talk of a tramp being seen leaving the woods on the afternoon of the murder.

Even as householders throughout Britain took in the details over the breakfast table, or on their journey to work, Ightham was being invaded by dozens of reporters, all of them desperate for an exclusive and eager to be among the first to report an arrest.

Superintendent Taylor's reinforcements had arrived and policemen drafted in from all over the county began to search the woods in the pouring rain, the dreadful weather which had been a feature of that August having returned with a vengeance. Local ponds were dragged in what proved a vain attempt to locate the murder weapon. Personal control of the investigation had now been assumed by Lieutenant Colonel Henry Warde, the Chief Constable of Kent.

By 1908 Warde had been Chief Constable of the county for thirteen years, but he was not a career policeman. During the late Victorian era it was not in the least unusual for the post of Chief Constable to be awarded to a retired army officer with good family connections but no experience of police work at all. (Captain Fullarton James of the Northumberland force was an identical case. Warde's immediate predecessor, Major Edwards, another retired army officer, just happened to be the son-in-law of the Chairman of Kent County Council.) By the end of the nineteenth century this practice was already attracting adverse comment so when news of Warde's appointment became known in 1895 there was, predictably, some criticism in certain sections of the press, where it was described as 'a piece of unscrupulous jobbery' with one writer questioning what a cavalry officer could possibly know about police work. In 1895, however, it was not what you knew, but whom you knew that counted.[13]

Henry Murray Ashley Warde was one of the Wardes of Squerryes Court in Kent, where he was born in 1850. His brother was Colonel Sir Charles Warde MP of Barham Court in Kent: both men were well known among the local gentry from whom were drawn the Justices of the Peace who played a part in the selection process for the new Chief Constable. Both were personal friends of Charles Luard and it is possible that Luard himself, who was both a JP and a county councillor in 1895, had a hand in Henry Warde's appointment. If so, then the saying that you get the policing you deserve can seldom have been more apposite, and in the long run General Luard's close connections with the Chief Constable would do him more harm than good.

In fairness to Henry Warde, the standards in place by the end of the twentieth century cannot be equated with those he encountered when he took up his post at the conclusion of the nineteenth. When Warde took over as Chief Constable, police recruits joining the Kent force received no basic training, and it was Warde himself who introduced the first voluntary classes in basic police law and procedure in 1903. He also led a drive towards greater discipline and fitness, instituting annual sports days from 1898 – although his various edicts with regard to marching, church attendance and the wearing of facial hair sound a note both militaristic and paternalistic to the modern ear. It was also Warde who, several years before the Luard murder, had initiated Kent's first 'Detective Branch', which consisted of four men led by Sergeant (later Detective Inspector) Edwin Fowle.

From this it can be seen that in 1908 the county force was still ill equipped to cope with a major manhunt, and Warde had not been involved for 24 hours before he decided to call in Scotland Yard.

By 26 August, the reporters besieging the district had plenty more copy to telegraph back to their papers. Local people were only too willing to talk about the late Mrs Luard, who according to the *Maidstone & Kentish Journal* was 'so well respected in the neighbourhood . . . it seems useless to suppose the murder was one of vengeance or spite. . .'.[14]

A local labourer told the press he had always had the greatest respect for Mrs Luard, who 'was one of those who would always speak to a working man, if she knew him. . . . when my arm was bad last year and I couldn't work, she met me twice and each time enquired how I was getting on and gave me something out of her purse. . . . she was a very kind lady and always had a pleasant word for me.'[15]

One of the Wilkinsons' tenants, whose cottage was next door to the one where Mrs Luard had once helped run the children's convalescent home, declared, 'Mrs Luard was a good lady. . . . She was so loved by the children, for she was very fond of them and would go out of her way to help them in any way she could.'[16]

The murder had taken place on the Frankfield estate and interviews had been obtained from various witnesses who lived there. The 'farm hand' who had heard the gunshots turned out to be Daniel Kettel, one of the gardeners on the estate. Kettel told reporters that he had heard the three shots while walking along the drive with a workmate. Although hearing shots was a common occurrence, his companion had said, 'Who's that shooting at the cottage?' Kettel had replied, 'I expect it's Mitchell, shooting squirrels.' Mr Mitchell frequently shot squirrels in his adjacent nut plantation and thus the two men thought nothing of it.

It is significant that although Kettel's companion queried who was shooting at the cottage, Kettel told reporters that he himself initially thought 'the shots appeared to come from a neighbouring farm' – an impression which makes perfect sense of his own reply. Kettel strongly denied reports which had appeared in some papers, claiming there had been a lot of shooting in the neighbourhood that afternoon. He had only heard three shots, the first and second of which were about half a minute apart. He reckoned he had walked about 60 paces between hearing the first and second shots.[17]

The 'woman in the garden' had also been tracked down and was pictured with her daughter, who had also heard the shots – the first shot having been followed after a brief interval by two more in quick succession. These witnesses were Anna and Edith Wickham, respectively the wife and daughter of the Wilkinsons' coachman Fred. Like Daniel Kettel, they lived in a cottage on the Frankfield estate, and happened to be out in their garden at the time of the shots. Some accounts had Mrs Wickham sitting in her garden, while others had her just stepping outside the front door for a breath of air. Whichever was correct, the Wickhams' cottage was the closest dwelling to the summerhouse by some considerable distance, so if the shots were fired while she was in the garden, Mrs Wickham would undoubtedly have heard them.

As half the male population of Kent seems to have numbered shooting either among its recreations, or else as a means of protecting crops from predators, or putting food on their table, the sound of gunshots must have frequently disturbed the silence of the countryside and yet, strangely enough, just as Daniel Kettel and his companion had exchanged remarks on hearing the shots, so these particular shots had also provoked comment from Mrs Wickham. She confirmed there had been a gap between the first two reports and added the information that the first shot sounded as if it had struck something hard and close up, leading her to remark to her daughter, 'What a peculiar sound.' After the second and third shots rang out, Mrs Wickham added, 'They meant to kill that thing well at any rate.'

Like Daniel Kettel, this witness was at pains to represent the afternoon as being particularly quiet up to that point. 'Even the jays weren't screaming.'

Mrs Wickham had something more to add in that she had been the first to encounter the General after he discovered his wife's body. He had arrived at her cottage in search of her husband: 'He was as white as death and his face seemed drawn and twisted in agony. He rushed into the garden and cried out for my husband. He could only speak in gasps and groans and broken snatches. Beyond that he wanted my husband, I couldn't make out what the matter was.'[18]

Mrs Wickham told the General that her husband was still at work up at the Frankfield stables, in which direction the distraught man now set out. The story is taken up by Fred Wickham, who told the *Daily Chronicle*'s representative, 'The General rushed into the stable yard, where I was cleaning harness. I asked him what was the matter but he could not speak. I took him by the arm and led him into the harness room.' Here Wickham found the General a seat, before fetching Herbert Harding, the Wilkinsons' butler, from the house.[19]

With the Wilkinson family all away, Harding was the most senior figure available and he did his best to take charge of the situation, attempting to calm the General and offering him some medicinal brandy, which was declined. Harding too gave his account of the affair to the press: 'I was called to the harness room, and found the General sitting on a box, in a terrible condition of grief. He seemed completely broken and on the point of collapse: so much so that we could not get any intelligible idea of what had happened to Mrs Luard.'[20]

It is impossible to be sure precisely what words passed between the General and Harding at this point. In some versions of the story, the General does seem to have gasped out the words 'Shot – at the Casa'. In others, Harding only begins to understand that a murder has been committed once the men were actually *en route* to the summerhouse, when the General suddenly burst out: 'The brutes. They have killed her.'

Nor is it clear at what stage Harding sent someone to notify the police. One account implies that this happened prior to his leaving the stable yard, but in others, including Wickham's interview published in the *Daily Chronicle*, it appears that the General and Harding returned to the summerhouse without summoning any outside assistance, and with Fred Wickham and one John Kettel trailing respectfully behind.

This is almost the only mention of John Kettel. He was never called to give evidence or interviewed by the newspapers, although if the *Daily Chronicle* is correct, he was a witness to these events. The farm steward on the Frankfield estate was called John Kettel and it is entirely possible that he happened to be in the vicinity of the main house or stable yard when all this excitement erupted. It is also possible that the newspaper had muddled him up with Daniel Kettel, the gardener who heard the fatal shots and would have been working reasonably close to the house. If, in fact, it was Daniel Kettel, rather than John, who accompanied this little party up to the summerhouse, then we have a situation in which the two witnesses who would provide vital testimony about the timing of the murder were also among the very first to be on the scene when the body was discovered. If Daniel Kettel was among the little crowd who had gathered up at the summerhouse, this might help explain how at such an early stage the press had got hold of the fact that the 'farm labourer' had heard the shots.

Both Wickham and Harding concurred that the General's grief was terrible to behold. He was groaning and crying and when they finally reached the veranda, he threw himself on to his knees beside his wife, seized her hand and cried out, 'She's dead, she's dead. Maggie, Maggie.'[21]

The alleged use of this name is somewhat confusing. Nowhere apart from the various newspaper accounts of this interview with Harding is there any reference to the victim's being called 'Maggie'. Maggie is not generally used as an abbreviation for either of Mrs Luard's names, which were Caroline Mary. Indeed, most sources claim that Mrs Luard was known to her family and friends as Daisy, and this was borne out by wreaths addressed to 'Daisy Luard' at her funeral. It is possible that the General did use the name 'Maggie', but it seems more likely that Harding misheard him, or else that the reporters misheard Harding.

Harding described the scene which confronted them in some detail: explaining that the body was lying face downwards, with a glove to one side and an umbrella to the other, while the lady's hat lay a short distance away. Harding considered that from the position of the body Mrs Luard must have been walking across the veranda when her killer struck. He speculated that this person had hidden in an angle of the building, then sprung out on Mrs Luard. There was no sign of a struggle, he said, and no footprints in the immediate area, where the ground was hard or moss-covered.

Even the General himself could not escape reporters, who waylaid him when he set out for a walk on the evening following the murder. It is impossible to say whether he was subjected to questions by a whole pack of pressmen, or whether the *Daily Telegraph*'s 'Sevenoaks correspondent' was one and the same as the *Star*'s 'special reporter' and the *Daily Mail*'s 'Special Correspondent'.

The General said he wished to thank the countless people who had sent him letters and telegrams of condolence. He had already received nearly forty telegrams. He could not discuss the crime as it was too painful, but praised the police and said they were doing their best – 'working splendidly and doing all they can' was the *Daily Mail*'s rather hearty version. Asked about the possible use of bloodhounds, the General said he rather favoured the idea, but would not sanction it without first consulting Colonel Warde. With regard to the evidence that a tramp might have been seen leaving the woods, the General said he 'cannot personally put much faith in this as tramps often leave the woods'.[22]

Aside from the various personalities involved, the press were at pains to explain the actual site of the murder to their readers. Photographs and sketches of the Casa from various angles began to appear in the papers, coupled with differing descriptions of the size and situation of the building. There was a distinct divergence of opinion between those who said the place was well known locally, standing just off a well-frequented bridle path, as represented by *The Times*, and those such as the *Maidstone & Kentish Journal* which said it was in such a secluded spot that a great many local people had not previously known of its existence.

The actual location of the summerhouse, the route of the Luards' walk to it and the General's return journey home were represented in a whole variety of ways, with some papers reproducing maps and diagrams, most of which were entirely speculative and inaccurate. Most agreed, however that the Casa was a bungalow which stood in private woodland on the Frankfield estate, which was the home of Mr Horace Wilkinson, an elderly stockbroker and friend of the Luards. The bungalow had several rooms and was used not only as a venue for teas and picnics, but also for overnight stays, when the family felt so inclined. At the time of the murder the Wilkinson family were away from home and thus the summerhouse had been locked up for several weeks. The building could only be accessed via private paths across Mr Wilkinson's land, so apart from friends such as the Luards who had permission to walk there, no one ought to have been anywhere near it on the day of the murder.

Some papers continued to contend that the murder had almost certainly been a robbery, carried out by the sort of dangerous tramps they supposed must habitually be roaming the neighbourhood. Mrs Luard's missing rings were described and were obviously of considerable value, particularly the antique setting of diamonds which was over a hundred years old and had belonged to her mother. This ring had a large diamond in the centre, surrounded by eight smaller diamonds; her plain gold wedding band and a gold ring inscribed in blue enamel with the word *ISHI* (which means husband) had also been taken. According to the *Daily Telegraph*, one unnamed villager knew that the summerhouse had been broken into and ransacked by tramps only a few months before,[23] while the *Daily Chronicle* reported that one of Horace Wilkinson's sons had been attacked by a group of poachers while lying in a hammock at the summerhouse.[24] Both these stories were unattributed and almost certainly apocryphal.

In the meantime other theories were already surfacing. The suggestion that Mrs Luard had known her assailant and therefore faced him without alarm or suspicion had been made the day before. Now a rumour flew round to the effect that Mrs Luard had been murdered by a woman: or else by someone who had stalked her through the woods, waiting for an opportunity when she was alone. Over the next few days, to these ideas would be added the theory that Mrs Luard might actually have met her killer deliberately. The information that Caroline Luard was much younger than her husband and still an attractive woman began to insinuate its way into the story.

Another element to emerge was the arrangements for the inquest, which was to be held at Ightham Knoll on 26 August. It was not especially unusual to hold an inquest in a large private house, particularly in remoter rural districts which sometimes had no other premises in the immediate vicinity with any sizeable rooms at all. However, this was not the case in Ightham, where public occasions could be accommodated in the biggest room at the George & Dragon Inn. Village inns provided regular locations for country inquests and the body of the deceased was not infrequently placed in the cellar or an outbuilding pending the event. As it was customary for the inquest jury to be shown the body, the inquest was always sited within a convenient distance of where the deceased was lying; but it was perfectly satisfactory for this to be in a separate building, a short walk away.

The decision to open the proceedings at Ightham Knoll would occasion much criticism.[25] Inquests were supposed to be public occasions with free access to the press and, in a case such as this one which had aroused nationwide interest, demand for press accommodation was likely to be high. Under such circumstances, there was an expectation that the proceedings would be held in as large a room as was available – and the dining room at Ightham Knoll, while a generously proportioned room in the domestic context, was completely inadequate to accommodate the numbers wishing to attend. Nevertheless, the inquest was scheduled to open there at 3.15 – the same hour as had been set for Mrs Luard's funeral on 28 August – which, as the *Daily Mirror* helpfully explained to its readers, was 'the exact hour at which Mrs Luard must have met her death'.[26]

10

'It was at 3.15 exactly'

On Wednesday 26 August the normally peaceful junction near the entrance to the General's property was the scene of unprecedented activity. A small crowd hoping to gain admission to the inquest had begun to gather at an early hour, and stood speculating over the various comings and goings as they occurred throughout the morning.[1]

Among the more interesting arrivals were Scotland Yard detectives Chief Inspector Scott and Detective Sergeant Savage. The availability of these specialist detective officers was a recent innovation. Just over two years previously the Home Office had issued a directive making the services of Scotland Yard available to all the county forces.[2] A few forces initially chose not to utilise this facility, being suspicious and resentful of outsiders, even though some forces still had no 'detective branch' of their own. In this instance Chief Constable Warde had sensibly decided to apply for assistance and Scott and Savage arrived by the morning train.

Their first port of call was Ightham Knoll, where they talked to General Luard at length before being driven away to examine the murder scene. It would appear that the investigations were being conducted from Ightham Knoll that morning, because Scott and Savage returned to the house several times, each time being driven away again, as the pressmen assumed, in pursuit of urgent clues. The local detectives, represented by Detective Inspector Fowle, Superintendent Ford of Malling and Sergeant Paramour who had been appointed Coroner's Officer for the case, were also observed entering and leaving through the General's gate.

Two police constables had been put on guard at the entrance to the drive, where some pressmen had taken up their station before noon, a rumour having already begun to circulate regarding the shortage of space for them inside. The house itself was tantalisingly out of sight, hidden by the shrubbery which grew alongside the sloping curve of the drive. The local and London press had invaded the area in force, and by 2.30 at least thirty photographers and journalists were crowding the narrow lane, which together with the nearby main road was lined with all manner of conveyances by which they had arrived. Within the next half hour their numbers had almost doubled, and were considerably augmented by a substantial group of villagers who entertained hopes of admission.

Together with the police officers and witnesses in the case, the seventeen jurors had to be ushered through this throng. Chief Constable Warde, his brother Colonel Warde the MP and Major Lafone the Deputy Chief Constable were among the early arrivals, driving up together in a dog cart. Then at a few minutes before 3.00, Superintendent Taylor came down to the gates to explain that as there was insufficient space to accommodate all the press, the Chief Constable had given instructions as to who was to be admitted.

It was occasionally the situation that an inquest into a sensational case had to be convened in premises too small to accommodate the numbers of pressmen who wished to attend. In such cases, the journalists invariably arrived at a gentleman's agreement whereby those who were admitted would freely share their notes with those who were not, the decision on which of them would hear the evidence generally being arrived at among the journalists themselves. There is no question that holding the inquest at Ightham Knoll when there were more suitable premises readily available nearby, coupled with the Chief Constable's high-handed approach to the journalists present, generated a considerable amount of resentment.[3]

The reporter representing the *Kent Messenger*, who was among the fortunate half dozen to gain admission, noted (possibly not without some satisfaction) that on learning of the Chief Constable's edict, 'Quite a scene followed at the gates. Some clambered over the low wall. Others tried to get past the constable on duty by ruses and excuses of all kinds.' When this did not work, and a 'strong petition' to the coroner having likewise failed, the crowd reluctantly dispersed.[4]

The *Sevenoaks Chronicle* reports that 'the police had to forcibly drive the unsuccessful applicants from the drive'. In their version of events, it was actually a member of their own staff, Mr A. Foster McAdam, who assisted in the selection of the lucky few who were permitted entry. Whichever was the case, the matter had been badly handled and a number of papers recorded their disgust the following day, pointing out that men from *The Times*, the *Daily Telegraph* and similar well-respected publications had been excluded in favour of 'three sensational half penny papers . . . and Sevenoaks reporters'.[5]

Holding the inquest in the General's house, while giving the appearance to outsiders of making things as convenient as possible for him, must in reality have increased his sensation of being under siege. Ightham Knoll was normally a very private place, a substantial creeper-clad house, set in large mature gardens and invisible from the road. Now it was being invaded by a host of curious strangers, who recorded for the edification of the general public how the wide hall was furnished with 'soldier souvenirs', such as panther skins. Not only did the intruders take over his dining room, but even the privacy of his wife's bedroom was violated when the inquest jury, accompanied it would appear by at least one representative of the press, trooped upstairs to view her body, which lay in a darkened room filled with flowers.[6]

The coroner and his assistant were late arriving. While awaiting him, the senior police officers occupied themselves in examining the bullets which had been extracted from Mrs Luard's head and were now lying in ointment boxes on the dining table. The dining room itself, which measured only around 25 feet by 15 feet, must have felt positively claustrophobic. In the centre of the room the dining table had been covered with a red cloth and the coroner, Thomas Buss, was seated at the centre of one side of it, with his back to the fireplace and his assistant on his left. A chair had been provided immediately to the coroner's right for the witnesses. Facing the coroner were the Warde brothers, Major Lafone, Detectives Scott and Fowle and Superintendent Taylor. Those members of the seventeen-strong jury who could not be fitted on to the window seat which occupied most of one side of the room were seated on cane chairs, borrowed from the local school for the occasion and placed against the wall at right angles to the window, while the last remaining half dozen seats at the opposite end of the room had been allocated to the selected members of the press.

Once the jury had been sworn in, the first witness was called.[7] This was General Luard, who entered the room slowly, accompanied by his faithful Irish terrier Scamp. In the day and a half since bringing his wife's body home, the General had been very busy. In addition to replying personally to all the messages of condolence, he had prepared an account of his movements on the day of the murder, which ran to several foolscap pages. Apparently he had hoped this would suffice in place of giving evidence, but Coroner Buss waved the written account aside and embarked on the proceedings in the usual way.

The examination began in standard fashion by confirming the identity and residence of the witness, before moving to establish various pertinent facts, such as the age of the victim, which was 58, and her state of health, which was good.

'You were on good terms with her?' asked Mr Buss.

'The very best', replied the General sadly.

The coroner then took him through the story of Mrs Luard's final afternoon. The General said they had left the house together at a little before 2.30, walking towards the golf links at Godden Green. A map was produced and, after donning his spectacles, the General indicated the route they had taken, leaving the main road at a point known locally as Seven Wents (because seven lanes and footpaths converged there) and following a private path (which was not included in these seven) through the Fish Ponds Wood on the Frankfield estate.

Thanks to the exclusion of much of the press and the publication of so many erroneous diagrams purporting to illustrate the Luards' route that day, a degree of confusion has always surrounded this part of their journey – the path in question entered the woods between the junction of the Maidstone to Sevenoaks road and the lane which runs down to Ivy Hatch. This path was so small and private that it was not marked on contemporary Ordnance Survey maps, and whatever path did exist is long gone. In 1908 there were no buildings in the vicinity, but a house now stands at the point where General and Mrs Luard left the road.

The General explained that they had walked through the woods along this path, passing the summerhouse known as La Casa and eventually reaching the junction with a 'narrow lane' which ran down to the Wickhams' cottage. (Today we would never dignify this bridleway with the term lane as it is too steep and rough to have ever seen any but foot and equine traffic.)

A wicket gate separated the path from this 'lane' and here the couple parted, as Mrs Luard wished to return home in time for a visitor who was expected to tea. The General watched her go a little distance along the path and when she was out of sight among the trees, he continued on his way to collect his golf clubs. He returned home by a slightly different route which did not pass the summerhouse.

When he arrived home at about 4.30, his wife's visitor Mrs Stewart had arrived, but Mrs Luard had not returned. They had tea, but Mrs Luard still failed to appear, so the General set out in search of her, again accompanied by his dog and also by Mrs Stewart, who particularly wanted to see Mrs Luard. They assumed they would meet her coming along the road, but when they reached the point where the Luards had entered the woods earlier and there was still no sign of Mrs Luard, Mrs Stewart had to return home as she was expecting someone by the afternoon train. That had been at 5.15, the General said. He knew this because the lady had checked her watch just before they separated.

He and Scamp re-entered the wood alone. As they reached the bungalow, the General caught sight of his wife on the floor of the veranda, as he initially thought in a fainting fit. As he got closer, however, he saw there was a lot of blood on the ground. His immediate idea was that she had burst a blood vessel, but then he realised that his wife's head and what he could see of her face were

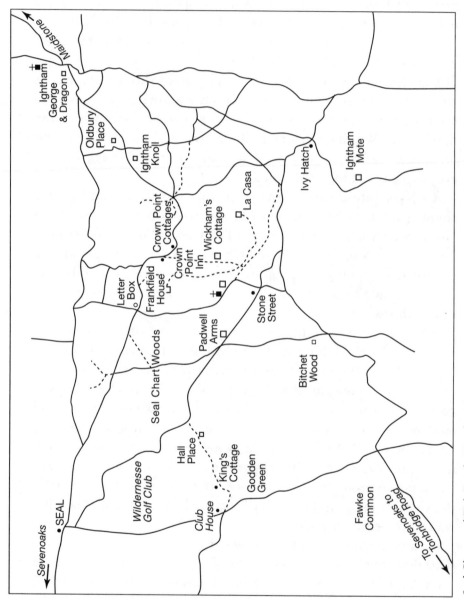

Seal Chart and Fish Ponds Woods.

covered in blood. On reaching her side he took one of her hands to feel for a pulse, but the hand was cold. At this stage in his evidence, the General was sufficiently overcome with emotion that he could only nod when Buss asked whether this was the moment he realised his wife was dead and must have met with foul play.

He had examined her dress, the General said, and observed that her pocket had been torn out and was lying on the veranda, as was one of her gloves, which appeared to have been torn off her left hand, from which three rings were missing. Mrs Luard had only worn rings on her left hand. He was unable to say whether she had any money with her, or how much, although he had subsequently checked the bureau where his wife's purse was normally kept and it was not there.

The General then told how he went to the coachman's cottage in search of Fred Wickham, then on to the stables, having been told by Wickham's wife that he would find the coachman there. At the stables the coachman had fetched the butler, who returned to the summerhouse with him, while the coachman 'made some arrangements'. In some reports, these arrangements imply summoning the police and a doctor, but others appear to suggest that Wickham was charged to arrange a conveyance of some sort.

Here the General's version of events diverges from the account already given to a newspaper by Fred Wickham, in which the coachman stated that he and John Kettel had accompanied the General out to the summerhouse. Certainly, some accounts of the inquest read as though no one went to notify the police until after Harding and the General arrived at the summerhouse together – and if this was the case, then a third person must have been there to go for help because it is plain that Harding remained with General Luard until the doctor and police arrived. Since even those papers whose reporters were actually present and taking notes at the inquest fail to agree with one another on every detail, a definitive answer to this is unlikely to emerge. Intriguingly the Frankfield farm steward John Kettel, who may well have known the true sequence of events, was actually one of the jurors at the inquest.

'Did you make an examination', the coroner asked, 'so that you could tell the nature of the injuries received?'

'No', replied the General. 'I saw quite enough.'

The coroner now wanted to know whether the General kept any guns in the house, to which the General replied in the affirmative. In reply to further questions, he said that the guns were not locked up, but that his wife was unlikely to have got hold of any of them. He corrected the coroner's impression that they had walked by the summerhouse every day, although he said they did walk that way quite often. He had not met anyone in the woods, either coming or going, and had not noticed anything unusual about the bungalow when he passed it that afternoon. In response to an enquiry as to whether he or his wife had anyone 'so unfriendly' that they might have been responsible for the crime, the General replied, 'I have no idea of anyone.'

The jury now had the opportunity to ask questions and one of them wanted to know if the General kept any ammunition in the house. The General said he did, but 'it's a strange thing but I no longer know where it is'. It had been in a cupboard upstairs, he said, in case of burglars. As his guns had become the object of so much interest, General Luard volunteered to fetch them and three revolvers were produced and laid out on the dining table, with the General again insisting that it was highly unlikely anyone would have had access to them apart from himself.

One of the jury wanted to know whether the General or Mrs Luard had any relations in an asylum who might have had a grudge against them. Looking bemused, the General replied that he did not know of anyone. In fact this question may have been prompted by a snippet of local gossip, from which had sprung a theory as to the identity of the murderer. Among the Luards' nearest neighbours was Sir William Boord, who lived at Oldbury Place, a large house with grounds extending to the junction opposite Ightham Knoll.[8] One of Sir William's sons suffered from some kind of mental illness and he was frequently confined to a 'mental home' or 'asylum'. At the time of the murder however, he happened to be at home with the family at Oldbury Place and rumour had it that Dr Walker had been called to attend him on the night of the murder, owing to his highly agitated state.[9] Could it be that a juryman was attempting to call the coroner's notice to this circumstance without actually naming names? At all events, the question led nowhere.

The General was then asked whether he had seen anyone while at the Golf Club. Yes, he said, he had seen both the groundsman and Kent, the club steward. Had he heard any shots that afternoon? This drew a negative. Another juryman wanted to know at what time the General had arrived at the clubhouse and at what time he left it, but the General said he did not know as he had not looked at his watch at all during the course of the afternoon. Which way had he come home? Via the main road past the post box, which was a shorter way, though less attractive, the General said. After satisfying this final enquiry, the General was permitted to retire to a separate room, supported on the arm of a friend.

The second witness was Daniel Kettel. It will be recalled that at the trial of John Dickman, evidence given by Wilson Hepple was called into question on account of his assumed 'great age'. If Mr Mitchell-Innes thought Hepple old at 57, he would have considered Daniel Kettel positively ancient. Kettel was 74 years old in the summer of 1908 and had been many years in the service of the Wilkinson family.[10] Kettel's age was not specifically mentioned at the inquest, although reporters did remark on his grey hair and beard.

Kettel told the inquest that at 3.15 on the afternoon of the murder he had heard three shots come from the direction of the summer-house. He was in the drive at the time, about a quarter of a mile from the Casa. Shots were often heard in the vicinity, so he thought nothing of it, assuming it was a local farmer. Between the first shot and the last two, he had walked about 30 to 40 paces. (A slightly shorter estimated distance than the '60 paces' which appeared in his newspaper interview.)

Superintendent Taylor wanted to know how Kettel had 'fixed' the time of the shots. Kettel said he had not been looking at his watch just then, but when he 'was getting down to my garden, about 5 minutes walk away, I looked at my watch and it was twenty past three'.[11]

Kettel confirmed that his duties had occasionally included cleaning the summerhouse and checking it was locked up. At the time of the murder it had been locked up and unused for several months. He had never seen a revolver there.

In reply to another question, he said he had seen no one about. The companion mentioned in the newspapers, with whom he had speculated that Mitchell must be shooting squirrels, was never mentioned at the inquest at all. The disappearance of this unnamed person, who presumably must have heard the fatal shots as Kettel did, is just one of several aspects of Kettel's evidence which was vague and unsatisfactory. It will be recalled that in the version he had already told the press, Kettel originally claimed he thought the shots came from a neighbouring farm. Yet by the time of the inquest the shots were 'coming from the summerhouse'. This radical change in his story over a period of less than 48 hours is disturbing, to put it mildly.

In addition, little effort seems to have been made at the inquest to establish Kettel's precise whereabouts at the moment when he claims to have heard the shots. As well as the main drive leading to Frankfield House, there were a number of carriage drives running through the estate. The main drive was considerably more than a quarter of a mile from the summerhouse – closer to double that distance at its nearest point. Kettel was apparently in 'his' garden within 5 minutes of hearing the shots, but did he mean his own cottage garden, which was at Crown Point, or the garden of Frankfield House? Where was he walking from and to, and how close to the murder scene did this place him? (It is worth noting that Fred Wickham, who was working in the stable yard adjacent to Frankfield House that afternoon, said he never heard any shots at all.)[12]

In a much later interview with another paper, Kettel would say that he had been on his way back to the Frankfield garden after carrying out some work in the churchyard.[13] (St Lawrence Church was part of the Frankfield estate and Mr Wilkinson took responsibility for its upkeep.) If this was the case, Kettel must have passed the now infamous wicket gate where the General parted from Mrs Luard, only a very short time before the murder. Yet he was not asked to clarify this point at the inquest, in spite of being a key witness.

Anna Wickham followed Daniel Kettel. Anna was 56 and had lived in the district all her life. Her husband Fred had been coachman to the Wilkinson family for most of his working life and like the Kettels the Wickhams had raised a large family on the Frankfield estate.[14] Their cottage was about 350 yards as the crow flies from the summerhouse, but separated from it by an orchard and a belt of woodland.

According to Anna Wickham, she was sitting or standing in the garden of their cottage on the afternoon of the murder when she heard three shots coming from the summerhouse. The first of these sounded strange, as though it had struck something hard at close quarters, with no sound afterwards. She had remarked on this oddity to one of her daughters, who was in the garden with her. Two further shots had sounded shortly afterwards: normal reports, not like the first one. She did not heard a cry, or any sound of voices before the shots, she said.

At 5.30 she saw General Luard come down the hill from the direction of the summerhouse. 'I could see from his manner he was in great trouble. He asked me if the coachman was in and I said "No. He is at the stables." I then said to him, "You are in deep trouble, Sir. Can I help you?" He did not answer, but went straight away towards Frankfield.'[15]

Asked at what time she had heard the shots, Mrs Wickham said, 'It was at 3.15 exactly.'

Had she seen anyone else come by that day, one of the jurors enquired. Anna Wickham said she had not. The only people who had passed by all day apart from the General were the postman and a labourer named Boreman, who had gone by at around 8.00 in the morning on his way to work, then again at around 6.00 on his way home.

The next witness was Herbert Hamilton Harding, the butler at Frankfield House. On the afternoon of the murder he had been called out to the harness room at a few minutes to 6.00 in the evening, where he found General Luard, who had been there for about 10 minutes and was in 'quite in a state of collapse. He said "She's dead, she's dead – at the Casa."' Harding asked if Mrs Luard had collapsed or fainted, to which he fancied the General had said under his breath, 'Worse than that'.[16]

Harding accompanied the General back to the summerhouse, an estimated walk of half to three-quarters of a mile. There they found Mrs Luard's body on the veranda in a pool of blood. Harding noticed that her dress was disarranged, with the pocket torn out and that one of her gloves was lying half inside-out beside her.

Harding's evidence gave no real indication one way or the other as to whether he and the General went to the summerhouse alone. What is clear is that they both remained there until Dr Mansfield and others arrived on the scene.

Was the body touched, a juror wanted to know, before the doctor arrived? 'The General took her hand in his; nothing beyond that.'[17]

Harding was asked whether it would have been necessary for Mrs Luard to leave the path and go on to the veranda, to which he replied in the affirmative, without elaborating. He also explained that it was only possible to see about 25 yards at most along the path, because the woods were very thick.

Dr Mansfield was the next to give evidence. He had arrived at the summerhouse at 7.40, having travelled there by car in response to a summons received by telephone. Assuming the urgency implied by this, and given that Dr Mansfield lived barely 3 miles away at Church Farm in Seal, it is difficult to believe that he received this message much before 7.15. If the alarm had been raised at around 6.00, when Harding and the General set out for the summerhouse, word of the tragedy must surely have reached Dr Mansfield well before that. The delay can only logically be accounted for by the fact that efforts to alert outside help were not set in motion until the Frankfield party reached the summerhouse, and finally appreciated the seriousness of what confronted them there.

Although he lived in Seal, Dr Mansfield's practice was in Sevenoaks, so he had never attended Mrs Luard in life. He described how Mrs Luard's body was lying prone on the veranda, with her right cheek resting on the ground. Her arms were lying by her sides, with their palms upturned. Her body was in line with the outer edge of the veranda and the wall of the bungalow, with the feet about 2 yards from the entrance on to the veranda and the head about a foot from the step part-way along it. There was a bullet hole in her left temple and on turning her head, he discovered a second bullet wound just behind her right ear. The bullets had both travelled upward on entry. On the left hand there were some very small abrasions on the fingers, consistent with the rings having been pulled off. There was no glove on the left hand and the woman was bareheaded. A large straw hat trimmed with blue ribbon was lying about a yard away and there were bloodstains on the back of it. One area to the back of the hat gave more easily to pressure, suggesting it had been damaged in some way. The clothing was not disarranged, except for a tear in the dress, as if something had been torn out. The body was almost cold. A small amount of vomit had been found close to the woman's head, and a clot of blood between the head and the wall of the bungalow.

Mansfield explained that Superintendent Taylor arrived while he was making his preliminary examination and that after Taylor had made some observations of his own, they agreed to carry the body inside. Under the circumstances there was little else the two men could have done. As it was, Dr Mansfield had to work by the light of candles fetched out of the Casa and a lamp from his car.

When the body was moved, Dr Mansfield observed the left hand glove, which had been lying inside-out underneath it, as if peeled off the lady's hand. Traces of blood inside the glove corresponded to the abrasions observed on the fingers. The clothing worn by the deceased on the afternoon of the murder was produced during this evidence, and it was noted that the dress pocket was missing. Dr Mansfield considered it likely that the pocket had been cut out of the dress, rather than torn, because the division was against the grain of the fabric.

On the morning after the murder, Dr Mansfield went to Ightham Knoll where he conducted a post mortem examination with Dr Walker (who practised in Ightham and was presumably Mrs Luard's regular practitioner). They found no bruising on the arms, legs, neck or trunk of the victim, although there was some bruising to the right cheek, nose and chin. There were powder marks around the bullet wounds, but no trace of powder in the left eye, indicating that Mrs Luard's eye must have been closed when that shot was fired. One of the bullets had been recovered intact. The other had fragmented, but all the pieces together represented an identical weight to the whole bullet. It was Dr Mansfield's opinion that if three bullets had been fired, only two had entered the body. An effusion of blood had been noted on the upper part of the head, which corresponded exactly with the damaged portion of the hat, leading Dr Mansfield to conclude that the victim had probably sustained a blow to the head.

When asked about this blow, Dr Mansfield said he thought it had been made with a large blunt rounded instrument. Asked whether it could have been made by a revolver, the doctor said he thought it could have been, though not with the General's service revolver which was still on the table. As Dr Mansfield's professional experience probably seldom extended to analysing the cause of blows to the head, he might have done better not to allow himself to be drawn on the subject.

The coroner then asked the doctor if he thought it possible the wounds could have been self-inflicted. At this point Mansfield would have done well to be succinct. The most sensible summation of his position was that it was 'most unlikely'. Alas, Dr Percival Aubertin Mansfield shared the tendency towards verbosity which seems to have been a characteristic of medical witnesses at the time, and he could not resist a long peroration, explaining that it was 'not impossible' for the wounds to have been self-inflicted. This could, for example, have occurred if Mrs Luard had held a gun in each hand and fired them simultaneously: or if the first shot had not done too much damage – which according to his post mortem it might not have done – then Mrs Luard might have turned her head and fired the second shot while lying on the veranda.

Eventually Mansfield was drawn back to reality, and gave his true opinion as to the interpretation of Mrs Luard's injuries. In his view she had first been hit on the head. The blow had been sufficient to knock her to the ground, where she had vomited. She had then been shot behind the right ear. That shot failed to kill her, so a second shot was fired into the left cheek.

Dr Ernest Walker followed Dr Mansfield. He had been party to the post mortem and agreed with all Dr Mansfield's evidence, apart from two points. He considered it beyond reasonable doubt that the injuries were not self-inflicted. He also disagreed about the blow to the head, which he felt had been sustained when Mrs Luard fell – he thought it possible that she had hit her head on one of the posts which formed the rail running along the edge of the veranda.

At this juncture Mr Buss decided to adjourn the inquest until 9 September, to be reconvened at the George & Dragon in Ightham.

Some interesting facts had emerged from the inquest, reports of which appeared in the following day's papers. Along with their accounts of the inquest, some editors and their staff included theories of their own, with the *Daily Chronicle* now opining that the theft of Mrs Luard's rings had merely been a blind to cover the true motive behind her murder.[18]

11

The Most Sensational Crime of the Age

There had been a suggestion of calling in bloodhounds from the very first hours of the investigation, and on the morning after the inquest a pair of bloodhounds named Solferino and Sceptre, accompanied by their owner Major Richardson, duly arrived at Wrotham station by the 8.00 train.[1] Major Richardson had been actively promoting the use of bloodhounds in crime detection for some time and appeared willing to travel to any part of the country at a moment's notice to put himself and his animals at the disposal of any police force that requested them.

Some six months after his involvement in the Luard case, Major Richardson would be called in by the Sunderland force to assist with enquiries into the murder of Herman Cohen, this time accompanied by Solferino and Waterloo. The episode was reported in the *Sunderland Daily Echo* and did little to convince a sceptical public of the potential benefits offered by the Major and his animals. The dogs had been allowed to sniff Cohen's body, which was still lying in the front room, and then been given free range all over the Yamkelowitzs' house. (What the victim's relatives thought about this is not recorded.) Richardson had declined to take the dogs out into the street, saying that the overnight rain had spoiled their chances and in any case 'pavement retains scent badly . . . it would have been better if there had been grass outside'. His conclusion – that the murderer left the house by the front door – no more than echoed what had already been established by routine police investigation.[2]

During the Major's visit, the police conducted tests to establish whether sounds made in the front room where Cohen had been killed were audible in the kitchen (which was where the rest of the family had been sitting). Richardson was an enthusiastic participant, volunteering to stand in the kitchen, while someone made sounds in the next door room. It became obvious that sounds did not penetrate the dividing wall when, after the police had shouted and banged about generally, Richardson called through to ask whether the test had begun.[3]

Major Richardson's involvement with the Cohen case underlines the role amateur sleuths and 'experts' frequently played in serious criminal investigations – and this certainly included the murders of John Nisbet and Caroline Luard.

In the Major's favour, there is no doubt that bloodhounds can be a useful tool in crime detection. As far back as the fourteenth century, they were known on the Anglo-Scottish borders as sleuth-hounds and were employed to track down border raiders: they have long been in use as part of the detection process in other countries, particularly in the United States. However there were considerable obstacles to their efficacy in Edwardian Britain, not least that there were seldom any trained bloodhounds available close at hand, which meant there was little likelihood of any such animals reaching a crime scene before evidence had been contaminated and the trail gone cold.

Moreover, Major Richardson's desire to achieve press exposure for his dogs' capabilities may have tempted him to become involved in cases where they could clearly be of no use at all, as with the Cohen murder in urban Sunderland. This resulted in Richardson turning up at crime scene after crime scene, then issuing statements to the press, explaining the reasons for his lack of success on that particular occasion. Unfortunately, this tended to create the opposite impression to that which the Major was trying to achieve.

In the Ightham case, the dogs were taken to the summerhouse and sniffed the spot where Mrs Luard's body had been discovered. They picked up a scent and followed it for at least a mile, before it was lost. The precise direction taken by the hounds (which were brought back to the summerhouse veranda and repeated the exercise without deviation) was the subject of contradictory descriptions in different newspapers, many of whose reporters were evidently hampered by a lack of familiarity with the local geography. One or two accounts have the hounds heading north towards Crown Point, but from Major Richardson and the police's comments, it appears they took a line through an area of open ground beyond the Casa, heading back into some more woods, before eventually emerging on the Tonbridge Road somewhere between Stone Street and Ivy Hatch.[4]

One point on which all sources agree is that the dogs began by heading for the place where Superintendent Taylor had observed broken down bracken on the night of the murder. Unfortunately, by the time the bloodhounds arrived several policemen, including Taylor himself, had stood close to the spot where Mrs Luard's body lay – perhaps even contaminating their boots with the blood which had flowed abundantly across the veranda floor, before walking across to inspect the spot beyond the stables where the bracken was broken down – though if this occurred to anyone at the time, no mention was made of it.

Major Richardson was at pains to explain to reporters that the bloodhounds had been called in much too late. The rain had spoiled the scent, ruining the hounds' chances of tracking the criminal beyond the main road. He was also overheard bending Inspector Scott's ear about the need to summon bloodhounds immediately, which cannot have endeared him to the Scotland Yard man, who had only been called in 24 hours earlier himself.[5] On 29 August the press published a somewhat indignant letter from Richardson, purportedly written with the intention of correcting some inaccurate statements which had recently appeared regarding the use of bloodhounds; but also taking the opportunity to criticise the police for being too slow in summoning their assistance and failing to protect the scene until they arrived.[6]

Not only was this hardly the way to instigate good relations with the police, but there was also an inherent lack of realism in Richardson's criticisms. Rural forces were short of manpower, training and means of communication. In the case of the Luard murder, no officer with sufficient seniority to call in bloodhounds would hear of the murder until at least six or eight hours after it happened. In addition, the crime scene had already been contaminated by a whole variety of well-meaning feet before the first policeman arrived. Even when his assistance was sought, Richardson had to travel by train from Stratford-on-Avon, where he happened to be staying at the time. In truth, the optimum conditions which Richardson required were seldom likely to exist in rural situations and, as the *Daily Telegraph* pointed out, bloodhounds had been tried out by Scotland Yard and found to be 'no use in towns'.

Chief Constable Warde responded to Richardson's criticisms by saying that the bloodhounds had only been called in to establish whether there was anyone still hiding in the woods, or if the murderer had committed suicide there.[7]

In the absence of much other hard news about the case, the bloodhounds provided a welcome diversion. Photographs of Major Richardson and his dogs were everywhere. The *Penny Illustrated Paper* devoted its front cover to a drawing of two bloodhounds straining at their leashes, accompanied by the headline: 'Bloodhound Detectives: Tracking a Murderer'. On an inside page the paper reminded its readers of 'the great public interest . . . centred on the attempts to obtain clues . . . by means of tracking with bloodhounds'. Bloodhounds had been used in two recent cases – that of Madge Kirby in Liverpool and of Mrs Luard near Sevenoaks. The lack of any tangible result in either case was, the paper explained, due to the fact that the dogs had been called in too late.[8] A full-page special was devoted to the use of bloodhounds, which inevitably included an interview with Major Richardson, together with an account of a specially laid on test to demonstrate the efficiency with which properly trained dogs could hunt a man down – given the right conditions. The *Daily Chronicle* had their own exclusive on 'Dog Detectives' which included pictures of a Mr Pakenham and his dog Tsar, which had been used in the Liverpool investigations.[9]

In the meantime plenty of other suggestions were being offered to the police investigators. Someone thought the murder might have been committed by a recruit who had escaped from the barracks at Caterham. Local geologist Benjamin Harrison advised a search of nearby prehistoric rock shelters, as he thought it likely the killer could be holed up there. Some people recommended that Mrs Luard's eyes be photographed: a notion based on the commonly held belief that the last thing a person saw before death was preserved as an image in their eyes – which also relied on the theory that Mrs Luard had faced her killer.

Dozens of letters had begun to arrive, addressed to just about anyone who had any connection with the case, including witnesses such as Anna Wickham, the investigating officers, inquest jurors and General Luard himself. Some contained suggestions and theories, others were cruel anonymous hoaxes; many were passed on to the police for time-consuming investigation.

Police efforts were further hampered by the small army of press reporters who persisted in following the investigating officers everywhere they went. Various ruses were employed to defeat this unwelcome attention. The police procured a bright yellow motor car, which became synonymous with the early stages of the investigation. It was an exceptionally fast car – but, needless to say, the reporters soon hired some fast wheels of their own and gave chase. This led to a feint in another direction. The detectives set out in Superintendent Taylor's usual pony trap, which the reporters allowed to gain a head start, knowing it pointless to follow closely by car. However, when they did set out in pursuit, they were immediately confronted by the trap returning, empty except for its driver, the detectives having transferred to the strategically parked yellow car and got clean away. Unfortunately, this sort of trick would not work more than once, so the police had to think up other strategies to evade the unwelcome pursuers. The *Sevenoaks Chronicle* reported that in spite of the shocking nature of the tragedy, some locals did derive a degree of amusement from the occasional discomfiture of the press pack, to say nothing of a mini-boom for those providing food, lodging and transport to the influx of London reporters.[10]

During these first hectic days, the police pursued numerous leads. They carried out a midnight raid on a hop pickers' encampment, but nothing was found. On 27 August, the *Daily Mail* stated that the 'tramp with a cast in his eye has now been traced and has accounted for his movements'. This was only one of a variety of tramps the police wished to interview. The Revd Arthur Cotton, the vicar of nearby Shipbourne, had given a description of a man he saw leaving the woods that afternoon, who had sandy hair, three to four days' growth of beard and 'the stamp of an East End loafer'. This man was also said to have a cast in his eye, but was described as being dressed in a suit, which hardly fitted the popular image of a tramp.[11]

John Martin, a local carpenter, had seen two men loitering close to the General's property on the weekend before the murder. Martin spotted them when he passed the General's gate on his way home for lunch and they were still there a couple of hours later, sitting on the bank at the side of the road. The carpenter had suspected they might be after one of the General's chickens, which were running about close to the fence. He saw the same men in the village shop the following evening, and two men fitting the same description were reported walking along the main road from Ightham to Seal at around 6.00 on the evening of the murder.[12]

An altogether more dramatic story had been provided by a Mrs Taylor of Sevenoaks. She was out walking on the afternoon of the murder when she observed a man behaving very strangely. This encounter took place about 100 yards along a lane leading towards the Ash Grove estate, just south-west of Sevenoaks. Something in the man's demeanour unnerved Mrs Taylor. He was leaning against the fence, standing in a curiously rigid posture, and as she drew nearer she could see he was breathing hard. When he turned in her direction, she was frightened by the look in his eyes, later observing that he had the appearance of a man at bay. Mrs Taylor was sufficiently alarmed that she hastily retraced her steps to the main road. On looking back, she saw the man running off in the opposite direction. He was of medium height and about 45 years old, with ginger hair and a sandy beard and moustache; and was wearing corduroy trousers with a belt, a soft-collared shirt, waistcoat and dark covert coat. He wore a flat cap and a heliotrope scarf.[13]

The timing and location of the encounter were significant. Mrs Taylor reached the almshouses on the main road at 4.30 and reckoned to have seen the man about 5 minutes beforehand. This happened just about 4 miles from the Casa, not very far from the point where a lane leading directly to Stone Street and Seal Chart Woods emerges on to the Tonbridge Road, south of Sevenoaks. If Mrs Luard's murderer shot her at 3.15, came out of the woods somewhere on the road between Stone Street and Ivy Hatch, then took the little-frequented lane across Bitchet Common and Fawke Common towards the main Sevenoaks to Tonbridge road, he would have arrived at the place described by Mrs Taylor at pretty much exactly the time she claimed to have seen the ginger-haired man behaving suspiciously.

The police 'investigated the story' and 'satisfied themselves that it was of no importance in connection with the unravelling of the mystery'.[14] No public explanation for this conclusion was offered. It has never been suggested that the man was identified and his alibi for the afternoon established. His involvement could not have been ruled out on the geographical grounds which eliminated the usual crop of 'suspicious men' reportedly seen at various places throughout the country that day. It is possible that the police considered Mrs Taylor an unreliable witness, although it is clear that she had not merely fabricated this story on hearing about the murder, because the incident upset her so much that she spoke about it as soon as she arrived home that afternoon – a point corroborated by her mother Mrs Bartholomew.[15]

A voluntary statement made at Tonbridge received similarly dismissive treatment. In this instance a local resident had gone into Tonbridge police station to report seeing a man 'apparently of the poorer working classes' leaving the woods near Crown Point, at about 3.15 on the afternoon of the murder. Although the police took down and circulated a description, this story likewise had 'no great importance attached to it'.[16]

In the meantime the police had been pursuing a suspect with actual links to the Luards. A gardener who had been dismissed by the General was detained by Dover police, but was able to prove he had been many miles away when the fatal attack had taken place.[17] This line of enquiry, coupled with an apparent disregard of the ginger-haired man seen by Mrs Taylor, and various other likely suspects, was increasingly leading the press to speculate that the police did not believe the murder had been a random robbery. The *Illustrated Police Budget* speculated that Mrs Luard might have been lured to her death, perhaps even drugged beforehand, citing the vomit as a possible indicator of poison and stating their opinion that 'there is more to this than meets the eye'.[18]

The *People* also aired its suspicions in print, stating point blank that 'police believe it was a deliberately planned crime . . . not the inspiration of the moment'. This paper was not alone in implying that the police were not being completely forthcoming about how much they knew. The *People* was typically more outspoken than most, complaining that 'the clues made public have proved valueless', and declaring that it was evident to those following matters closely that the police knew much more than they were revealing. They reported that Chief Inspector Scott had returned to London to consult with his superiors; 'should an arrest be determined the outcome would be followed with breathless interest the length and breadth of the land'. According to the *People*, this consultation was necessary before 'a definite move' was made against the killer and in the meantime the police were still seeking evidence and a motive: from which readers were left to surmise that the killer's name was known to the police, and that his identity would cause a far greater frisson than that of any mere tramp or disgruntled ex-gardener.[19]

The day of Caroline Luard's funeral saw no let-up in either the intrusive press interest or the atrocious weather. Persistent rain failed to deter a huge attendance: the church was packed, leaving many mourners to stand among the gravestones in the pouring rain. The *Kent Messenger* noted that the 'working class and gentry alike were in black'.[20] A long procession of cars and carriages discharged representatives of every well-known family in the neighbourhood, including Horace Wilkinson, the owner of Frankfield, who with his family had returned home for the occasion. Retired military and naval officers, political figures past and present, stockbrokers, landed gentry and members of the minor aristocracy had turned out in force. Journalists scribbled down the names of the more notable among them, to be listed in the extensive reports of the proceedings which appeared in both local and national papers in the following days.

Family mourners were conveyed from Ightham Knoll in a funeral omnibus, which followed the horse-drawn hearse at a respectful distance. Caroline's married sisters, her brother Thomas Hartley, nieces and nephews had all come down to Ightham for the funeral, some of them travelling more than 300 miles to get there. The General's family were also present in force: his half-sisters Sybil, now married to Sir William Church,[21] and Beatrice who had married paper mill magnate Alfred Willink,[22] together with his half-brother Bertram and various Luard cousins, were there to support him and pay their respects. Floral tributes continued to arrive up to a few minutes before the cortege departed, so that by the time they left the house, Mrs Luard's coffin was invisible under a mountain of flowers. Village shops had put up their shutters and blinds were drawn all along the route. In the lane outside Ightham Knoll, policemen stood to attention as the cortege passed and villagers lined the way to the church, the men bareheaded in spite of the heavy rain.

The coffin was carried into the church amid the melancholy tolling of the church bells, with the General walking behind it alone. The General was escorted to the front left-hand pew, while the remainder of the family and Mrs Luard's servants took up seats in the pews reserved for them to the right of the aisle.

The service was conducted by the Revd Bertram Winnifrith, vicar of Ightham, and the Revd Julian Guise, a friend of the family who had a living at Addingham. The Revd Shaw Hill Scott, the clergyman who had comforted the General at the scene of the murder, assisted them. The Revd Guise gave the address, his voice occasionally betraying the emotion he undoubtedly felt: the choir chanted the 39th Psalm and the congregation sang 'Jesus lives! No longer now, Can thy terrors, death, appal us'.

As the service progressed it became necessary for the participants to compete with the increasing ferocity of the gale and accompanying downpour. The storm reached its vicious climax as the party made their way back into the churchyard, where the coffin was lowered into the grave already occupied by the Luards' younger son. The Revd Winnifrith read the remainder of the burial service while the General looked on, sheltered beneath an umbrella held for him by his brother-in-law Thomas Hartley. During the committal he dropped a bunch of daisies on the oak coffin. At the conclusion of the ceremony he stood looking intently into the grave for a few seconds, before walking slowly back towards the church gates, guided by Thomas Hartley.

One or two reporters complained that the dignity of the occasion was somewhat marred by photographers loosing off their flash-bulbs to capture images of the hearse and the chief mourners. However, most of the newspapers that covered the event had no compunction about publishing images of Mrs Luard's coffin being conveyed through the village, juxtaposed with the tragic figure of her top-hatted husband leaning on the arm of a relative or, worse still, standing bareheaded at the graveside.

Once the principal mourners had departed, the police had to marshal the crowds waiting to peer into the grave and examine the cards on the wreaths – almost a hundred had been sent and these were laid out across the churchyard and pored over by reporters who noted down messages for reproduction in their papers, accompanied by the Revd Guise's funeral address and lists of the mourners.

These messages of sympathy were touching in their simplicity and sincerity. Many were affectionately addressed to Daisy Luard; length of friendship was a common theme; love a frequently expressed sentiment. The General's own wreath was singled out as particularly beautiful, made up of arum lilies and white chrysanthemums. There can be no doubting the affection and respect in which Caroline Luard was held by her friends and relations, or the genuine grief her untimely death evinced.

All this was in stark contrast to the way the rest of the world was coming to perceive the Luard case. In 1908 it was still customary for many people to work a six-day week. When Sunday 30 August dawned bright and clear, literally hundreds of people spontaneously decided to spend their day off travelling down to Ightham, prompted by a ghoulish curiosity to view the place they had been reading about ever since news of the murder had broken on Tuesday morning.

Attempts to view the murder site were thwarted by the local police, who threw a cordon round the Casa in anticipation of the invasion. The nearest sightseers got was the now famous wicket gate, where a policeman stood guard against all-comers. One cannot imagine that most of those who 'picked their way through mud and puddles and essayed the steep climb' along the bridle path or 'lane' from Crown Point derived much satisfaction from their endeavours.[23] Many took home twigs and leaves as souvenirs of their expedition. Considerable numbers made their way to the churchyard and inspected Mrs Luard's grave, some arriving early enough to gawp at the General as he attended the morning service on the arm of a friend.

Not everyone was denied access to the murder scene that day. A reporter from the *Kent Messenger* was allowed up through the woods, where he observed that since his previous visit the police had washed away the bloodstains from the veranda. He noted the bright flowers blooming in the narrow strip of garden to either side of the summerhouse (protected from the depredations of rabbits by a surrounding fence of wire netting) and the wonderful view from the balcony, which he speculated Mrs Luard may have paused to admire just before she was struck down. Meantime, in the surrounding woods and fields the police were busily cutting down and pitchforking away the surrounding bracken in the hope of uncovering fresh clues.[24]

While standing on the veranda the reporter found he could hear the voices of people talking to one another in the Wickhams' cottage garden, and on making enquiries with the Wickham family he learned that conversely from their garden they could sometimes hear people speaking on the veranda of the summerhouse: the obvious inference being that Mrs Wickham and her daughter could not have failed to hear any screams uttered by Mrs Luard.

Police experiments would shortly be carried out which proved that a revolver fired at the Casa could easily be heard from the Wickhams' garden.[25] Unsurprisingly, some amateur detectives had already undertaken a similar exercise, in the presence of a reporter from the *Westminster Gazette*, but their tests only cast fresh doubt on the issue. Using woodland 'approximating the thickness of that on the Frankfield estate', a revolver was fired at a distance of 300 yards from waiting listeners. The listeners claimed to hear only five of the six shots fired, which sounded 'more like the cracking of sticks close at hand' than gunshots, leading these amateur sleuths to question whether the sounds allegedly made by the revolver that fired the fatal bullets had actually been the much louder shots of a gun employed by a sportsman shooting nearby. The *Westminster Gazette* pointed out that if doubt was cast on the exact time of the murder, it would 'give a new turn to the enquiry'.[26]

It would be another ten days until the resumption of the inquest, but the frenzied reporting of what was being described as 'the most sensational crime of the age' continued unabated.

Many of the weekly papers which appeared on Fridays, Saturdays or Sundays devoted several pages to the 'Summerhouse Murder': some even advertised that they would be including special articles about the case. Violent death has always sold newspapers, but this particular tragedy was a gift to editors with space to fill. The General's Huguenot antecedents, his military service and grand connections with Ightham Mote were easily discoverable and filled newspaper columns much more readily than a common or garden suburban murder ever would. The murder, inquest and funeral had all taken place within the previous week and there were plenty of photographs available to accompany the story – including views of the summerhouse from various angles, a stolen shot of the front of Ightham Knoll and the personalities involved in the case – from Scotland Yard detectives to mourners at the funeral. In one account Sir William Church became an Admiral and the General was elsewhere variously gifted with a brother called William and a third son he never had. What did it matter if reports sometimes failed to get things quite right? The gratuitous thrill, the horror and the mystery of it all, those were the key to unlocking the public's purses.

Fresh developments helped to keep the story in the headlines over the next few days. Some of these were generated by the press coverage itself, for most of the letters which continued to pour in from all over the country were undoubtedly prompted by what people read in the papers. A letter from Manchester claimed that its anonymous author had murdered Mrs Luard in revenge, after waiting three years.[27] The revenge killing became a popular theme and several more letters arrived retailing the rumours generated by reports of the original Manchester letter.

Not all the letters making headlines came from cranks or amateur detectives. In response to the widespread criticism over the exclusion of the press from the inquest proceedings at Ightham Knoll, Coroner Thomas Buss was moved to write to the papers on 28 August, exonerating himself of any blame:

Sir,

My attention has been drawn to . . . references to the exclusion of large numbers of the Press . . . and I feel compelled to state the facts.

It was not until after I had concluded my inquiry that I was made aware that any representatives of the Press who had asked for admission had been refused, and as reporters have always been allowed free access to my Courts I had no reason to suppose there was any necessity for the complaint alleged on the present occasion.

I must say at once, therefore, that I disclaim all knowledge of the order in question and as I consider this is a gross interference with my powers and discretion, I am making inquiries so as to ascertain, if possible, who is responsible for this unwarrantable action, that I may take such steps as I consider necessary to prevent a repetition of the offence.

I must express my regret for the treatment received by the Press on the occasion referred to.

I am etc

Thomas Buss

Coroner for Kent, Tunbridge Wells[28]

As it had been clearly stated in a number of reports that the order to exclude the press emanated from Colonel Warde, there can be little doubt that Coroner Buss knew perfectly well who was responsible for the 'gross interference' and this letter was perhaps as close as the coroner dared come to openly criticising the Chief Constable.

Nor were local newspapers slow to intimate dissatisfaction at the Chief Constable's handling of other aspects of the case. The *Tunbridge Wells Advertiser* said, 'Attention is being directed to the fact that at the crucial period . . . the aid of Scotland Yard was not immediately asked for', going on to make the uncomplimentary if truthful point that by the time this expert help was applied for, 'inexpert local men [had] trodden out or failed to notice clues which would have been seized on by the expert'.[29]

Not everyone contented themselves with limiting their involvement to writing a letter. A man walked into Sevenoaks police station claiming to know where the murderer was – he had put his son under a 'fluence' and the boy told him the murderer was then in the Riverhead district and gave a full description of the man. A London clairvoyant claimed she too had 'seen' the murderer, but the culprit she described was a woman. As the *Sevenoaks Chronicle* wryly observed, 'they cannot both be right'.[30]

On 3 September a man walked into Bow Street police station and confessed to the crime, but no sooner had this sensation hit the news-stands than the man retracted everything and said he had never been to Sevenoaks in his life. Police soon satisfied themselves that he had nothing to do with the case.[31]

Then there was the 'Pembury' suspect, who unintentionally succeeded in sustaining police interest for several days. This minor drama began on the day of Mrs Luard's funeral, when a man walked into the police station at Tonbridge claiming to have lost his memory. On being questioned, he explained that he had found himself at Paddock Wood railway station, having no idea where that was, or how he had got there. He asked directions for the nearest town and walked the 7 miles into Tonbridge. He was untidy and mud-spattered and used the few coppers he found in his pockets to get shaved before giving himself up to the police.

There was no documentation or means of identification about his person, so after being questioned he was taken to the hospital wing of Pembury Workhouse, where Superintendent Taylor soon arrived to interview him. As this encounter revealed very little, he was put under police supervision while attempts were made to establish his identity. Although the press hoped to associate the Pembury suspect with Mrs Luard's murder, it is evident that the police were equally concerned lest the man had independently been the victim of some sort of foul play.

Enquiries revealed that the mystery man was Alfred Pearson of 150 High Street, Tottenham. Taxed with this, Pearson reluctantly admitted it was true and eventually that his whole story of amnesia had been a fabrication, with the intention of getting a bed for the night. It appeared that Pearson had absented himself from home as he was in some kind of trouble there.

The 'Pembury Workhouse Man' had diverted precious resources from an overstretched enquiry team and the Kent force were not amused. Alfred Pearson was brought before the magistrates at Tonbridge on 2 September on a charge of obtaining relief by making a false statement and malingering at the workhouse. Pearson pleaded guilty and apologised, saying that it had never entered his head that the police would suppose he had anything to do with the Ightham murder. The bench sentenced him to fourteen days' hard labour in Maidstone, remarking that he had 'put the county authorities to a great deal of trouble by shamming'.[32]

On the same afternoon Chief Constable Warde, his deputy Major Lafone, Chief Detective Scott, Superintendent Taylor, Superintendent Ford and a handful of other officers joined Mr Edwin Churchill, a firearms expert, as he conducted tests to determine whether shots fired at the summerhouse could be heard at the Wickhams' cottage.[33]

In the week and a half since the murder, few fresh clues had been uncovered and several apparently promising leads had come to nothing. A Tonbridge pawnbroker called Mr Peters had generated considerable excitement when he arrived at the police station bearing a diamond ring, which fitted the description of the one taken from Mrs Luard. The ring, estimated to be worth about £100, had been pawned two days after the murder by 'a respectable looking woman'. The ring was given to Colonel Warde who took it to Ightham Knoll in person, but the General said it was not his wife's ring, which was 'much more valuable'.[34] A second diamond ring discovered in London proved to be another false lead.[35]

One item genuinely connected to the murder had turned up. This was the pocket of Mrs Luard's dress, which had been found by a housemaid at Ightham Knoll on the day before the funeral. Many papers reported this discovery – some noting that the pocket had been missing presumed stolen from the scene, others merely stating that the pocket had been found in General Luard's house, both of which comments only added a further layer of mystery to the proceedings.[36]

Scraps of torn paper discovered near the summerhouse during the original police search turned out to be nothing more exciting than a list of villages, which was assumed to have been discarded by someone who had been using it to navigate their way through Kent – possibly some holidaying cyclists, the police thought.

Rumours of a connection between the case and a man who had committed suicide at a rest home in Wrotham during the week of the murder proved to be completely without foundation, as did the story of someone seeing a man throwing a revolver into the Medway on the night of the murder – although not before that story had been widely reported, leading a London firm of specialist divers to offer their services to the enquiry.

The revolver-in-the-Medway story was linked to that of a man who had reportedly visited a public house in Larkfield on the evening of the murder. Apparently in an agitated state, after calling for brandy he offered a ring for sale for 5s, but there were no takers. The public house in question was almost 10 miles from the scene of the crime, but even so it seems unlikely that Mrs Luard's killer would have risked attempting to sell one of her rings in such close proximity. If robbery was the motive, we may assume that even the least savvy of criminals would have appreciated that his booty could be fenced for rather more than 5s.

More time was wasted when two men approached the police with a story that they had seen someone breaking into the Casa on the afternoon of the murder and stealing a rug. They said they had not seen Mrs Luard and knew nothing of her murder, but felt they should approach the police as the man seen stealing the rug was literally on the point of departing for Canada. The police raced to the railway station and detained the man named, who turned out neither to have entered the Casa nor to be going to Canada. Horace Wilkinson confirmed that no rugs, or indeed any other items, were missing from the summerhouse (in fact police records already showed there had not been a break-in). The time-wasters in this case appear to have been let off more lightly than Alfred Pearson.[37]

The *Daily Graphic* was among those that picked up the story of a woman (conveniently unnamed) who had once worked as Mrs Luard's cook.[38] Allegedly this ex-employee visited her old mistress not long before the murder, and during their conversation Mrs Luard mentioned that she had become quite nervous about walking alone in the woods as she had recently been 'molested' there and asked for money. It seems extremely odd that Mrs Luard would confide this information to an ex-employee yet never mention it to any of her family or friends – odder still that a woman who was nervous about walking in the woods alone should continue to do so on a frequent basis. Indeed it would emerge from the General's evidence when the inquest resumed that Mrs Luard quite often walked alone through the woods to the Casa – and had done so only a few days before she died in order to meet her husband when he was returning from a game of golf at Godden Green.[39]

Among all these stories some potentially important new witnesses went almost unremarked. Two woodcutters, who had been working several fields away from the summerhouse on the afternoon of the murder, came forward to say they had heard two shots, immediately preceded by a shrill squeal, which they thought sounded as if a weasel had got hold of a rabbit.[40] Although this has generally been accepted as corroboration of the Anna Wickham/Daniel Kettel testimony, in reality it contradicts it. Neither of the two witnesses who gave evidence at the inquest spoke of hearing any sort of cry before the three shots, whereas the woodcutters reported two shots, preceded by a squeal. It is therefore possible that what these two witnesses actually heard were some completely different shots – and this may have been the conclusion reached by detectives at the time, because although these men had come forward by 31 August (when their story is recounted in the press) neither of them was called to give evidence when the inquest reconvened.

The *Daily Chronicle* was among the few papers which picked up that 'an artisan' had told the police about a man he saw leaving the vicinity on the day of the crime, but the police 'were not placing much reliance on it'.[41] Like the woodcutters, this man was not identified by name at the time; but there is good reason to believe he was George Skeer, a local labourer, who would later claim that he approached the police with a story of meeting a black man in a lane close to the scene on the afternoon of the murder. According to Skeer, the man was very agitated and asked directions for the nearest railway station. In response to Skeer's seeking clarification as to where he wanted to go, the man replied, 'The quickest way to a railway station. I have just shot a woman.'[42]

The police refused to listen and told Skeer to clear off, which is perhaps not very surprising. Like the story of the man who called for brandy at Larkfield, this tale fails to ring true. Most fleeing murderers do not announce their recent actions to a stranger casually encountered in a nearby lane, then ask directions to help effect their escape.

One of the worst hoaxes was yet to come. Fresh headlines were derived from the discovery of a coat and a pair of boots near the lake in Regent's Park. Beside the discarded clothing was a note which read:

My dear father,
I can bear the suspense no longer. The Ightham affair has preyed on my mind. I fired the shots while the devil was in me. By the time you get this I shall be beyond human aid.

Your unfortunate son
Jack Storm

The lake was dragged but with a negative result.[43] 'Jack Storm' was evidently educated enough to produce an accurately spelled, grammatically correct suicide note, and well heeled enough to spare a pair of boots and a jacket on a cruel practical joke. Like the invasion of Ightham on the Sunday following Caroline Luard's death, this episode illustrates the way in which one family's tragedy had become a public entertainment for the masses.

Not all the newspapers followed the sensationalist line. The weekly *Maidstone and Kentish Journal*, a publication whose tone tended towards the religious – in its pages the murder was not the most 'sensational', but rather the most 'wicked', and the 'mark of Cain' was upon the murderer – sensibly summed up the situation in their 3 September issue with the words: 'Ten days have passed since the murder . . . there was no clue then and there is no clue now. . . . Trails here, trails there, but all brings us back to what is after all the only known fact in this maze of mystery, that a kindly lady was cruelly done to death in the woods of Ightham at three o'clock on an August afternoon. All else is surmise. . . .'

The paper went on to complain that village gossip in pubs was starting false trails. The story of the revolver being thrown into the Medway with the subsequent dragging of the river and employment of a diver was dismissed as 'fantasy'. All the letters received to date were liable to be hoaxes. The rumour that a woman was known to have killed Mrs Luard was 'absurd'. The paper pointedly reminded its readers that among the many rumours flying around the neighbourhood, it had been falsely stated on several occasions that an arrest had been made.

The Luard case continued to dominate the headlines throughout September. On the 8th of the month, the General himself added to the copy available by writing a letter to the editors of various local papers, which was quickly picked up and reproduced by many more.

Sir,
I should be very much obliged if you will permit me, through your columns, to acknowledge the very large number of telegrams, letters, and cards which I have recently received, expressing such deep sympathy for me.

The public at large has been deeply stirred by this awful crime and I may have some right to ask if the time has not arrived for clearing away from our roads, our lanes, and our woods, the many thousands of unemployed people, many of them in a desperate state from want, who may give way to temptation and commit the worst of sins.

I am sir, yours truly

C. Luard

Major-General

Ightham Knoll, September 8th 1908[44]

12

A Hearty Welcome and a Surprise Ending

The inquest into the death of Caroline Luard reconvened in a large room at the George & Dragon Inn in Ightham.[1] On the wall above the seat occupied by Coroner Buss a large sign proclaimed 'A hearty welcome to one and all'. Other decoration included a series of drawings showing the kings and queens of England, interspersed with brewery advertisements and photographs of local cricket teams.

Before calling any witnesses, the coroner expressed the hope that all the press had been accommodated, and on hearing to the affirmative, first read over the evidence heard at the previous session before recalling General Luard.

At his wife's funeral, the press reporters had seemed divided between those who felt the General looked an old and broken man, and those who commented on his upright military bearing. On this occasion they were almost unanimous in describing him as old and frail in appearance. He entered the room on the arm of a friend, walking slowly, and to some even appearing uncertain of his surroundings.

After briefly explaining that he intended to put some additional questions to the General, the coroner asked: 'First, is there any incident in the lives of the deceased and yourself, which in your opinion would cause any person to entertain any feelings of revenge or jealousy towards either of you?' After a pause, the coroner added, 'Do you follow the question?'

The General apologetically said that he did not. The coroner repeated his question and this time the General replied that he could not think of anyone. The coroner then asked if the Luards had ever received any letters suggesting that someone entertained bad feelings towards them. Again the General seemed almost bemused by the question, eventually replying that he did not think so.

Buss then asked, 'Did your wife recently before her death receive a letter from anyone, making an appointment to see her?'

'You mean invitations – oh yes, there were invitations of all kinds.'

The coroner explained that he meant some sort of 'obscure' invitation.

'Oh no. She would certainly have told me if she had.'

Buss then moved on to the whole question of Mrs Luard's walking through the woods alone and cutting across the summerhouse veranda. Was this not going out of her way? The General said it was not. Returning from the direction of St Lawrence to Ightham Knoll it was quicker to leave the path and cut across the veranda, which was what he and his wife habitually did. He confirmed that both he and Mrs Luard used the route frequently, and in answer to the direct question of whether Mrs Luard was in fear of anyone using violence towards her in any way, the General replied firmly that she was not, and had in fact walked that same way alone only a few days before she died.

The coroner also wanted to know whether the General or his wife were acquainted with anyone who suffered from homicidal mania, or any kind of insanity; whether there was anyone likely to benefit by Mrs Luard's death, and whether the General ever carried a revolver with him, and if so, whether he had done so on the afternoon of his wife's death. To all these questions the General responded in the negative.

The jury were now invited to ask questions. One man wanted to know more about the dog which had accompanied the Luards that day. Was he likely to have given warning, if there had been anyone about in the woods? The General replied that he thought so – 'Yes, most certainly.'

From further questions it was elicited that no one was likely to have known that the Luards intended walking that way on 24 August, and that the General had not heard any shots after parting from his wife.

At the conclusion of his evidence, General Luard retired from the room, again supported on the arm of a friend.

The second witness was Thomas Jordan Durrant, the 53-year-old manager of Blythe's Brewery, who lived at Manor Cottage, Sevenoaks. Durrant's evidence was straightforward. On 24 August he had left home at around 2.30 to walk to the Padwell beerhouse, accompanied by his wife and their fox terrier. Near Hall Farm he met General Luard, who was walking in the opposite direction with his dog, an Irish terrier. In response to a question about the General's manner, Durrant said the General looked happy and contented; he had smiled and for a moment Durrant thought he was going to speak. Their dogs had run off together. The General was walking quite quickly, at a rate of perhaps 3 to 4 miles an hour.

When Durrant reached the Padwell he had checked his watch, which said 3.40, but he habitually kept it 10 minutes fast and thus the time was actually 3.30. He reckoned he had seen the General about 10 minutes before reaching the pub. Durrant himself had not been walking as fast as usual, he explained, on account of having his wife with him.

Did Durrant know the area well, the coroner enquired. Durrant said he did, though when asked how far from the Casa he had seen the General, he said he did not know where the Casa was. He knew St Lawrence Church, however, and estimated it to be about 15 minutes' walk away from where he had seen the General. In complete contrast to the evidence of Mrs Wickham and Daniel Kettel, Durrant said he had heard a lot of shooting going on that afternoon.

The jury wanted to know why Durrant kept his watch 10 minutes fast and were not greatly enlightened by his explanation that this was 'for brewing purposes'. One of the jurors questioned whether it might not have been slightly more or less fast that afternoon, but Durrant insisted it was always kept precisely 10 minutes fast as 'we brew by the clock'.

The next witness took the General's progress towards the golf club a little further. This was Ernest King, a labourer in his mid-twenties, who had been working near the path the General took between Hall Farm and the golf links. King had observed the General between 3.25 and 3.30, walking in the direction of the club-house and again about 10 minutes later, returning with his golf clubs. King said he had only just looked at his watch the first time General Luard passed him, at a point which he estimated to be about 400 to 500 yards away from the place where the previous witness had encountered the General, and about 350 to 400 yards from the clubhouse at Godden Green. The General had not spoken to King, or given any indication that he had seen him.

Harry Kent, the sub-postmaster at Godden Green, who also acted as steward at the golf club, was the next person to give evidence. Kent particularly remembered that he had been an hour late going out to feed his poultry on the afternoon of the murder. When he checked the clock just before leaving the house, it was almost 3.30. On his way to feed the chickens, Kent saw the General approaching; he had seen him again a few minutes later in the clubhouse, where the General greeted Kent just as usual.

A touch of glamour was introduced to the proceedings by the appearance of the next witness. 'All eyes were turned to the door', according to the *Sevenoaks Chronicle*, as Mrs Mary Alice Stewart entered the room.[2] This was the visitor for whom Mrs Luard had been returning home on the afternoon she died: a fashionably dressed lady whose entire demeanour was in contrast to the preceding witnesses. Mrs Stewart was the wife of Frank Stewart, a retired solicitor, and they had been residing in Ightham during the summer months.

Mrs Stewart began by telling the court how on 9 June shortly after arriving in the district, the Stewarts had called on General and Mrs Luard and finding them out had left their card in the usual way. Subsequently, Mrs Stewart heard that Mrs Luard was surprised they had not called – apparently Mrs Luard was unaware of the Stewarts' call as their card had been mislaid. Mrs Stewart therefore wrote to Mrs Luard, telling her the date of their call, and received a letter back inviting them to tea on 24 August.

Mrs Stewart had arrived at Ightham Knoll at 4.20 on the appointed day, and was conducted to wait in the drawing room as neither General nor Mrs Luard was at home. Mrs Stewart was sure of the time because she took a seat facing the clock. The General arrived home about 5 minutes later. 'He apologised for Mrs Luard's not being at home and said he expected her every minute.' They waited about 5 minutes before having tea.

'Did General Luard then suggest that you should go to meet his wife?' asked the coroner.

'No. We had tea and then he looked at his watch and suggested that he should go and meet her. I said I would go with him, as I wished to speak with Mrs Luard.'

The General and Mrs Stewart walked to Seven Wents, where Mrs Stewart had to leave him as she was expecting a friend. They parted at 5.15. She had no doubt about the time, because she had asked the General to check his watch owing to her concern about meeting her friend. (Although the General and Mrs Stewart contradicted one another regarding whose watch was referred to, it seems reasonable to accept that one way or another they established the time was 5.15.)

Did Mrs Stewart know the Casa well, the coroner wanted to know. Mrs Stewart said she did not know it at all and had never been there. The jury were then asked whether they had any questions for Mrs Stewart, as she had an appointment and therefore wished to leave as soon as possible. There is more than a suggestion of Mrs Stewart's being a reluctant participant in the proceedings: a newcomer to the area, who in fulfilling her social obligations had been dragged into a sordid enquiry that entailed statements to the police and attendance at a public house, where she was gawped at by every Tom, Dick and Harry who cared to attend.

Harriet Huish, the parlourmaid at Ightham Knoll, was the next witness to be called. Miss Huish had worked for the Luards for the past six years and when questioned about her employers stated that they had been on good terms with one another. On the afternoon of the murder she had seen Mrs Luard go up to her bedroom 'to dress' (effectively to put on outdoor things, such as appropriate gloves and a hat) at about 2.20. When the General and his wife left the house at approximately 2.30 they seemed just as usual. In response to a question, Miss Huish confirmed that she had known the General was going to the golf links and Mrs Luard intended to walk part of the way with him.

Miss Huish confirmed that Mrs Stewart was expected to tea and said she had arrived at 4.15. The General returned to the house at exactly 4.30. He was in his usual cheerful state of mind when he came in.

When the jury and the coroner had finished with Miss Huish, one of the observers sitting in the hall got his turn. This was the Revd Arthur Cotton, who had already sought permission to ask a question of the witness, but been asked to wait until the official examination was finished. Cotton, who was a witness himself, asked the parlourmaid to confirm that the General and his wife had been accompanied by a dog when they left the house, which she agreed had been the case. Quite why the Revd Cotton imagined there was an urgent necessity to obtain Miss Huish's confirmation on this point is unclear. It had already been established in the evidence offered by both General Luard and Thomas Durrant that the Luards had taken their dog with them – and more bizarrely, Mr Cotton would shortly testify to the dog's presence himself. It is possible that the reverend gentleman saw some significance in this issue which was lost on everyone else, or perhaps he was just a pompous windbag, who could not resist asking a question however irrelevant.

After the parlourmaid came the housemaid, Jane Pugmore, who had also been in the Luards' service for six years. When asked about her employers' marriage, Miss Pugmore stated they were on 'the very best of terms'. Asked about guns in the house, she confirmed that she had been aware of three guns, kept in various locations, one of which had been in the bathroom.

While keeping a gun in a bathroom has a very strange ring to modern ears, it is unlikely to have created much surprise among those gathered in the George & Dragon that day. The Edwardian attitude to guns was extremely casual and a household such as the one at Ightham Knoll would have been exceptional in not having a gun somewhere about the premises. The gun in the bathroom was probably the one the General kept upstairs to deter burglars.

The coroner then examined Jane Pugmore about the discovery of Mrs Luard's dress pocket. She explained that she had found it among the sheets when she was clearing up in the room where Mrs Luard's body had been laid out. She had shaken out the sheets and the pocket had been lying loose among them. The coroner then wanted to know if the witness had seen anything of her employers on 24 August; to which she replied she had not.

The jury were not so easily satisfied on the matter of Mrs Luard's pocket. At the first inquest they had been told the pocket was missing and Mrs Luard's clothes had been produced for their inspection without it. Now the missing pocket had reappeared and, according to the housemaid, she had found it in plain view among the bed sheets. In fact there was an easy and obvious explanation to the pocket mystery, but a question and answer session with an evidently nervous witness did not elucidate the matter much.

One juryman wanted to know whether anyone had previously looked over or shaken out the sheets prior to Miss Pugmore's doing so. 'I cannot say', the maid replied. 'I was not in the room before that.'

Was the pocket in the clothing or rolled up? To this the witness answered that it was rolled up – but of course this did not entirely clarify whether it was rolled up in the clothing or among the sheets, leading another juror to ask who had charge of Mrs Luard's clothing from the time of the post mortem.

'It was left in the bedroom. My fellow servants had more to do with the clothing than I did.' On this slightly unsatisfactory note, Jane Pugmore's evidence concluded and the Revd Arthur Cotton got his chance in the spotlight.

The Revd Cotton, a bald, bespectacled clergyman with a beard and moustaches, had already achieved fame as the man who had seen the sandy-haired fellow with the 'stamp of an East End loafer' emerging from the woods. In 1908 Arthur Cotton was 75 years old and living at The Grange in the nearby village of Shipbourne. The Revd Cotton and his wife (who was thirty years his junior) employed six live-in servants, to say nothing of a butler, several gardeners and a coachman who all lived in cottages nearby;[3] from which it can be construed that, like the Luards, the Revd Cotton well and truly belonged to the local gentry and, sure enough, when asked if he was acquainted with General and Mrs Luard, he confirmed that he was.

On the afternoon of 24 August he had been out for a ride in his motor car, driving some visitors to admire Seal Chart Woods, where they stopped to take photographs. At 3.55 one of the ladies in the party had looked at her watch because she was timing an exposure. About 10 minutes after that, Reverend Cotton and his party saw the General approaching up the road, carrying his golf clubs and accompanied by his dog. He looked rather hot and tired, so the Revd Cotton offered him a lift. General Luard declined for himself, but put his golf clubs in the car and continued his walk unencumbered.

The photographic party subsequently returned to the car and overtook the General as he was turning on to the main road. The Revd Cotton stopped the car and again offered a lift, which this time was accepted. They dropped General Luard at his gate at about 4.30. Questioned further, the Revd Cotton thought it might have been nearer 4.10 when he first saw the General and about 4.20 when he picked him up, as it was 'not more than a 10 minute run' from there to the General's gate.

The General's precise return route from the golf links was never clarified at the inquest. It is evident that he walked back along the footpath to Hall Farm and turned right along the lane towards Stone Street. Returning by road he could either have turned up the lane running through the middle of Seal Chart Woods, or taken the lane which passes St Lawrence Church, joining the main road at a crossroads about half a mile further east.

When asked to describe his route, the General merely said he had returned by road, passing the postbox on his way. In 1908 there was a postbox at the easterly of these two crossroads (it is marked on contemporary OS maps and is commemorated by the fact that the lane running to Styants Bottom is now called Pillar Box Lane), but since taking either of these aforementioned lanes would have entailed the General passing the pillar box, this leaves us none the wiser. Although both lanes ascend towards the main road, the western route involves a steeper climb, which was probably a consideration for a man carrying a set of golf clubs. Moreover, in mentioning the pillar box, the General may have intended his listeners to understand that as the point where he emerged on to the main road.

The Revd Cotton's account is not particularly helpful either, in that points on both these lanes might be considered 'roughly half a mile from the scene of the murder' – nor can we be certain whether the Revd Cotton knew precisely where the Casa was. If he was taking St Lawrence Church as a marker, then he almost certainly encountered the General in the lane running through the centre of the woods, rather than the one which passed the church – and in favour of this argument is the fact that although a steeper climb, it was undoubtedly a slightly shorter way home for the General. If so, then the second meeting with the General must have taken place at the crossroads not quite a mile and three quarters from the gates of Ightham Knoll. To take 10 minutes to cover this distance, the Reverend or his driver must have been travelling at the stately pace of 10mph – an entirely likely proposition, given that the maximum speed limit had only been raised to 20mph in 1903 and the road between Seal and Ightham then included a couple of hairpin bends.

The Revd Cotton was the last of the witnesses who had anything to add to the story of the events of 24 August. The remaining evidence would come from those involved in the case in a professional capacity – but would end with a touch of drama, as befitted 'the most sensational murder of the times'.

In his deposition the London gunsmith Edwin John Churchill stated that he had received and examined the two bullets (presumably a whole one and the collected fragments of the second) which had been recovered from Mrs Luard's body. He concluded that they had come from a .320 revolver, which had been fired when the gun was no more than a few inches away from the victim's head.

When shown the three guns recovered from Ightham Knoll, Churchill said they could not have fired the .320 bullets: one was a Webley, one was a Colt, both of which fired .450 or .455 ammunition, and the third was a toy revolver. An air gun was produced and this too was dismissed as incompatible with the bullets recovered from the scene. None of them, Churchill said, could possibly have been the murder weapon. He was asked to examine some ammunition recovered from the General's house, which he did, and said that it was the wrong size to match up with the revolver used to kill Mrs Luard.

He confirmed that when making a close inspection of the murder scene two days previously he had discovered a large number of bullets embedded in the upright posts supporting the veranda roof. These were smaller bullets than those used in the murder and were accounted for by a gentleman having used the posts for some target practice. He had also discovered a dent in the veranda floor, which had not been noticed on the evening of the crime because the area had been obscured by blood. There were traces of lead in the mark, which was close to where Mrs Luard's head had been, and he considered it to represent the point where a bullet had hit the floor, before presumably ricocheting into the woods. This of course represented the 'missing' third shot.

Churchill had been taken to the place where Mrs Wickham and her daughter heard shots on 24 August, and had interviewed Mrs Wickham. He considered that the sound described by Mrs Wickham was due to the first bullet having hit something very close to the point from which it was fired. As to the theory that the wounds were self-inflicted, Mr Churchill dismissed this absolutely.

The jurors put quite a number of questions to Churchill, including whether the bullets used and the type of gun from which they were fired were of a very common type. Churchill confirmed that they were. A cheap foreign revolver taking .320 ammunition could be purchased for about £1, he said: it was a very common size of gun. To prove the point, the gunsmith casually produced a .320 revolver from his pocket, at which Superintendent Taylor smilingly enquired whether the gun was loaded – and was no doubt relieved when he received a response in the negative.

Could Mr Churchill say whether the gun had been fired by a left- or right-handed man, another juror wanted to know. Demonstrating with his own gun, Churchill showed that it was impossible to say. Nor was it possible to state at what angle the gun had been held when the fatal shots were fired. Several of the jurors' questions led back to the guns found at Ightham Knoll; one man, clearly wondering about the bullet which had disintegrated, wanted to know whether a .450 bullet would weigh the same as a .320 one. Churchill said it would actually weigh almost twice as much. Another juror asked whether Mr Churchill had been invited to examine any of the ammunition used in the smallest of the pistols. Churchill said he had not, but reiterated that the weapon in question could not possibly have been employed to fire the bullets which killed Mrs Luard.

Superintendent Albert Taylor followed Edwin Churchill. Taylor said that he first learned of the murder at 7.00 in the evening. When he arrived at the scene about 50 minutes later, Dr Mansfield was already there examining the body, which was still *in situ* on the veranda. He took the court through the subsequent events, the removal of Mrs Luard's body and the limited search operation under darkening skies, explaining that the only trace of footprints was a trail which led from the Casa to a gate leading to some stables. Beyond the stables, which were about 40 yards from the summerhouse, the bracken had been trodden down to the hedge, a distance of about 30 feet. It appeared that the person who had made this track had been heading in the direction of Crown Point, but there was no trace of any trail beyond the line of the hedge.

Superintendent Taylor was quizzed on the 'footprint' evidence, which the jurors clearly hoped might hold some vital clues. When asked about the nature of the footprints, however, Taylor said there had not been any distinct footprints, only a trail where someone had trodden down the bracken. It is a little surprising that no one took the Superintendent up on this. His own evidence referred to 'footmarks . . . leading from the Casa, through the gate to some stables'.[4] Although bracken covered the area behind the stables, the area between the gate and the Casa was not obscured by bracken and either there were footmarks there, or there weren't. Three possibilities seem likely here. Either there had been so much careless trampling in the proximity of the summerhouse before Superintendent Taylor arrived that it was impossible to be sure who had made any footprints; or perhaps whatever marks had existed when Taylor arrived were inadvertently obscured by the police during the early stages of the search. However, bearing in mind that Herbert Harding told the original inquest that the ground around the summerhouse would not have retained clear footmarks, perhaps the third and most likely explanation is that Taylor had discovered the broken-down bracken and inferred the presence of 'footmarks' extending the trail logically to the Casa, even though no actual footmarks were visible. A final note on this point is that Taylor had already mentioned that the enquiries had been hampered by an almost continuous downpour, so perhaps this would account for the disappearing footmarks.

One of the jurors wanted to know if the footprints led in the same direction as that taken by the bloodhounds, but Taylor said he did not know as he had not accompanied them.

Taylor then confirmed that he had undertaken some experiments regarding the General's walk between Ightham Knoll and the clubhouse at Godden Green, having walked the route taken by the General twice. On the first occasion he determined that the full distance took one minute over an hour. On the second he had specifically timed the route from Ightham Knoll to the Casa, which had taken 30 minutes and from the Casa to the clubhouse, which had also taken 30 minutes.

If the jurors were content to accept the inherent contradiction in Superintendent Taylor's non-existent footmarks, they were not going to let the issue of the vanishing pocket go so easily. The foreman of the jury wanted to know when Taylor had taken possession of Mrs Luard's clothing. Taylor responded that he had taken possession of Mrs Luard's dress and hat after the post mortem, which had taken place on the day after the murder.

'Was there', the foreman enquired, 'any possibility of the pocket being in the dress at that time?'

'There can be no doubt that it was', replied the Superintendent.

This was a ridiculous answer which can only have muddied the minds of the jury still further. When Taylor collected Mrs Luard's garments immediately after the post mortem, the rogue pocket was certainly not with the clothes, having by then become entangled in the bed sheets. Superintendent Taylor probably intended to convey the reassuring message that the pocket had never really been missing at all, because it had obviously been carried back from the crime scene among Mrs Luard's clothes, then temporarily mislaid among the bedding. However, in suggesting that it was with the clothes he collected from Ightham Knoll on 25 August, Taylor was completely at variance with the facts – and of course the jury knew very well that the pocket had not been with the clothes when they were produced at the first inquest.

Taylor did try to clarify the matter by adding rather hopelessly, 'You see, it was dark when we brought the body home.'

Another juror wanted to know about the removal of the pocket – had it been cut or torn out? Taylor felt it had been cut. Someone wanted to know why the murderer would have cut it out. Taylor, missing the point, said he felt sure the murderer had abstracted whatever money was in the pocket, then dropped it on the veranda before fleeing the scene; but what the juror was clearly driving at here was why anyone would bother to take out a knife and cut the pocket away from the dress, when it would only take half as long simply to put his hand inside and extract whatever was there.

At least one of the jurors was still not satisfied about the pocket's temporary disappearance and asked Taylor what conclusion he drew from the fact that the pocket had not been found at the time of the murder, and 'How was it that the murderer put the pocket back?'

'I don't think he did', said Taylor. 'I think he must have left the pocket lying there and when the body was moved, it was picked up with the clothing.'

Taken in isolation, it is perfectly clear what happened to Mrs Luard's pocket – but this sequence of events was not presented to the jury systematically. The pocket evidence became obscurely entangled among various other aspects of the case, just as surely as the pocket itself had become entangled among the sheets at Ightham Knoll.

The first mention of the pocket had come in the General's evidence at the first inquest: during his account of finding his wife's body, he described how she was lying on the veranda: 'I made an examination of her dress and found that her pocket was cut open and lying exposed on the veranda. One of her gloves was lying inside out, as though it had been wrenched off her hand.'[5]

Another two witnesses were heard, then Herbert Harding took the stand. He also described seeing Mrs Luard's glove lying alongside her, but when Dr Mansfield took the witness's chair he stated, 'Under the body, I found a left-hand glove, half turned inside out.'[6]

How had the glove managed to shift itself from alongside the body to underneath it? The answer is fairly clear. While General Luard awaited the arrival of the doctor, he may have attempted to lift or cradle his wife and, in so doing, unwittingly shifted her body slightly, thereby concealing the glove beneath it. Alternatively while making his preliminary examination, Dr Mansfield himself may have disturbed her position more than he realised – Mrs Luard was wearing a floor-length dress, so a glove lying alongside her could very easily have disappeared under its folds. The General's evidence reads very much as though the pocket, like the glove, was originally lying in full view alongside the body, but presumably within minutes of Dr Mansfield's arrival, if not before, the pocket had become hidden among Mrs Luard's skirts.

No description of Mrs Luard's dress or gloves survives, but it is reasonable to assume that the gloves were of a different colour to the dress, whereas the pocket matched it. Thus, in the gathering dusk, Dr Mansfield spotted Mrs Luard's glove, but not the torn-out pocket. By the time Mrs Luard's body was lifted on to a mattress and carried into the Casa it was almost dark. The place where her pocket had been cut or torn out had left very obvious damage to the dress and as the pocket was not lying on the veranda, Superintendent Taylor assumed it was missing, when in fact it had been unwittingly gathered up among the folds of the dead woman's skirts.

The next morning Drs Mansfield and Walker presented themselves at Ightham Knoll to carry out the post mortem. No doubt Mrs Luard's body has been respectfully covered by a sheet, as was customary after death. The doctors drew back the sheet and by unlucky chance the pocket caught on it and was dragged unseen to the foot of the bed, where it then lay concealed among the bedding until the day before the funeral, when the undertakers lifted Mrs Luard's body into her coffin and Jane Pugmore was instructed to shake out the sheets which had been used for the laying out.

In order to carry out their examination, the two doctors had removed Mrs Luard's clothing, which had been taken away by Superintendent Taylor in case it yielded further clues. When the clothing was produced at the first inquest, the pocket was declared missing, along with Mrs Luard's purse and rings; but the very next day Jane Pugmore discovered the pocket and naturally this was reported to the police. There may have been some red faces at this point. Clearly, the original examination of the crime scene had not been as thorough as it should have been and Taylor had jumped to the conclusion that the pocket was missing. Under the circumstances, the police may have preferred to gloss over the whole episode, but in reality this sequence of events should have been made much clearer for the benefit of the jury when the inquest reconvened – not least because some of them evidently remained both uncertain and uneasy about the affair of the pocket.

The final witness that day was Chief Detective Inspector James Scott of Scotland Yard. Scott explained some of the efforts made to date to solve the crime, including the wide circulation of descriptions of the missing rings. He confirmed that, during the experiment conducted by Mr Churchill, he had heard the shots fired at the Casa while standing on the spot where Mrs Wickham said she heard the shots on the afternoon of the murder. Not only did he hear them clearly, but he considered they would have been audible a good deal further away. He confirmed that the shots fired during this experiment were made by a revolver using .320 ammunition.

When questioned about the summerhouse itself, he said it had been established with Mr Wilkinson that the building had not been used by the family or their friends for several months. The keys were kept at Mr Wilkinson's house and no one had entered the bungalow since 27 July. It had been examined thoroughly and there were no signs of recent occupation or break-in: the locks, doors and windows had not been tampered with.

In response to a question about fingerprints, Scott explained that there was no fingerprint evidence available. (In 1908 fingerprinting was not generally employed unless a villain had helpfully dipped his fingers into blood, paint or some similarly obvious substance, then plastered his prints all over the scene. It was, however, clear from the jurors' questions regarding such things as fingerprints and whether it could be determined that the murderer was right- or left-handed that real-life police work had not kept pace with the detective fiction with which they were evidently familiar.)

At the conclusion of Chief Detective Inspector Scott's evidence, Superintendent Taylor stood up and requested a further adjournment to enable the police to continue their enquiries. This came as a surprise to everyone present. The reporter writing for the *Kent Messenger* noted that he had expected the inquest to conclude 'in a humdrum way' – by which he presumably meant a verdict of murder by person or persons unknown.[7]

Coroner Buss was equally taken by surprise and hastily conferred with Chief Constable Warde, on whose orders Taylor was clearly operating. After a brief private conversation, the coroner addressed the jury. 'You have now heard the whole of the evidence and I was in hopes that it would have been possible to conclude this enquiry today, so far as this court is concerned. But from the information which has been given to me, I understand that the Chief Constable of the County thinks that the interests of justice will be furthered if another adjournment takes place for a fortnight. That is to say, the Chief Constable hopes, as we all hope, that someone will be found who is responsible for this crime. In that case it is in the interests of justice that any further evidence should come before this court. In the circumstances, I am under the necessity of asking you to attend once more on 23rd of this month at the same hour and place, and I hope we will then be able to conclude this enquiry.'

The coroner then thanked the jury for their attendance and the hearing concluded on this somewhat ambiguous note.

13

Ogled by an Idle and Cruel World

On the day following this second adjournment, a small body of amateur sleuths arrived from Lancashire, claiming that they would be able to solve the crime by dowsing with wire rods. The party consisted of Mr Berry the diviner, Mr Wilkinson the treasurer and an unnamed 'engineer'. They 'followed the rod' from the Casa to St Lawrence Church, informing those reporters still in Ightham that they were confident they would be able to find the murderer.[1]

This episode was contemptuously dismissed by the *Sevenoaks Chronicle* as 'the divining rod absurdity – and the least said about that the better for all concerned'.[2] In fact the Lancashire 'wire diviners' were not discouraged and returned a month later, basing themselves at the Wheatsheaf in Kemsing while they conducted further 'research' in the vicinity of the murder scene. This second visit was not picked up by most of the national dailies, which had now largely lost interest in the summerhouse murder (by the middle of October clues had dried up and the General was dead), but it was reported in the local press. Although their antics were both unproductive and distasteful, the 'diviners' did inadvertently help to clarify one aspect of the evidence given at the first inquest.

The *Sevenoaks Chronicle* reported that on Saturday 10 October, Frank Wickham (then aged 33, although the report refers to him as a 'lad' and 'young Wickham') was sweeping leaves from the path in St Lawrence churchyard when a gentleman he took to be 'someone in authority' came up and asked him where the rings and the pistol were. Frank Wickham replied that he did not know. This man then asked permission to search Frank Wickham's lodgings, to which Wickham assented, although no search was carried out.

203

Frank Wickham was one of Fred and Anna Wickham's sons and was employed as an under-gardener on the Frankfield estate. At just before 6.00 on the Monday evening following the encounter in the churchyard, he was working in the Frankfield gardens with Daniel Kettel, when another stranger called him to one side and asked whether Wickham knew who he was. Wickham said he did not, but believed him to be one of the wire diviners. The man then blew a whistle, which summoned the other two men in the party. According to Frank Wickham, 'they said I stood in rather queer shoes and asked me to tell them the whole truth about the murder. I said I had spoken the truth and did not know anything about it.'

The three strangers then asked Wickham to accompany them up to the Casa, which he did. They asked how many times he had been there since the murder and he told them three, although as he explained to the press later, he had really only been there once, to assist Daniel Kettel, when they boarded the place up on Mr Wilkinson's instructions. Wickham was alarmed by these questions and the more so when he saw 'a black man' standing nearby in the gathering dusk. Afterwards he reported the whole episode to Superintendent Taylor.

The local paper was at pains to point out that Frank Wickham was a chorister at St Lawrence and had worked for Mr Wilkinson for fifteen years. When approached for a comment, Frank's father Fred Wickham said: 'I call it a scandalous and cruel bit of work.'

The reporter was 'unable to see Mr Wilkinson' (on whose land the whole episode had been enacted) – it is a marked feature of the newspaper coverage that the Wilkinson family managed throughout to elude all the news-hungry reporters; their house stood well within the estate boundaries and the presence of a butler and other staff made it almost impossible to doorstep them.

Daniel Kettel's cottage at Crown Point was easily accessible, and perhaps he was less reluctant to see his name in print than were his employers. At all events, he confirmed Frank Wickham's story about being approached that Monday evening, adding that Wickham had been with him on the afternoon of the murder, when they had been working in the graveyard of St Lawrence Church, after which they walked down the pony drive together towards the big house, reaching the garden at about 3.20.[3]

From this we learn that the 'mate' Kettel omitted to mention at the inquest was Frank Wickham, and that the 'drive' they were walking down when they heard the fatal shots was the pony drive which ran between Frankfield House and the wicket gate where the General and Mrs Luard parted. From the point of view of hearing the shots while walking down a 'drive' this made perfect sense. There was a potential difficulty, however. Those who knew the geography would know that the 5 minutes it took Kettel and Wickham to get half-way down the pony drive was pretty much the same length of time it would have taken Mrs Luard to walk in the opposite direction from the wicket gate to the summerhouse. Logically, therefore, all parties ought to have been at the wicket gate at roughly the same time – and yet Kettel never saw Mrs Luard or the General, whose route to the golf links would have taken him a few yards along the same bridle path which the two gardeners must have used to come from St Lawrence Church.

This sort of contradiction kept the local rumours churning. From the very outset, the whole issue of the timing of the General's parting from Mrs Luard had been the focus of theories. Although the General never actually specified at what time he had separated from his wife, he said it had been at the half-way point in a walk which began at 2.30 and took an hour, and from this is was deduced that the General and his wife parted at 3.00. In spite of attempts to keep sightseers away from the summerhouse, plenty of people (including the wire diviners) had managed to make their way along the path and knew it took nowhere near 15 minutes to reach the Casa from the wicket gate. Thus, if the General was telling the truth, the theories had it that Mrs Luard must have waited at the summer-house for some reason.

A prolonged pause to admire the view seemed unlikely because Mrs Luard was not only familiar with it, but supposedly in a hurry to get home. She would not have sat down to rest because the veranda was entirely devoid of furniture. Nor had she been waylaid by a gang of ruffians, because surely she would have called out for help and any raised voices would have been heard by Edith and Anna Wickham.

The idea that Mrs Luard had arranged an assignation with a lover gained considerable currency. This may have started outside the district: perhaps among those who had noted from the press coverage that Mrs Luard was one of that suspicious species 'the much younger wife'. Very few newspapers had managed to obtain an up-to-date photograph of Mrs Luard, showing the jolly, middle-aged lady she undoubtedly was.[4] Some had described Mrs Luard as looking 'young for her years' – which in fact she did not. From such crumbs grow rumour and legend. According to some stories, Mrs Luard had been shot by her lover – according to others, she was shot by the General because she had a lover. In a variation on the theme, the General shot Mrs Luard because he had a lover.[5]

In this climate of suspicion and speculation, the General continued to receive literally dozens of letters, some accusing him of the crime, others suggesting that he knew more about the affair than he was choosing to reveal. The most hurtful of these must have been the ones with local postmarks. The General also found himself the object of continued curiosity. Writing not long afterwards, the rector of Ightham, the Revd Bertram Winnifrith, noted how everywhere he went the General was 'ogled by an idle and cruel world'.[6]

General Luard had assumed himself to be a well-respected figure within the local community, but the way in which local opinion divided against him is admirably reflected in Monty Parkin's booklet, *The Seal Chart Murder*, in which Mr Parkin published the collected reminiscences of those who could still remember the murder, or had been told about it by relatives who were involved.

It is clear that for everyone like Mr Winnifrith, who obviously thought it absolutely ridiculous that anyone could suspect General Luard, there was someone like Rose Miles, who lived at Stone Street in 1908 and was convinced that the General's frequent excursions to the golf club were a front for an affair she assumed he was having with a woman there.[7] One of the differences between Bertram Winnifrith and Rose Miles was that while the latter knew General Luard only by sight, as a member of the local gentry who passed her cottage frequently on his way to play golf at Wildernesse, Bertram Winnifrith knew the Luards personally in his capacity as their local parish priest. General Luard was one of his churchwardens and church business aside, the Winnifriths may have dined and socialised with the Luards.

Whether or not they were convinced of his innocence, the General's friends and neighbours rallied round. After bringing home his wife's body, the General sat up all night writing letters to notify his numerous friends and relatives of the tragedy. After that he never spent another night at Ightham Knoll, preferring to accept the stream of invitations from sympathetic friends nearby, including Sir Thomas Colyer-Ferguson at Ightham Mote, Sir William Boord across the road at Oldbury Place, and the Colletts at St Clere.[8]

Within a fortnight of his wife's death he had decided to leave the district altogether. Some sources said he planned to take rooms near his London club, others that he was going to reside with his brother-in-law Thomas Hartley at Armathwaite Hall in Cumberland. Whichever was correct – and it may have been a combination of these two – the General advertised the remaining eight years of the lease on Ightham Knoll, 'house, stable, cottage & 8 acres – rent £200'.[9]

The contents were to be auctioned by Hamptons. The home he and Caroline had shared for more than twenty years was to be dismantled and sold off, piece by piece. The sale included bedsteads, bedding, wardrobes, and chests of drawers in mahogany, satin, walnut, ash and birch. There were old oak gate-legged tables, a carved oak settle, a finely carved bureau and a Venetian cabinet; couches, easy chairs, tapestry and other curtains and a spinning wheel, Turkey pile and Brussels carpets and rugs. The twelve Old English mahogany dining chairs and extending mahogany dining table were considered fine enough to merit advertisement in capital letters, as was the antique oak hall cabinet and a finely carved oak bookcase. There was an inlaid writing table and some Queen Anne armchairs, together with other tables, chairs, bookcases and clocks. Almost everything was to go, right down to books, china, glass, kitchen utensils, stable implements and house plants.

The sale was scheduled for 24 September at the property, commencing at 1.00 p.m. 'precisely'. Understandably, the General did not intend to be present. His surviving son, Captain Charles Luard (known in the family as Elmhirst, to avoid confusion with his father) had been given leave and was sailing home from South Africa. He was due to arrive in Southampton on 19 September, where his father planned to meet him off the ship, after which the two men had been invited to stay with friends in Dulverton.

In the three weeks following the murder, General Luard spent most of his days at Ightham Knoll, supervising the packing of those personal items he intended to retain, and dealing with his correspondence: for example, writing personally to everyone who had sent flowers to his wife's funeral. Each evening he left for the sanctuary provided by various hosts, dining and sleeping at the grandest houses in the neighbourhood, never much more than a mile or two away from his own home. Every morning he returned, often to be confronted by more of the letters described by the Revd Winnifrith as 'vile effusions' which continued to arrive in the post.

Once he had decided to accept the invitation to stay in Somerset, he wrote to Coroner Buss, asking to be excused from attending the third session of the inquest, which was scheduled for 23 September, but Buss replied that this was not possible.[10]

Among those who had offered hospitality was Colonel Charles Warde MP, brother of the Chief Constable: but Warde lived at Barham Court, some 8 or 9 miles away, which was not very convenient for returning to Ightham Knoll each day to take care of all the arrangements which had to be made.

A few days after Mrs Luard's funeral, Charles Warde had arranged to take the General out for a drive in the hope of raising his spirits. After this excursion they had tea at Ightham Knoll, and it was then that the General informed Colonel Warde that he had already decided to leave the area. He said he planned to take furnished rooms near his club and to sell all his own furniture, except a family sideboard and his late wife's writing desk, which he thought Elmhirst might like to have.[11]

When he spoke about the kindness of those friends who had provided him with hospitality since his wife's death, Warde again pressed him to stay at Barham Court, but the General was uncertain. He thought he would probably have finished his packing by Tuesday 15 September, which left three days before he set off to meet his son at Southampton; but he had already promised another dear friend that he would spend 2 days with him before he left – even so he thought it might be possible to go to Barham Court on Wednesday 16 September. The two men agreed to confirm these arrangements closer to the time, and accordingly Colonel Warde wrote to General Luard on Tuesday 15 September, to ascertain whether he would in fact be coming to stay the following day. He received a telegram in reply from the General (in the days before the widespread installation of private telephones, the upper classes frequently used telegrams as a swift means of routine communication): 'Will stay with you Thursday night. Can you send car at six o'clock on Thursday?'

Colonel Warde replied that he would collect the General personally and drove over to Ightham Knoll late on Thursday afternoon. When he arrived General Luard was making his final preparations and taking a last look round to ensure he had not forgotten anything. According to Warde's subsequent account, the General's manner was absolutely calm and natural and he said, 'I will be ready in a few minutes.'

As the two men left the house together there was, said Warde, 'a most brilliant sunset – the most brilliant I have ever seen'. The General remarked on it two or three times as they drove away.

During the journey the General spoke about going to his friends in Dulverton. He had wanted to take his son straight there, he said, thus avoiding a return to Ightham; but he had to return for the inquest. He had written asking to be excused, but had received a courteous letter back, explaining that new evidence might crop up, requiring information from him. He went on to complain about the 'scandalous questions' which had been asked of him at the earlier hearings.

He was evidently upset about this, so to change the subject Warde said, 'I wonder why it was adjourned, because of course whatever verdict is given, police enquiries will go on.'

The General replied, 'Yes indeed. I should hope they would.'

After this, said Warde, the conversation turned to other more commonplace subjects.

After dinner that evening at Barham Court, Mrs Warde retired early, leaving her husband and their guest smoking and talking. When it was time for the men to go upstairs, the Colonel walked his guest to the door of his bedroom, where they bid each other goodnight.

The General had asked to be called at 8.00 next morning and at 8.10 Bernard Kelly, one of the Barham Court footmen, took the General a cup of tea. Kelly found the General sitting up in bed. The footman noticed nothing unusual about him and the General did not speak, except to say 'Come in' in response to Kelly's knock at the door.

The Wardes sat down to breakfast, but were somewhat surprised when their guest failed to appear. In due course they sent the butler, Joseph Wolff, in search of him. Wolff went first to the General's bedroom but found it empty. He then began to look in other parts of the house and make enquiries of the servants. One of the housemaids said she had seen the General come downstairs and leave the house by the garden door.

When Wolff conveyed this information to his master, Colonel Warde went into the garden in search of his guest, only to be confronted almost immediately by two policemen, who informed him that a body believed to be that of General Luard had been discovered on the railway lines near the Teston level crossing.

The news that General Luard had taken his own life caused a second press exodus in the direction of rural Kent. Just when the summerhouse murder had begun to run out of steam it suddenly became headline news again, with many papers taking a second opportunity to regale their readers with an account of the late Major General's career, ancestry and a reprise of his wife's murder.

The *Penny Illustrated Paper*, never a publication to allow issues of taste to stand in the way of a good story, devoted the front page of its 26 September issue to an artist's impression of the General throwing himself in front of a train, complete with inset photographs of the late

General Luard and his son. Other pictures included a photograph of the spot on the railway line, marked with an 'x', where the General's body was found. A number of reports mentioned that the General had left a suicide note saying, 'I cannot face my son'.[12]

The General's body was conveyed from the spot where he died to the South Lodge of Barham Court and the inquest arranged for the following day at the Village Room in Teston. Coroner Buss was presiding and had taken particular care of the arrangements for the press, even taking the unusual step of engaging a shorthand writer in order to avoid the usual delay while evidence was taken down in longhand (thereby earning the gratitude of reporters, who needed to wire through details for their evening editions once proceedings were completed).

The coroner's table had been positioned on the platform at one end of the room, with a chair placed alongside it for the witnesses, which *The Times* observed was 'occupied during the greater part of the enquiry by Colonel Warde'.[13]

Indeed, as with the inquest into the death of Mrs Luard, the presence of the Warde brothers loomed large over the proceedings. Both Colonel Warde the MP and his brother the Chief Constable were in attendance, together with Assistant Chief Constable Major Lafone, Captain Charles Luard, who must have been inwardly reeling from the shock of this double bereavement, and Thomas Hartley, the dead man's brother-in-law. Mr Boorman, the Mayor of Maidstone, got in on the act by asking permission to make a little speech, saying how grieved the town was at the recent events and extending sympathy to the Luards' relatives and, of course, to Colonel Warde.

Before the first witnesses were called, the jury were driven to the South Lodge to view the body – a singularly unpleasant task as it had been badly mutilated. –

The first witness was footman Bernard Kelly, who had little to say about his brief morning encounter with the General; nor did the butler Joseph Wolff detain the jury long with his account of searching for the General that morning. It was a different matter with the third witness, Colonel Charles Warde.

Warde had already given lengthy interviews to local reporters, which had been taken up in varying forms in both the national and provincial dailies. Once seated in the witness chair, he asked Buss's permission to read a statement instead of answering questions in the usual way. When faced with an identical request from General Luard during the original inquest at Ightham Knoll, Thomas Buss had refused to deviate from normal procedure. On this occasion he acquiesced to Warde's request; possibly because the circumstances were entirely different, although there may have been other factors at play.

Ever since the press had been excluded from the first inquest on Chief Constable Warde's orders, there had been a degree of animosity between Buss and Warde. As already mentioned, Buss had written to the papers after the episode at Ightham, describing what had taken place as 'a gross interference with my powers and discretion', and although he had not specifically named the Chief Constable, it was a very public slap on the wrist and probably needled Warde.

It is therefore possible that when Warde intervened to request an adjournment at the George & Dragon, he may have been partly motivated by a desire to show Thomas Buss that he could exert influence over the proceedings, whether the coroner liked it or not. Certainly, the circumstances engendered by Chief Constable Warde made it almost impossible for Buss to conclude the inquest that afternoon, as he had clearly intended to do.

Then on the day of the General's death, another salvo had been fired in the coroner's direction. Evening editions of newspapers all over Kent and beyond carried interviews with the Chief Constable's brother, Colonel Charles Warde, which stated that the General had been upset by the 'scandalous questions' asked of him at the previous inquest – something which could have been read as personal criticism of the coroner himself.[14]

At all events, thanks to Coroner Buss's decision to deviate from the usual protocol at the Teston hearing, all those present (and the public at large via the newspapers) received a lengthy, coherent account of the events leading up to the General's suicide. If there was a problem with this, it was that Warde had been a personal friend of the General and was plainly intent on putting a particular slant on his evidence. It also led some of those who had been following the case to the inescapable conclusion that the General's powerful friends had succeeded in imposing themselves and their version of events on to the proceedings.

Charles Warde told his story of the General's final evening and the summons to the railway line. On his way to the line, he had been overtaken by Wolff, who on returning to the room used by the General had discovered three letters on the desk, one of which was addressed to Colonel Charles Warde.

18-9-08

My Dear Warde,

I am sorry to have returned your kindness and hospitality and long friendship in this way, but I am satisfied it is best to join her in the second life at once, as I can be of no further use to anyone in this world, of which I am tired and in which I do not want to live any longer.

I thought my strength was strong enough to bear up against the horrible accusations and terrible letters in reference to that awful crime, which has robbed me of all my happiness, and so it was for a long time. The kindness and sympathy of so many friends has kept me going on somehow. Now in the last day or two something seems to have snapped: the strength has left me and I care for nothing except to join her again. So goodbye, dear friend.

Yours very affectionately

C.E. Luard

PS. I shall be somewhere on the line of the railway. Please send the enclosed telegrams to Elmhirst my son; my brother-in-law and my maid.

The three telegrams read, respectively:

Agent Union Castle Line, Southampton. Immediately 'Norman' arrives send message Captain Luard to go to Barham Court. General Luard.

Hartley, Armathwaite, Bassenthwaite Lake. Come to Barham Court near Maidstone. I have now joined her. Charlie.

Miss Huish, The Knoll, Ightham. Not returning today. Capt Luard goes Barham Court.

Colonel Warde went on to explain that he had not sent these telegrams, thinking it better to substitute them with telegrams of his own. When he returned to the house, he made enquiries with the footman, who confirmed that the General had consumed the tea and bread and butter taken up to him that morning. The sponge and towels in the General's room were still damp, indicating that he had taken his bath.

'I cannot help thinking', Warde expounded, 'that as he said in his letter something must have snapped. He must have hurried into his clothes and written these letters and telegrams. I calculate that he had 35 minutes to do that before being seen by the housemaid, leaving the house by the garden door.'

Warde continued in this vein for some time, reiterating his belief that the suicide had been a spur of the moment act and recalling various small incidents to support this idea. He also wished to mention, he said, a letter he had come across only recently from Mrs Luard, writing about her husband in affectionate terms. Finally, 'speaking with some warmth', he wanted to state how horrified he had been by some versions of the General's letter to him, which had appeared in the press the previous day – in particular the line 'I cannot face my son' – which was a complete fabrication.

In pressing his own opinions regarding the General's suicide, some people may have felt the Colonel was overstepping the mark. It was for the jury to decide whether this had been a deliberately planned act, or one which had been committed while of unsound mind. Deliberately planned suicide was widely considered a sin (unsuccessful suicides were still liable to prosecution) and burial in consecrated ground was sometimes denied. Warde's urging that the General had taken his life during a fit of momentary madness because 'something had snapped', while understandable, nevertheless encroached beyond the usual role of a witness.

One of the jurors wanted to know when Colonel Warde considered the three letters had been written. Warde said this must have been between 8.10 and 8.45. The letters were dated for that morning and the General could not have written them before daybreak, or after retiring the night before, because the candles in his room were so little burned down.

The next witness was Robert Wright, who was employed on the Barham Court estate. Wright had seen General Luard go through the gates at the South Lodge just before 9.00 that morning. He had looked absolutely as usual and wished Wright 'Good morning' as he went by.

Frederick Bridges, the driver of the 9.00 Maidstone to Paddock Wood train, described how the General suddenly jumped out in front of his train, giving no opportunity to apply the brakes in time to avoid hitting him. The train had not actually knocked the General down, Bridges explained, rather the General had put his hands up in the air and fallen in front of the engine, which then ran over him. Bridges had applied the brake as hard as he could, throwing some passengers out of their seats, but it had been too late. The train had come to a standstill near the level crossing, where some platelayers were working, and these men walked back to the body with the signalman.

Richard Harper, the signalman at Teston Crossing, told the court that after walking back to the body on the line he had fetched a constable from the village. The constable had examined the dead man and established his identity. Harper said that after leaving Barham Court the General would have had to climb two gates and cross a field to reach that point on the track.

The first policeman on the scene was PC Masters. On searching the body he found a linen mark on the shirt 'C.E. Luard' at which point it occurred to the men that the body was probably that of the General. When they reached the South Lodge, a more thorough search was made and Masters discovered an unsealed envelope in a jacket pocket, on which was written 'General Luard's body. To be taken to Colonel Warde's Barham Court 18-9-08'.

Superintendent Ford then gave evidence that he had searched the General's bedroom at Barham Court, in the presence of Colonel Warde and the Chief Constable. On the dressing table he had found £1 0s 11d in cash, a gold watch and chain, a small compass and two bunches of keys. On the writing table was a pair of spectacles, a pipe, a tobacco pouch, several postage stamps, a photograph of Captain Luard, two sealed envelopes addressed to 'Capt Luard DSO to await arrival' and 'T. Hartley Esq to await arrival' and finally a telegram torn into six pieces, which when put together read:

> Willink, Burneside, Kendal. I have gone to her and the other life. Goodbye. Something has snapped. Charlie.

(Beatrice Willink was one of the General's half-sisters and why he changed his mind about the telegram notifying her of his death remains a mystery.)

The two letters addressed to the General's son and brother-in-law had been handed to the coroner unopened. In a moment of pure theatre, Thomas Buss now handed the letter addressed to Mr Hartley across to its intended recipient, who opened and read it in silence, before passing it back to the coroner, who then read it aloud to the court.

Barham Court
18-9-08

My Dear Tom,
Something has snapped at last. My strength has gone and I have gone to join her. I had left her everything, but have now made a new will (at Atkins) leaving everything to Elmhirst and you as sole executor. Goodbye dear brother.

Ever yours
C.E. Luard

PS. It is all the horrid letters (destroyed) and insinuations that have been made.

The doctor who examined General Luard's body gave his evidence before the final act in the drama, when the coroner invited Captain Luard to enter the hall. Buss apologised for calling on Captain Luard to attend, but explained that the letter found addressed to him might contain information which had a bearing on the proceedings and might therefore need to be disclosed. He asked Captain Luard whether he wished to open the letter himself and, on receiving a positive reply, handed the letter over.

There was silence in the hall while Captain Luard read the letter or, as close observers noted, what appeared to be two letters, one of which was written on paper edged with a black border. When he had finished, Captain Luard turned to the coroner and said, 'There is nothing here that would interest you.'

'May I look at it?' asked the coroner. After a moment's hesitation the young man handed the letter over and it was Mr Buss's turn to scrutinise it in silence. Having done so he announced that he did not intend to reveal the contents, which contained nothing 'pertinent to this enquiry' being merely 'domestic matters' which concerned the General and his son. This announcement was greeted with cries of 'Hear, hear' from several of the jurors.

The moment had now arrived for the coroner to sum up. He made a long speech, which included recounting episodes from the General's 'distinguished' military career. He alluded to the General's service to the community, his time as a magistrate and a county councillor, and his work with the Patriotic Society, all of which sounded rather more like a eulogy given at a memorial service than a summing-up of the evidence at an inquest. Coroner Buss then spoke of the death of Mrs Luard and mentioned the 'many base insinuations in the shape of anonymous letters' sent not only to the General, but to everyone involved in the case, including himself. (Those he himself had received had been consigned to the wastepaper basket.)

He reminded the court that it was a principle of English justice that a man was innocent until proved guilty – which rousing sentiment drew further cries of 'Hear, hear'. The letters written to the General, 'a sensitive and honourable man', had made his life all but intolerable and had no doubt been a great factor in inducing the General to take his own life.

Buss dwelt on the theme of the letters for some time, stating that the writers had contributed to the General's death, and concluding, 'Let us hope that although they treated him so badly in the last remaining time of his life, they will respect his memory now and utter no more lying and baseless and unfounded insinuations.'

From the letters he moved seamlessly into the issue of remarks made regarding questions asked of the General at the inquest. 'I do not feel bound and have no reason to defend my conduct in any way', said Buss. In spite of this, he went on to explain at some length that in the light of the rumours which had been flying about, he deemed it his duty to call the witnesses who testified at the second inquest, in order to demonstrate that the General had accounted for his movements on the day in question; which showed 'he could not possibly have been present and committed this act'. He had done this not least, he said, because 'the General had no other tribunal where he could give his evidence'.

Eventually the coroner reached the crux of the matter in hand. There could be no doubt from the evidence they had heard that the General had committed suicide. However, 'If you take into consideration the tense strain which he had undergone, I think I may suggest to you it was enough to unhinge anyone's mind.'

The jury could hardly have been given a clearer indication of the verdict expected of them, and took a very short time to return a verdict of 'Suicide during temporary insanity'.

The foreman announced that the jury wished to express their deep sympathy for Captain Luard and to thank Colonel Warde for his statement and the way he had 'contradicted so many falsehoods' which had been in circulation. To this the coroner added his thanks as 'we are all greatly indebted to Colonel Warde'. A rather cloying note on which to conclude, considering that Colonel Warde had done no more than provide a witness statement, and use the inquest as a platform from which to lambaste certain sections of the press.

14

A Delicate Affair

On Sunday 20 September 1908, the Revd Bertram Winnifrith preached on the text from I Corinthians 13:13, 'And now abideth faith, hope, charity, these three; but the greatest of these is charity.' The congregation in St Peter's Ightham listened soberly as the Revd Winnifrith spoke of the great tragedy which had lately been enacted in their midst. There had been a terrible lack of charity shown, he said, and a great many cruel and baseless accusations had been made. He echoed Coroner Buss's reminder that a man is innocent until proven guilty. When they thought of the sixth commandment, he said, few people considered that it was possible to murder a man by taking away his good character. He had no doubt that this second death could be styled as much murder as the first, except that it had taken a crueller and more harrying form. 'What can possibly be more contemptible than for one calling himself a man to write under cover of anonymity to one already smarting under the cruellest blow that could possibly be inflicted, accusing him of a deed which he would scorn to commit – a deed which bereft him of a trusted and loving partner who had been all in all to him for thirty-three years.' Whose heart would not go out to that young soldier who had arrived home to learn of this second terrible blow, the rector asked.[1]

In one sense at least Captain Luard did not return home. Colonel Charles Warde went to meet him at Southampton, from whence Warde had arranged for them to travel to London on the mail train in order to evade press attention. Even this did not enable them to completely evade reporters, who managed to get a glimpse of the shocked, pale visage of Captain Luard as he disembarked from the *Norman* early on Saturday morning.[2]

From London, Colonel Warde and Captain Luard travelled on to Barham Court, where the young officer stayed pending his father's funeral. In the meantime Ightham Knoll was not deserted. Reporters who turned up there on the day of the General's suicide, hoping for a story, discovered the house under police guard and were told that Superintendent Taylor was inside, making a search for any letters and documents which 'might throw light on the matter'.[3] It was rumoured that the police had exhumed the remains of a dog, shot by the General two years previously, but discovered the animal had been dispatched with a shotgun.[4] It cannot have gone unnoticed that on hearing of his old friend's suicide, the Chief Constable had dashed to Barham Court in order to be present when the bedroom so lately occupied by General Luard was searched by Superintendent Ford.[5] None of this activity really squared with assurances at the inquest that everyone concerned in the investigation was convinced of the General's innocence.

Similarly, there cannot have been much faith in Colonel Charles Warde's notion that the General's suicide had been a sudden, impulsive act. A man does not suddenly conceive the notion to end his life, dash off a small pile of correspondence, leave his belongings neatly set out on the desk and his bedroom tidy – not forgetting to have his bath and drink his morning tea, all in a matter of half an hour. When a momentarily doubting juror asked Colonel Warde when he thought the General had written all those letters, Warde glibly stated that this must have taken place in a time window of precisely 35 minutes.

Major General Luard left three letters, all of which had to be written and placed into sealed envelopes, each of which he addressed. In addition to this he had composed four telegrams and written out the envelope issuing instructions that his body be taken to Barham Court. The precise wording of these communications is all known, apart from the text of the letter to his son. Experiment has shown that it takes 15 minutes to reproduce the text of the known communications and the envelopes – assuming that the writer does not pause at all. The longest communication where the contents are known is the letter to Charles Warde, which occupied

6 minutes of the 15. If the letter to Captain Luard was of a similar length (as it apparently ran to a second page, it may have been substantially longer), then the General must have spent at least 21 minutes at his writing desk that morning, unless some of these missives were composed in advance. This timescale presupposes that the General knew precisely what he intended to write and never hesitated over a word. In the remaining 14 minutes, he had to get out of bed, remove his night attire, take a bath, get dressed, drink his morning tea, eat his bread and butter, quietly leave his bedroom and get down to the garden door. Although not impossible, it is a somewhat unlikely scenario.

The General's behaviour that morning was both considered and orderly: the possessions laid out in the bedroom, the identifying envelope found in his pocket, his customary polite good morning to the employee at the Lodge Gate. It is the calmly unhurried behaviour of a man carrying out an act which has been carefully planned. Additional evidence that General Luard fully intended to end his life that morning can be found in his behaviour during his final day at Ightham. He visited the Mote, the house which had first brought him to the district and of which he remained so fond. This was followed by a visit to the church, where it was later discovered he had signed his name in the Visitors' Book – a singularly unusual act for someone who had been a regular worshipper there for more than twenty years.[6]

The General's funeral was set for 3.15 on Monday 21 September.[7] Contrary to expectations, the body was kept in the South Lodge at Barham Court, rather than brought home to Ightham Knoll. At shortly after 9.00 on the morning of the funeral, the hearse arrived from Ightham to convey the body straight to St Peter's Church. The coffin was placed on a bier in the aisle, next to the pew the General had customarily occupied in life. His son and Colonel Warde followed the hearse in a motor car. After seeing the coffin placed in church, they returned to Ightham Knoll to await the other family mourners. The house must have presented a desolate prospect: a great many items had already been packed in readiness for the General's departure to London.

Although the weather was much kinder, the funeral did not draw such enormous crowds as had attended when Mrs Luard was buried, just over three weeks earlier. Even so there was a larger crowd than could be accommodated inside. Once more the extended family had journeyed considerable distances to attend, and reporters who managed to obtain a position inside the church noted their obvious distress.

Captain Luard sat in the pew his father had occupied for Mrs Luard's funeral, with his uncle Thomas Hartley next to him, and Colonel Warde on the other side of Mr Hartley. Family friend the Revd Guise had again been invited to assist the Revd Winnifrith at the funeral, which was a noticeably simpler affair than that of Mrs Luard. There were no hymns and no funeral address. The only military links were provided by names on some of the numerous wreaths. The local gentry had turned out in force and messages on their wreaths were full of sympathy, affection and regard for the deceased.

At the conclusion Captain Luard tossed a bunch of chrysanthemums, said to have been the General's favourite flowers, on to the coffin: other relatives added a bunch of clematis and a simple posy of violets. It was like a melancholy replay, with Captain Luard standing in for his father at the head of the grave.

The inquest into the death of Mrs Luard resumed at the George & Dragon two days later.[8] All the witnesses who had given evidence at the two previous hearings were in attendance, with the exception of the General himself and Mrs Stewart. The coroner opened by reading through all the statements previously made, which took up a considerable time.

All the witnesses concurred to their evidence as it stood, with the exception of Dr Mansfield, who said he wished to add something. At the first session Dr Mansfield had indulged in some fanciful speculations as to how Mrs Luard's death might possibly have been suicide; he had also diverged from the opinion of his colleague Dr Walker by saying that the effusion on the back of Mrs Luard's head was due to a blow being struck with some object, whereas Walker thought it had been caused by a fall. After giving the matter further thought, Mansfield had decided the effusion was, after all, the result of a fall. 'If it had been a blow, there would have been a small effusion. This was an enormous effusion.'[9] (Dr Mansfield apparently failed to appreciate that an 'enormous effusion' might equally be the result of the victim's having sustained a heavy blow.)

When he had finished a full recital of the proceedings to date, Coroner Buss turned to Superintendent Taylor and asked him if there was any further evidence.

'No sir', Taylor replied. 'We have not been able to find any further evidence to bear upon this matter. The clues we had at the last adjournment have been followed up and nothing further has occurred which we can bring to your notice.'

At this point it may have occurred to some people to wonder why on earth the inquest had been adjourned on 9 September. Apart from the single intervention by Dr Mansfield, this third sitting had been no more than a pointless revision of what had gone before, bringing the proceedings to precisely where they had been at the end of the previous session. Working men had been summoned to attend, losing an afternoon's pay in the process, and apparently all for nothing. Before summing up, the coroner addressed this issue saying, 'I would like to refer to the reason for the adjournment of the inquest until today. You may remember that on the last occasion, at the request of the Chief Constable, it was stated that the police wished for further time to make other enquiries.' Some press reports, he continued, had suggested this was because the Chief Constable had some definite clues in hand which might lead to the arrest of some particular individual. He wished to assure them that this had not been his understanding of the matter, and that any suggestions that an arrest had been imminent were based on this misapprehension of the situation. 'You have heard the statement of Superintendent Taylor', he reminded the jury – they had heard all the evidence there was to hear – there were no other clues.

Buss then summed up the evidence. He reiterated the respect in which Mrs Luard had been held by 'all classes' and the fact that no motive had been established to explain why anyone should wish to harm her. Suicide was not a possibility. All the evidence showed that Mrs Luard and her husband had been on excellent terms. 'Certain questions' had been asked of General Luard, he said, 'the object of which had no doubt been clear to the jury' – namely to establish whether anyone other than the General had any motive for killing Mrs Luard. The guns kept at Ightham Knoll had been shown to be incapable of firing the bullets which killed the victim.

He spoke of the anonymous letters which had caused the General such immense anguish: he hoped the police would be able to trace and punish the senders. The police, he declared, had carried out their investigation under 'the most disadvantageous circumstances' – the murder scene being at a remote spot, a long way from their headquarters in Sevenoaks.

In his twenty-five years as coroner for the county he could not recall a case where the police had been so much in the dark. It was 'one of the most mysterious crimes that have been perpetrated in Kent'; it had been 'most cunningly conceived and daringly executed'. Naturally everyone still hoped the perpetrator would be brought to justice, and although the matter was completed as far as this court was concerned, the police would still be pursuing their enquiries.

The jury retired to consider their verdict and returned after about 10 minutes to pronounce a verdict of murder by person or persons unknown. The verdict had evidently not taken them long because they had occupied some time in preparing a short written statement, which with the coroner's permission was read aloud by their foreman:

> We wish to enter our most emphatic protest against those persons who have written or forwarded anonymous letters and postcards to various members of the jury, with a view to influencing their minds; and we should hail with pleasure any action which may be taken to bring such persons to justice. We also wish to convey our sympathetic condolences to Captain Luard in the great trouble which has befallen him. We also express our sincere appreciation of the difficult exertions of the Kent constabulary and the Scotland Yard Detectives.

Chief Constable Warde took this as his cue to rise and make a brief statement. In the light of the coroner's comments today and at the Teston inquest on Saturday, he said, he wished to state that the police 'had ascertained beyond doubt that there is not the slightest foundation for any of those rumours or accusations made by letter or otherwise'.

The coroner wound the inquest up by declaring himself in agreement with the jury's verdict and in complete sympathy with the sentiments they had expressed after giving it.

The verdict had finally been given – to many it must have seemed not just 'murder by person or persons unknown' but a resounding 'not guilty' in respect of General Luard.

For the local people, the words spoken from the pulpit that Sunday and in the inn on Wednesday may have carried an additional subtext. Not only those who had written the vile anonymous letters to the General were to be condemned, but seemingly anyone who had written anonymously to others involved in the case – perhaps even people who had no more than written to the police, offering what they genuinely assumed to be helpful suggestions. Nor was it just letter-writers who fell within this net of condemnation – those who had gossiped and spread rumours were equally culpable. Where did discussion end and gossip begin? Now there was talk of the police seeking out and punishing anyone found guilty of this behaviour. The message to the lower classes was loud and clear – there was to be no further speculation regarding General Luard's role in his wife's murder.

The last weekend in September saw what might be termed the grand finale as far as press coverage of the Luard affair was concerned. The weekend papers had two inquests and a funeral to cover, and while not on the scale of the original murder, these events provided a mass of material which was eagerly seized upon. Some emphasis was placed on the terrible loss suffered by Captain Luard ('a tall soldierly gentleman, with a fair moustache'),[10] but for most editors the real focus remained the extremely mysterious nature of Mrs Luard's murder, coupled with disparaging denunciations of the letter-writers who had driven the General to his death. Any connection between the anonymous letter-writers and the sensationalist coverage deemed appropriate by the newspapers themselves was conveniently overlooked – although the papers which had not printed the 'I cannot face my son' version of General Luard's letter lost no time in sniping at those which had.

The *Maidstone & Kentish Journal* adopted a typically lofty tone, stating that the General had been driven to his death by anonymous slanders. In a long, rambling article which summarised the story to date, the *Journal* emphasised how mysterious the case was, particularly since it involved a woman of Mrs Luard's position in society. Joining the universal condemnation of the letter-writers, the report said that 'two murders have been committed in Kent this month. Mrs Luard was killed with a pistol; General Luard was killed with a pen.' As for the identity of Mrs Luard's murderer, ''Tis not likely the answer will be given until the leaves of the Judgement Book unfold.'[11]

During the following week many newspapers reproduced a letter written by Thomas Kennion, one of Caroline Luard's nephews, protesting about the anonymous letters which had driven the General to take his own life. While Kennion's anger was justified, it is difficult to envisage how he imagined the police might be able to trace and punish those who had sent the letters – not least because they had all been destroyed. Nonetheless, Mr Kennion wrote: 'I urge that some means be found whereby these pests can be dealt with. At the present moment it seems anyone . . . in the public eye is open to the frenzied attacks of any maniac or criminal who can afford a penny stamp.'

He went on to say of the General that 'Few people had so unclouded a married life as he and his wife had. . . . No friction existed between them, or had ever existed; no motive whatever has been alleged and it was absolutely proved at the second inquest that the General could not have been anywhere near the scene of the crime when the shots were fired and yet there have been men and women who have written to everybody concerned in the case, the vilest slanders against the bereaved husband himself.' He ended by urging that the Home Office 'should deal severely with those who have used and are using the postal service for such infamous purposes'.[12]

From then on, the aftershocks of the summerhouse murder would sound more quietly. When the Malling Petty Sessional Court opened at the end of September, at the commencement of business a statement was read out to the effect that the Justices had lost a respected colleague in General Luard. They wished to record their sympathy for his son and deprecate the 'deliberate, unscrupulous, venomous attacks . . . by anonymous letter writers' whom they too hoped would be identified and punished. Several of the signatories, such as Major General Goldsworthy and Sir Mark Collet, had been near neighbours of the Luards; the first name on the list was that of Colonel Charles Warde MP.[13]

In mid-October some local papers reported that shortly before his death General Luard had made a generous gift to the Patriotic Society.[14] Around the same time, a brief flutter of local interest was occasioned by 'the divining rod absurdity'. In November one or two publications had to quell rumours printed in some Sunday editions that police had turned the focus of their enquiries to Plymouth, where the ring inscribed *ISHI* had been found. According to the Kent Constabulary there was no truth in this whatever.[15]

After this the summerhouse affair dwindled into silence until the first anniversary of the General's suicide when, in a sensational development, a man was arrested and charged with Mrs Luard's murder.

The man in question was 62-year-old David Talbot Woodruff, or Woodruffe. According to the *Kent Messenger* Woodruff had seen better days, having once been in regular employment as a gardener. He had been twice married, but both his wives had died and so had all his children, except one who had gone abroad. Woodruff had fallen a long way since his days as a family man in regular work. For the last few years he had been on the road, picking up casual work as and when he could.[16]

On 12 May 1909 he had been admitted to Bromley Union Workhouse, where a revolver was discovered among his possessions. He was accused of pointing this weapon at the workhouse labour master and attempting to discharge it at him. Woodruff denied the charge, but was found guilty and sentenced to four months' hard labour.[17]

Although it was customary for prisoners to be released first thing in the morning, on the day Woodruff was due to be discharged from Maidstone Prison he was detained there without explanation until after lunch. Eventually, Superintendent Albert Taylor arrived and charged Woodruff with the murder of Caroline Luard. (To which Woodruff later commented, 'I was never so astonished in my life.')

Taylor escorted Woodruff by train to Sevenoaks, where he was subsequently brought before the magistrates with a request that he be remanded in custody for seven days to enable the police to make enquiries. Mr House, the solicitor who had been charged with defending the accused man, objected strongly to this. He said the police had had four months in which to make enquiries, and that there was not a shred of evidence to connect Woodruff to the Luard murder, apart from the discovery of a revolver among his possessions. The police, he said, had arrested Woodruff 'for some reason best known to themselves' and he felt so strongly on the matter that he was 'in danger of committing an indiscretion before the Bench'.

Taylor responded by saying that the police had only recently become aware of certain facts and thus had not had time to make their enquiries. The magistrates were not at all happy with the situation, and as the warrant for arrest had been issued at the instigation of Chief Constable Warde, Warde was required to enter the witness box himself. Warde swore that the 'evidence' had indeed only come to the attention of the police during the preceding few days, but he was reluctant to elaborate as to what this evidence comprised.

The chairman of the bench, Mr Crosbie Hill, said that if a man was to be detained, they required some evidence to be placed before them to justify it. Warde continued to prevaricate until Mr Crosbie Hill asked him point blank whether he was prepared to bring any evidence before them that day.

Warde replied, 'Not today sir. Of course, I can give certain facts which came to my own knowledge, which caused me to have the prisoner arrested, but I should be very loath to do that just now, as it would affect the case. The hands of the police are very much tied. They want to make certain enquiries before the facts are made public. If they were made public, they would militate against justice.'

The magistrates retired to consider the matter. When they returned, it was to state that insufficient evidence had been provided to warrant detaining the prisoner. There was some applause at the rear of the court.

Woodruff walked free. He was given a meal at the police station and put on the train to London, but not before he had given a brief interview to a local reporter. He again denied the charge of threatening the labour master at the workhouse, declaring that he had never pointed the gun at anyone and was only 'minding it, for a pal in London'. As for the Luard murder, he remembered what he had been doing at the time clearly. On 13 August 1908 he had been sentenced to one day's imprisonment for sleeping out. On his release, he went to Tunbridge Wells, from there he had gone to Hildenborough and from there by train to Orpington. By 24 August (the day of the murder) he was in Farnborough, where a fire he made by the roadside was kicked out by a policeman. On 25 August he had returned to London, where he read about the murder in the newspapers. This was the sum total of his knowledge of the crime.

Woodruff was never re-arrested and the evidence Chief Constable Warde claimed to possess about the matter was never revealed. The issue did not end with Woodruff's release, however. Mr House felt so strongly about the matter that he put it before a local MP (presumably not Colonel Charles Warde) and it became the subject of a parliamentary question. Mr House told the papers he thought the matter ought to be looked into and 'mentioned generally the action of the Kent police in connection with the Luard case'.[18] This latter rather implies that the Woodruff arrest had not been the first instance of heavy-handedness in connection with the enquiry.[19]

More telling yet were the contents of an interview published in the *Kent Messenger*, in which the Revd Jackson, one of the magistrates who heard the Woodruff case, openly criticised Warde and expressed the opinion that his actions ought to be the subject of a full enquiry. The Revd Jackson claimed to have fifty years' experience as a magistrate and said that during that time he had never come across anything comparable. He stressed that the situation was entirely the responsibility of Colonel Warde – Superintendent Taylor and the Sevenoaks police were 'in no way responsible'. A warrant for arrest was not normally approved without there being some evidence to justify it, and the warrant for Woodruff's arrest had only been issued on the strict understanding that evidence would be forthcoming at the proper time. The Revd Jackson felt very strongly that the charge should not have been made and that such a serious charge called for the utmost care and caution.

Although the Revd Jackson would never have used such an expression, even if he knew it, it is perfectly clear from his remarks and those of Mr House that there was a strong suspicion Chief Constable Warde had attempted to 'fit up' David Woodruff – and that in reality no evidence at all existed to implicate him in the Luard murder.

Warde responded to all this adverse comment with a lengthy piece of bluster, informing a press representative that:

> I do not take any notice of personal criticisms of my conduct as Chief Constable of the county, raised by individuals or by the Press. If no person was ever arrested on suspicion, few criminals would be detected at all and hardly any crime would be solved . . . certain suspicious facts were within my knowledge, which explained the action I saw fit to take.
>
> The magistrate who granted the warrant and the clerk to the justices knew these circumstances privately from me, before I swore the information on which this warrant was granted. I must confess I was surprised at the action of the magistrates, for it is usual to leave a matter of this kind to the Chief Constable . . . as it is, the county have been put to considerable expense.[20]

Not only does Warde display an arrogant sense of his own importance here, but the very fact that he felt able openly to imply that in cases where he was personally involved the rules simply did not matter, is disturbing to put it mildly. Warde had evidently obtained an arrest warrant under false pretences, expecting the magistrates to go along with him simply because they were part of the same upper-class 'club' where the word of one of their caste was good enough to set aside the tiresome niceties of the law.

Warde finished up by complaining that people failed to appreciate the great difficulties faced by anyone at the head of a criminal investigation, adding that 'the Luard case has been a particularly delicate and difficult task from the first'.

In the same week, prompted by Mr House's concerns, Mr Pickersgill MP put a question to the Home Secretary, asking whether a prisoner was entitled to be released in the morning. The Home Secretary replied that although prisoners were usually let out in the morning, the prison authorities were entitled to keep them for the full duration of the last day of their sentence if they elected so to do. In this particular instance, they had elected to do so at the request of the police.[21]

After this the Woodruff affair petered out. There was no enquiry into the Chief Constable's actions, but nor were there any more arrests in connection with the Luard murder.

The arrest of David Woodruff may be one of the strongest indications that Chief Constable Warde actually believed General Luard had been the guilty party. Woodruff was an expendable dupe, whose conviction would have helped silence rumours against the late General, thereby restoring not only his own reputation, but by association the reputation of his class.

Anyone who doubts that a man in Warde's position would be capable of such duplicity need look no further than the case of Oscar Slater. Although the Kent force was not involved in the Slater affair, it has elements which are strongly reminiscent of the Luard–Woodruff episode. Slater was a Jewish immigrant who until convicted of the murder of a wealthy Glasgow spinster named Marion Gilchrist had nothing more serious on his record than a couple of petty gambling convictions. His death sentence was commuted to life imprisonment on appeal, after which he served almost twenty years before being released on a technicality. The case papers have subsequently revealed that senior police officers knew from the outset that Slater was an innocent man. The real killer was a man whose family connections numbered among them the Glasgow Procurator Fiscal – Slater's arrest and trial were nothing more than a means to divert attention from the real culprit. Miss Gilchrist was murdered in December 1908 and Slater was tried and convicted the following year – just a few months prior to David Woodruff's lucky escape.[22]

15

Unbreakable?

The summerhouse murder created a massive sensation in 1908 and would eventually pass into the annals of Britain's most famous unsolved murders. Over the next half-century numerous accounts of it were published and theories aired. In the early 1960s it appeared that the solution had been provided by the C.H. Norman memorandum. Post-Norman, amateur and professional sleuths continued to bend their minds to the case, and local people continued to discuss it.

Local opinion seems to have been polarised between those who accepted the General's innocence absolutely and those who were utterly convinced of his guilt. For many years after the murder, however, the latter group seems to have been reluctant to voice their opinions beyond their immediate family – a reflection, perhaps, of the degree to which locals heeded the denunciations and threats of retribution which had issued from pulpit, coroner and police in the immediate aftermath of the General's suicide.

One or two people claimed to have first-hand information which might have helped either convict or exonerate General Luard. A local man who had been 12 years old at the time of the crime claimed to have seen the General running through the woods on the day of the murder, presumably attempting to establish an alibi by arriving at the golf club at 3.30.[1] In fact the General's walk between the summerhouse and the golf club was so well supported by independent witnesses that this story is unworthy of serious consideration.

Similarly improbable is the rumour that Mrs Luard was murdered by Sir William Boord's mentally unbalanced son: a story which probably reflects the widespread suspicion attached to mental illness at the time rather than any real evidence that he was the culprit. Since no one actually saw the young man commit the deed, this suspicion is at best based on the coincidence of his being missing from the house at the time of Mrs Luard's death – an absence from home which only 'rumour' has ever suggested.

This particular scenario called for Sir William's son to have evaded the rest of the household long enough to obtain a revolver, carry out the crime and then, presumably, return home. If he had left the house hoping to shoot someone, the normally deserted Fish Ponds Wood was not the most obvious place to seek a victim. Any notion that he deliberately followed the Luards, shadowing them through the wood and lying in wait for Mrs Luard's return to the summerhouse, is frankly ridiculous. This would have required not only some very clever scouting techniques, but also the foreknowledge that Mrs Luard *would* be returning alone to the summerhouse. Nor could the young man have seen the Luards leaving their home from his windows at Oldbury Place – he would have needed to be in position near the gates of his father's property to observe the Luards emerge from Common Lane, and then to have stalked them without their noticing for some distance along the main road, until they turned into the wood at Seven Wents.

It is pertinent to ask where this unlikely theory might have had its genesis. Since the story goes that the Boords hushed the matter up, Sir William's family can certainly be excluded as the source. Dr Walker (who was also the Luards' doctor) would be bound by medical confidentiality, and if he had entertained any suspicions at all, he was surely more likely to have breached his professional code of conduct by informing the Chief Constable, rather than spreading a rumour around the neighbourhood. This leaves understairs gossip. Traditionally family servants are supposed to have known everything that went on 'upstairs', but in reality the lower servants in even quite modest households might go for days without setting eyes on their employers, and were not generally in the confidence of those trusted senior servants, who were in a position to overhear things – but among whom discretion was an absolute watchword.

(It will be recalled that Jane Pugmore, the housemaid at Ightham Knoll, had not seen either General or Mrs Luard at all on the day Mrs Luard died – and Oldbury Place was a much larger, grander establishment).[2] It may well be that a whisper in the scullery about summoning Dr Walker grew into an entirely unwarranted suspicion that the murder, which coincidentally took place on the same day, was in some way connected.

There can be little doubt that many local people suspected that the General had killed his wife. There was a widespread belief that the police net had been closing in on him and the General was tipped off that his arrest was imminent. Rather than face the disgrace of trial, arrest and the hangman's noose, the General was assumed to have 'fallen on his sword'. According to one rumour, this course had been suggested to the General by a police sergeant, chosen for the delicate task because General Luard had helped him get into the police force in the first place, his father having previously worked as the Luards' gardener. This story had supposedly come from the mother of the police sergeant himself: though why a personal friend of the Chief Constable would need to have the situation spelt out by a lowly sergeant is not at all obvious – nor is there evidence that any serving police sergeant in 1908 was descended from any of the Luards' various gardeners.[3]

In the absence of any other motive, it was suggested that the General had a lover. No candidate was named for the role and no evidence has ever been provided to link his name romantically with anyone other than Mrs Luard herself. This may have been a case of chicken and egg. The General was assumed to have killed his wife and therefore he must have had a motive and the most likely motive was that he *must* have had a lover.

Perhaps because the General was approaching 70, a more popular theory ran that the slightly younger Mrs Luard had a lover. In this set-piece melodrama, the summerhouse became the scene of their trysts – the fact that it was locked and there was not so much as a bench available on which the lovers could canoodle notwith-standing. One name was bandied about in connection with

Mrs Luard – that of Dr Cecil Bosanquet – but it seems to have been linked to hers only long after she was dead.

Dr William Cecil Bosanquet was the bachelor son of Admiral George Bosanquet, whose house, Bitchet Wood, was a little south of Stone Street.[4] The Bosanquets moved in the same social circles as the Luards, and had there been anything in this story, the Casa might have provided a useful meeting place because it was roughly half way between Ightham Knoll and Bitchet Wood.

This version of the tale has the General shooting Mrs Luard because of her affair with young Bosanquet. There is a huge problem with this theory in that by 1908 Dr Bosanquet had long ceased to live at his father's house in Kent. He ran a medical practice from Upper Wimpole Street in London, was a senior physician and medical tutor at Charing Cross Hospital, an assistant physician at Brompton Consumption Hospital, the author of numerous medical works and editor of others. Aside from the difficulties of being based 25 miles away, it is hard to see when Dr Bosanquet would have found the time to engage in an affair.[5]

His father Admiral Bosanquet is scarcely a more likely candidate. He was 73 years old at the time of Caroline Luard's murder and would only live another five years.[6] Arguing even more strongly against the General's entertaining the least hostility towards any member of the Bosanquet family is the fact that the Admiral was the 'dear friend' with whom Charles Luard had promised to spend two days before leaving Ightham for good – something probably not known by those who originated this rumour.[7]

This story comes directly from the servants at Bitchet Wood, or rather from one servant in particular – Edith Wickham. Edith Wickham was standing in the garden alongside her mother Anna Wickham when the fatal shots rang out from the summerhouse on the afternoon of the murder. This made her one of the witnesses on whom the General relied for his alibi – yet Edith Wickham was convinced of the General's guilt.[8]

Edith did not go to work at Bitchet Wood until some time after the murder, but while she was employed there as a parlourmaid she once stumbled across something which provided her with a sharp reminder of it. According to Edith, when she was clearing out a room one day she discovered a hidden revolver. It was not all that unusual for the gentry to leave firearms in various nooks and crannies about their homes, but Edith, mindful of the possible link between the Luard murder and the house where she now worked, was so alarmed by the discovery that she concealed the gun about her person until she finished work, then secretly removed it from the house, and threw it into a nearby pond. She told her family that she did this rather than bring the weapon to the attention of her employers as she was afraid she might get into trouble and lose her situation.

Edith's behaviour appears bizarre to the modern reader, while her suspicions of the General are downright peculiar, since she above all people ought to have been convinced of his innocence. Yet amid the contradiction of Edith Wickham's behaviour lies an important truth about the summerhouse murder, a factor which was surely one of the reasons the General fell under suspicion – and an integral part of the untold story behind the tragedy.

In his book *Kent Tales of Mystery and Murder* W.H. Johnson commented that while it might be possible for the General to have murdered his wife in circumstances such as a sudden loss of temper, during which he battered her to death with the nearest blunt instrument available, it would not have been '. . . in this curiously calculated way, by taking her into the woods . . . making his way to the golf club . . . and engaging himself in all that followed'.[9]

To understand the suspicions which attached themselves to the General it is necessary to approach the situation from a completely different angle. In the event that for some reason unknown Charles Luard had in fact decided to murder his wife, clearly the one thing he could not do was simply batter her to death with the nearest blunt instrument. The Luards employed three servants and screams from their mistress would bring them running. If the General had conceived a plan to murder his wife, it would have to be at some distance from the house, where there were no servants to provide inconvenient witnesses. Ightham Knoll stood in 8 acres of garden – but they also employed a gardener, who might inconveniently blunder upon the scene and whose cottage at the gate afforded a handy vantage point from which the gardener's wife could give an assurance that no one but the General had entered the garden all afternoon.

Where then if not the house and garden? Of the various walks regularly undertaken by the Luards, the one providing the greatest degree of privacy was undoubtedly the path through Fish Ponds Wood to the Casa. Not only was there a screen of trees, but unlike the Seal Chart Woods which were common land, Fish Ponds Wood was private property. True, a couple of public bridleways ran through the Frankfield estate, but these were little used except by the Wilkinsons and their employees. With the Wilkinsons known to be away from home, the Casa was probably the most suitable spot available, if the General had murder in mind.

In order to carry out the deed, the General had first to lure his victim to the spot – this was the easy part – his wife would have accompanied him on their walk, suspecting nothing, completely unaware of the gun concealed about his person. There would be no witnesses to the murder. Shots would ring out, but this was such a frequent occurrence that the General could safely surmise they would not attract any curiosity.

The most difficult part was the return home, because under normal circumstances the couple would return together. If the General arrived back at the house alone, with some hollow excuse about feeling tired and turning back without Mrs Luard, rats would be smelt at once. What the General needed was a reason for parting from his wife, something which made it perfectly logical for each to conclude their walk separately.

The golf clubs and the guest provided the perfect solution. Few other scenarios would have fitted so well. If Mrs Stewart had not been expected, then it might reasonably have been asked why Mrs Luard had not gone all the way to the golf club. General Luard could have said she had become tired and decided to turn back early – but this was not so solidly convincing as Mrs Luard actually needing to return home, and therefore being unable to accompany her husband any further.

Moreover, if the General wanted to establish an alibi, proving that he really had gone to a particular location for a specific purpose, the golf club was ideal, inasmuch as he could virtually guarantee he would be seen and recognised there, not only by the steward, but also possibly by any members who happened to be playing there that afternoon. Far from the location of Mrs Luard's murder arguing for the General's innocence, it was actually a powerful argument for his guilt.

Another layer of suspicion would be ignited by the General's own behaviour in the latter part of the afternoon. When the Revd Cotton dropped the General off at 4.30, he appeared to be his normal, cheerful self. At that stage there was no reason for him to be otherwise, but on entering the house, the General discovered his wife's guest waiting alone. No doubt he was tired and thirsty, and good manners dictated that his guest be offered refreshments, so he instructed that tea be brought in – nevertheless, there is something rather peculiar about the scene from this point onwards.

It is 4.30 and Caroline Luard is an hour overdue. Her devoted husband knows she was walking alone in the woods. What is he thinking, as he sits drinking tea with Mrs Stewart? A twisted ankle? A fainting fit? An accident of some kind, surely? Yet he did not immediately set out in search of his wife, or initially give any impression that he was in the least concerned.

At around 5.00 he set out with Mrs Stewart and they walked together along the road to Seven Wents: a point which Caroline Luard should have passed long before – the woman was getting on for 2 hours late – surely a cause for some anxiety? There was no likely explanation except an accident of some kind. Yet when the General parted from Mrs Stewart, he did not ask her to summon help, just as he had not sent one of his servants with a message soliciting help to search for Mrs Luard; just as he did not deviate from his route to enquire at any houses along the main road, in order to check whether his wife had sought assistance there because she was feeling unwell. On the contrary, the General set off into the woods – one might almost begin to wonder if this is where he knew he was going to find his wife.

Then the terrible discovery at the Casa: it must have been obvious even from a cursory examination that Mrs Luard was dead. What does a man do when he finds his wife has been murdered? He needs to get help, and with Mrs Luard beyond medical aid, this is clearly a police matter. The police had to be summoned and that meant a telephone call. Did General Luard hasten to the nearest house he knew of with a telephone? He did not. He hastened to the cottage of his neighbours' coachman.

In the sense that the Wickhams' cottage was the nearest habitation to the scene, and thus the most likely place to locate someone who could help raise the alarm, this was an entirely logical thing to do. When the distraught man found only womenfolk at home, he decided to go off in search of the coachman, completely ignoring young Edith Wickham, who could so easily have been sent off to fetch a constable. It is fair to say that the General may have been in deep shock: a man of Victorian principles, he may have considered the Wickham women too liable to feminine sensitivities to be involved in such tasks as summoning police assistance – although women of the servant class were not generally such a protected species as their middle-class sisters. Whatever his reasons, the General dashed away to solicit masculine help, revealing nothing of the tragedy to Mrs Wickham.

By the time Herbert Harding came out to the Frankfield harness room, between 20 and 30 minutes had elapsed since the discovery of Mrs Luard's body. By this time one might expect the idea of summoning the police to have become uppermost in the General's mind, shock notwithstanding; but here the bereaved man's actions took another inexplicable turn. Instead of directing Harding to summon the police, the General set off for the Casa with Harding in tow.

This business of fetching Harding out to look at the body (probably accompanied by at least two other servants), whether deliberately or inadvertently, had two detrimental effects on the subsequent enquiries. First, it delayed the arrival of the police by at least 40 minutes, increasing the likelihood that they would not arrive in any great numbers until the light was failing. Second, it ensured the presence of someone other than the General at the crime scene, long before the police arrived.

Forensic science was in its infancy, but a rudimentary search for footprints and possibly the use of bloodhounds would obviously form part of the immediate investigations. There had been recent rain – but by the time the General had tramped back and forth and Harding had approached to view the body, any other prints leaving the summerhouse veranda might arguably have been confused or destroyed. Luard's actions would have had to be very calculated indeed for him to have foreseen the advantages of introducing another man on to the scene – but then again, why did he not initiate a call to the police?

To a modern observer, it seems odd that Herbert Harding did not suggest this course of action immediately. Here was a tiny, yet potentially important piece of circumstantial evidence. Harding was accustomed to taking orders from his betters – and Charles Luard was customarily in a position of command. If the General suggested Harding accompany him to the summerhouse, Harding would have done so – even if all his instincts told him that the correct course of action was to call the police. The one set of circumstances when their customary roles might have dissolved would have been an occasion on which Harding recognised that the General was in such a state of shock that he hardly knew what he was doing. In this situation, Harding might have ventured to suggest it was appropriate to seek external assistance, but although this was a singular set of circumstances the servant–master relationship prevailed. To a 1908 audience this suggested that General Luard remained in control of the situation – and thus that any failure or delay in summoning the authorities lay with him alone.

Appearances were not helped by the decision to hold the inquest 'behind closed doors' at Ightham Knoll, circumstances exacerbated by Warde's clumsy handling of the press. No doubt Chief Constable Warde's personal involvement in the case was no more than that due to a serious enquiry, but to the lower classes it looked like a case of the gentry sticking together, with the well-publicised friendship between the General and the Chief Constable only serving to heighten the sense that the General was being helped out by friends in high places.

The official line was that the General could not possibly have murdered his wife because he had an unshakeable alibi. Yet local people continued to suspect him of the crime. Was this based on a stubborn refusal to accept hard facts, or did locals have a better insight into the General's 'cast-iron' alibi than investigators have given them credit for?

The General's alibi relied on timing. He was seen at the golf club at 3.30 and thus he could not possibly have fired the fatal shots at 3.15.

The crucial evidence which appeared to exonerate the General emerged in the public domain at a remarkably early stage. On the evening of the murder, a reporter from the *Sevenoaks Chronicle* raced to the murder scene on the basis of a tip-off. When describing his journey to the summerhouse, he wrote: 'Going through Seal, groups of villagers were standing about, discussing the shocking discovery, it not then being known who the victim was.'[10]

These bystanders did not receive confirmation of the victim's identity until the reporter himself paused to tell them, when he was driving back to Sevenoaks. It is clear from this that on the night of the murder specific details about the incident had not filtered far beyond the confines of the Frankfield estate. With information apparently so scarce, it is quite surprising to read such compre-hensive accounts in newspapers published the following morning: accounts which gave such definite information as the time the General and his wife parted at the wicket gate, and mentioned the existence of two witnesses who had heard the fatal shots.

What was the source of this information? Certainly it was not common knowledge around the pubs and on cottage doorsteps, where even the name of the victim was not known. It is unlikely that any other reporters made it to the scene that night. The man from the *Chronicle* was the only one on the spot. His own paper was a weekly, not due out until Friday, but there can be little doubt that this man was the source of a great deal of the information wired to the London dailies that night.

The *Chronicle* reporter reached the scene not long after Superintendent Taylor. He got there just as '. . . Dr Mansfield of Sevenoaks was . . . bending over the body, which was lying prone on the veranda, face down. . . . It was a weird ghastly spectacle, as night was closing round and all the light available was a motor lamp from Dr Mansfield's car and two or three candles. . .'.[11] The reporter was enjoying the scoop of a lifetime and he must have derived most of his information that night from people 'in the know' at the crime scene: a helpful policeman perhaps, and one or two of the staff from the Frankfield estate.

The *Chronicle*'s reporter got there before Mrs Luard's body had been moved inside and before the police had had time to organise an adequate cordon to keep the curious at bay. Presumably they had not had time either to take proper statements from witnesses, and yet someone was able to inform the *Chronicle*'s reporter that the shots which killed Mrs Luard had been heard by two people. How was it that these witnesses had been identified at such an early stage? A clue comes further on in the account of the reporter's experiences. By the time he had made his notes and was ready to leave the scene, darkness had fallen, but fortunately help was at hand to 'pilot' him back to the road, in the shape of '. . . the coachman Mr Wickham, who has been in the employ of Mr Wilkinson for the past 40 years. . . .'.[12]

By 26 August, the estimated time when the shots were heard had been honed down from the originally published 'around 3.30' to a very precise 3.15. Just in case anyone was in any doubt about the matter, the time of death was reinforced in two comparatively unusual ways. The inquest into Caroline Luard's death was opened two days later at 3.15, and the funeral on Friday 28 August was also arranged for 3.15, with the press helpfully noting that this was to coincide with the exact time she died.

Both these events were necessarily arranged before the inquest officially opened. Seldom can the actual timing of a murder (particularly one where there were no eye-witnesses) have been so publicly and firmly set in stone before a coroner has had the opportunity of questioning any potential witnesses. The funeral arrangements were indisputably a matter at the discretion of the dead woman's husband; and since the proceedings were scheduled to take place at his home, the timing of the inquest may also have been at General Luard's discretion: it is reasonable to surmise that the coroner would have conducted the proceedings at a time mutually agreed with the householder.

During these proceedings, Coroner Buss questioned the witnesses who had seen the General on his walk to and from the golf club, asking each of them how they could state the time they had sighted the General so confidently. Durrant knew his time of arrival at the Padwell pub, from which he could make an educated guess as to the time he had met the General. Ernest King explained that he happened to check his watch only a minute or so before the General appeared. Harry Kent had looked at a clock only moments before seeing the General. These sightings all dovetailed beautifully. On the return journey, we have King again, then the lady timing her photographic exposure in the woods, followed by the Revd Cotton giving the General a lift, and confirmation from Mrs Stewart and the servants, that the return home took place at 4.30. It all fitted perfectly. The men from Scotland Yard walked the route themselves and their timings only served to confirm the General's.

At this point most people's suspicions of the General have ground to a halt. His alibi has repeatedly been described as unbreakable. Yet that is not so. The General's alibi is like a plank bridge, resting on two separate piles of bricks – if either pile of bricks were to be demolished, the bridge would collapse in an instant.

The first pile of bricks represents the timing of the General's journey. The General indisputably made a journey on foot, over a particular route. He was seen at various points along the way by a whole series of witnesses, and piecing their evidence together it is possible by inference to place the General to within a couple of hundred yards at any time from around 3.05 to 4.30 that afternoon. The timing of the first half of his walk is much less certain, because there were no witnesses in respect of that part of the afternoon. This did not matter, however, because there was no question of the General being able to walk – or even run – at sufficient speed to cover the ground between the Casa, where his wife was shot at 3.15, and Hall Place where he was seen by Thomas Durrant at 3.20 – and thus he could not have been the man who fired those shots.

It is now time to look at that second pile of bricks. The first pile is made up of a group of witnesses, each of whom helps confirm the accuracy of the others. King's timing helps support Durrant's, and so on. The other half of the General's alibi relates to the timing of the shots which killed Mrs Luard. Here we are not relying on a solid stack of bricks, each supporting and reinforcing the other. The evidence relating to the shots relies on a much smaller number of sources. We have two women standing in a garden, a pair of woodcutters and a couple of gardeners. All of these people heard the shots and in spite of the fact that hearing shots was for them an everyday occurrence, which would not normally occasion any comment, these witnesses could apparently state, with remarkable precision, the exact time they heard those shots when asked to recall it several hours later. It is a feat of collective memory little short of miraculous.

If not miraculous, then at least highly fortuitous for the General. The scenario would have been rather different in the event that these witnesses had been vaguer: for example, if they had admitted to having no real idea at what time they had heard the shots – maybe estimating it at 'around 3.00 to 3.15'. If the General shot Mrs Luard at 3.05, then hurried along the path and out into the lane, he could still have been seen by Durrant at 3.20. If the shots were actually fired at 3.05, or even slightly earlier, then the rest of the General's alibi matters not one whit – in truth, if the 'shots at 3.15' half of the alibi collapsed, all the evidence about the remainder of the walk suddenly shifts to support a case against the General; because the collective evidence of Durrant, King and the rest would then place General Luard within yards of the Casa at the time of the murder. In reality there was nothing to confirm the General's story that Mrs Luard actually reached the wicket gate that afternoon.

When assessing the evidence of the witnesses who heard the shots, it is important to consider how many of them can genuinely be called 'witnesses' at all. Although most subsequent accounts of the murder mention that 'half a dozen' witnesses corroborated the timing of these shots, only two ever gave formal evidence to this effect.

The woodcutters so often mentioned as witnesses did not testify at the inquest. Their evidence survives because it was reported in the newspapers, where most contemporary versions of their story simply do not tally with Mrs Wickham's, inasmuch as they heard a cry of some kind (which they attributed to an animal) immediately before the shots; they heard only two shots rather than three; and, finally, they did not state a precise time at which they heard the shots. It is unclear exactly where these two men were working, but if the testimony of Thomas Durrant is to be believed, there was 'quite a lot' of shooting going on that afternoon – so it is entirely possible that what these men heard was some other entirely unrelated shooting.

Four other people are known to have heard the shots – Daniel Kettel and his workmate Frank Wickham, and Anna Wickham and her daughter Edith. Neither Frank nor Edith Wickham were called to give evidence. Edith was then 19 and Frank 33, so this was certainly not on account of their extreme youth.[13]

Oddly enough, both Daniel Kettel and Anna Wickham were most insistent that there had been no other shots that afternoon – conveniently ensuring that there could be no question about which particular shots they heard at precisely 3.15.

During Mrs Wickham's evidence, she was asked by the coroner whether she was sure of the time, to which she replied 'It was at 3.15 exactly'. How does one know the exact time when standing in a cottage garden? Did Mrs Wickham own a watch? Was she within earshot of a chiming clock? Coroner Buss had asked other witnesses to explain how they could be so sure of the time, but he did not seek any clarification from this one.

The other witness to the timing of the shots was Daniel Kettel. He was invited to expand on how he could be sure of the time, and said he had looked at his watch 'about 5 minutes later': but as we have seen, there were discrepancies in the story Daniel Kettel had told the press and the story he told at the inquest. To the press Kettel said he thought the shots had come from a neighbouring farm – yet at the inquest, he thought they had come from the summerhouse.

In the first press reports, shots had been heard at about 3.30; by the inquest this had altered to precisely 3.15. In those first reports, the shots had been heard by two witnesses: the 'woman in her garden' and the 'labourer'. There cannot be a shadow of doubt as to the identity of these people, and we can therefore conjecture that the original 3.30 'guesstimate' came from them.

It is possible that Kettel and Mrs Wickham were absolutely confident about the time of the shooting from the outset. In the heat of the moment, newspaper reporters have been known to note things down wrongly. Or could they have been influenced by the public assertions that Mrs Luard died at precisely 3.15? It would be a bold witness who would go before the coroner and contradict the established facts, once they had been published in a newspaper and acknowledged by the timing of an inquest and a funeral.

The witnesses who supplied General Luard with an alibi that day are often described as 'independent', yet in one sense the witnesses who testified to hearing those shots were not independent at all. The Wickhams lived in a tied cottage on the Frankfield estate, which they could lose at a moment's notice on the whim of their employer Mr Wilkinson, who happened to be a close personal friend of General Luard. The gardener Daniel Kettel was in exactly the same position. Years later Edith Wickham would go to elaborate lengths in order to hide a gun she found in the home of an employer, for fear that even querying what she should do with it might lead to dismissal. This is the level of fear and awe which their employers inspired in these key witnesses.

To be on the staff of an estate like Frankfield meant safety and security beyond the wildest dreams of many. Good employers not only provided wages and housing, but took a paternal interest in the families on their estates. The relationship between employers and employed sometimes stretched back several generations. It was not unusual for son to follow father as estate carpenter or coachman, with other children being found 'good positions' in service as well. There is strong evidence that many were content with their lot, in spite of the long hours and an expectation of unquestioning loyalty to one's employer. Few estate families would contemplate any act of disloyalty – many were bound by gratitude for the perceived largesse of the family up at 'the big house'. Economic realities also played a part – employees could be dismissed at a moment's notice without a reference, and no domestic or estate worker without a 'good character' had any hope of obtaining similar employment elsewhere.

It was a cold world outside the confines of the estate. In 1908 the destitute and unemployed were trudging through Kent in their thousands, many submitting to the ultimate degradation of the workhouse after failing to find work picking hops. David Woodruff, the man arrested for Mrs Luard's murder in 1909, had once been a gardener, but had fallen on 'hard times' – for a 62-year-old without regular employment this meant sleeping rough and picking up work as and when he could.

Daniel Kettel was still working at the age of 74. In 1908 a parliamentary bill to introduce old age pensions was under discussion. It was proposed that a pension be paid to men who had reached the age of 70, but it was not to be a universal provision: those already in the workhouse or in receipt of other 'poor relief' would be excluded.[14]

Nor was it exclusively the elderly who had reason to fear unemployment. In October 1908 there were hunger marches, culminating in a demonstration in Trafalgar Square. Mounted police charged the marchers, amid cries of 'Cossacks' and 'Russia' from 'certain sections of the crowd'.[15]

In the same week in which Coroner Buss opened the inquest into the death of Mrs Luard, his colleague Coroner Murton held inquests into two infant deaths in other districts of Kent. The first was of a child who weighed 7lb: less than half the expected weight for its age. The second, a child of 17 months, weighed a mere 13½lb. Both children were severely malnourished. Both had died bereft of all but the most basic medical assistance. The first, Annie Callaghan, was the baby daughter of a London porter. The second, Arthur George Peters, the child of a costermonger. Each family was evidently in such desperate straits that they had travelled down to the hop fields in search of work, in spite of having very sick children.[16]

In 1908 no one needed to have these facts spelled out for them. People not only in Ightham but throughout the land understood perfectly the significance of the General's station in life in comparison with that of Daniel Kettel and Anna Wickham, those two 'independent' witnesses in the service of one of his greatest friends.

Those who were already sceptical about General Luard's 'perfect alibi' must have considered their suspicions justified when he took his life on 18 September. It is entirely possible that some authors of the poison-pen missives, far from experiencing remorse, actually considered themselves vindicated. Many people privately looked to the General's friendship with Chief Constable Warde and surmised that the Wardes 'knew something' and had recommended their old friend to take the honourable way out, before it was too late.

One argument in favour of the theory that the General was being 'leaned on' comes in the particular location and timing of his death. Charles Luard had impeccable manners. It has been suggested that one of the reasons he did not immediately set out in search of his wife was his reluctance to abandon Mrs Stewart, before observing the usual courtesy of offering her the afternoon tea for which she had been invited. This simply does not square with committing suicide at a friend's house, knowing full well that one's mangled carcass and all the associated unpleasantness of a sudden death will inevitably have to be dealt with by that friend. Luard's own suicide note mentions what a poor repayment of hospitality and friendship his actions represent.

Nor was there any need for him to involve his friend at all. Charles Luard owned several guns. He could have taken his own life at home, in house or garden, or if he did not wish to upset his faithful servants, he could have walked out and shot himself in the woods, leaving a note in the house explaining where he could be found. If for some reason he particularly wanted to effect his end by jumping out in front of a railway train that too could easily have been accomplished from Ightham Knoll. The house stood within less than a mile and a half of a railway line, and we know he was capable of walking this distance and more.

The General could have committed suicide in exactly the same way, taking exactly the same trouble to ensure his body would be found, and his letters and telegrams reach their intended recipients, without involving Colonel Warde at all. Yet he chose to accomplish all this in a very particular way. Contrary to the insistent claims put forward by Colonel Warde that the suicide was a spur of the moment decision, everything about that final day and a half of the General's life suggests the intending suicide made his preparations carefully, making farewell visits to the places in Ightham which meant most to him, preparing correspondence, pinning a note to his clothes, taking a bath and making a final meal of tea and bread and butter: even commenting several times on what must have seemed a symbolic sunset, as he was driven away from Ightham for the very last time.

Why involve his friend Colonel Warde? Why go to so much trouble to ensure his body was taken back to Warde's house? It does rather appear as though he may have been sending a message to Warde – this is what you wanted, now you can clear up the loose ends.

Although in every respect Charles Warde did take on the role of the good friend, even travelling down to Southampton to meet Captain Luard off the boat, there is just one matter in which a degree of resentment might possibly be detected. The note found on General Luard's person instructed that his body be taken back to Barham Court. In the event, Colonel Warde instructed that the body be brought back only as far as one of the lodges; there it stayed until it was conveyed back to Ightham for the funeral. It was certainly within Warde's power to have the body brought back to lie in the house – that he did not do so may be a clue to his true feelings.

It is significant that in spite of protestations that General Luard was not a suspect, Charles Warde summoned his brother the Chief Constable to be on hand when the General's room was searched. Nor did it go unnoticed that police invaded Ightham Knoll as soon as they learned of the General's death. Were Charles and Henry

Warde really so utterly convinced of Charles Luard's innocence? They may have said this repeatedly in public, but their behaviour simply does not tally with these verbal assurances.

Perhaps the strongest example of this is provided by the strange conclusion of the second session of the inquest into Mrs Luard's death, when the proceedings were adjourned at the instigation of the Chief Constable. At the time it was generally assumed that the police had obtained some significant evidence which they would be able to bring before the inquest when it reconvened: but when the proceedings resumed, Thomas Buss was at pains to deny that this had been the reason for the adjournment.

The official line was that the inquest had been adjourned to give the police longer to carry out their enquiries. This was something of a nonsense and Buss knew it. Police enquiries were independent of the coroner's inquest, and would continue regardless. Where a murder had been committed and the culprit not identified – a common occurrence – the jury brought in a verdict of murder by person or persons unknown. This was precisely the 'humdrum' verdict anticipated by the reporter from the *Kent Messenger*.[17]

To understand why the Chief Constable intervened, the progress of the second inquest needs to be considered in some detail. During this session, the 'missing' pocket had become the focus of a great deal of attention. The sequence of events by which the pocket was discovered, mislaid and rediscovered, is clear enough when the facts are set out in their logical order, but unfortunately that was not the way the matter had been presented to the jury. At the first inquest they had been told the pocket was missing, presumed stolen by the murderer. At the second, they were told it had now been found. Jane Pugmore was called upon to describe how and where she had found it. The coroner then moved to a separate line of questioning about another issue; but some jurors were clearly not satisfied and during their turn to ask questions revisited the discovery of the pocket, asking who had had access to the dead woman's bedroom and clothing.

The situation might have been clarified at this point, if General Luard had confirmed, as his evidence seems to suggest, that he had actually seen his wife's pocket lying on the veranda floor on the evening of the murder – but General Luard had left the room after giving his evidence, and was probably completely unaware of the ridiculous complications arising out of what was in reality a trivial misunderstanding.

Miss Pugmore was allowed to stand down, and that had been the end of the pocket for a while, because the Revd Cotton was called next, and his evidence took everyone back to Seal Chart Woods. Then came Mary Alice Stewart, who again had no connection with Mrs Luard's pocket. She was followed by Superintendent Taylor, but once he had been asked about the distance from the Casa to the golf club and the footprints found at the scene, the foreman of the jury suddenly returned to the issue of the pocket, enquiring of Superintendent Taylor what had happened to Mrs Luard's clothes after the murder.

After Taylor had managed to create further confusion with his misleading claim that the pocket had been with the dress all the time, the questions moved on to the method used to separate the pocket from the dress; but before long another member of the jury was probing around the original question again, asking, 'What conclusion did you come to, when the pocket was not found at the time? How was it that the murderer put the pocket back?'

At this point, General Luard's supporters must have seen the way the land was starting to lie with some members of the jury – for who could possibly have had access to Mrs Luard's bedroom, to 'put the pocket back', other than the General himself?

Superintendent Taylor replied that he did not think the murderer had put the pocket back. This may or may not have satisfied the jurors. To Chief Constable Warde, however, the lines of questioning taken by some of the jurors had given out disturbing hints that they were entertaining suspicions against General Luard, particularly in the way they kept returning to the mystery of the pocket, worrying at it like a dog with a bone.

Taylor was the penultimate witness. He was followed by Chief Detective Inspector Scott and as soon as Scott stood down, the Chief Constable initiated his surprise application to have the hearing adjourned for a further two weeks. The police subsequently stated that they had had no particular leads to follow up at that point, so any notion that in another fortnight they might be in a position to produce evidence with a bearing on the inquest verdict was sheer fantasy, as was the suggestion that in holding over the verdict, the interests of the enquiry 'would be better served'.

There was no question of the jury bringing in a verdict of suicide – the logical verdict was one of murder by person or persons unknown – and there was nothing in this verdict which would have hampered the police investigations in any way. It was a perfectly normal, appropriate verdict and Warde had no reason whatever to prevent it. The only logical assumption is that Warde feared the jury might bring in a verdict of murder by Major General Luard. In 1908 a coroner's jury were allowed to bring in a verdict of murder against a named individual, and their verdict carried the same legal authority as that of a magistrates' court. Hence if the jury had brought in a verdict of murder by General Luard, it would have automatically ensured that Luard stood trial for the crime.

It appears that whether or not Warde himself believed the General had killed his wife, he thought there was a better than outside chance that the inquest jury did, and he was not prepared to risk them getting as far as a verdict. He therefore intervened in a way which left the coroner little option but to adjourn the proceedings – thereby effectively preventing the jury from returning any verdict at all for another fortnight.

Ultimately the jurors did not pronounce Major General Luard guilty of murdering his wife. It may be that they never had the slightest intention of doing so – possibly Henry Warde misread the situation completely. It is equally possible that some of the jury did have their doubts about the General, but between the two sessions at the George & Dragon a number of things happened to influence them. To begin with the General himself was now dead and nothing could possibly be gained from pursuing him. There had been time, too, for even the slowest thinkers to clarify the pocket evidence in their own minds; but most crucially of all, public opinion was officially outraged at the way the General had been treated. After the Revd Winnifrith's condemnation from the pulpit and the words of Colonel Warde and Coroner Buss, what man in Ightham would openly voice the opinion that General Luard had murdered his wife?

If the inquest jury at one time entertained doubts about the General's alibi, there also exists the awful possibility that Chief Constable Warde shared their views, and did go so far as to intimate that his old friend should take the honourable way out, rather than face the ignominy of arrest and trial.

Warde was closely involved with the investigation from the outset. He would have been among the very few people who knew exactly what was happening on the Frankfield estate in the hours immediately following the murder. Mrs Luard's body was scarcely cold before two people belonging to the estate had presented themselves as having heard shots coming from the approximate direction of the summerhouse earlier that afternoon. Perhaps they initially estimated having heard those shots at about 3.30. Unless anyone really had just happened to check the time, it is highly unlikely that they would remember at *precisely* what time they heard the shots.

As soon as the events of the afternoon were pieced together, the police would appreciate the significance of the timing of those shots. A time of 3.30 would have been excellent for the General, because he was then in clear view several miles away at the golf club. The problem was that by then Mrs Luard ought to have been back at Ightham Knoll; she had no reason to be at the summerhouse at 3.30 – which meant that this was almost certainly not the time the fatal shots were fired – and once there was any element of doubt about the timing, it would inevitably be useless from the point of view of providing the General with an alibi. Moreover, if 3.30 was accepted, wild speculation would inevitably commence about what Mrs Luard had been doing at the summerhouse all that time. How much more convenient it would be if the shots had actually been heard at precisely 3.15. The General still could not have fired the gun, but it cut down on Mrs Luard's unexplained delay in the woods.

It would not have been difficult to suggest to either witness that approximately 3.30 must really have been 3.15 – after all, that *was* the time Mrs Luard must have been at the summerhouse surely? If these witnesses were encouraged to beef up their evidence, the Chief Constable would surely have been aware of it – and therefore have known that the 'unshakeable alibi' was seriously flawed.

This scenario might also explain why Edith Wickham was not convinced of the General's innocence in spite of herself and her mother being among those who 'proved' it.

There is no suggestion that anyone coerced these witnesses, or threatened them with the consequences of saying the wrong thing at the inquest. There would have been no need. Daniel Kettel and Anna Wickham understood perfectly the implications of their respective positions and the dangers of doing anything which might offend the gentry. Both were probably overawed by the prospect of sitting in the General's dining room to give their evidence and terrified of putting a foot wrong in front of all those important people.

If any confirmation of the biddable nature of the Frankfield employees is needed, a perfect example is provided by the episode involving Frank Wickham and the wire diviners. Young Wickham was working in the churchyard when first confronted by a member of this party, whom Wickham assumed to be 'someone in authority' because he was smartly dressed. Wickham therefore answered questions posed by this complete stranger and even agreed to have his lodgings searched. When this man or one of his companions subsequently approached Wickham, and instructed him to leave his work in order to accompany him and other men into the woods, the gardener obediently complied. The subsequent reporting of these events does not imply that Wickham was thought particularly foolish or gullible in so doing – on the contrary, he was merely showing the appropriate level of cooperation expected from someone of his class.

Among families such as the Wardes and the Luards, there undoubtedly existed an honour code which required that any kind of scandal be hushed up at all costs. Throughout the Luard case there is a distinct suggestion that someone was pulling the strings. There was the decision to hold the original inquest in the General's home, which ensured the exclusion of most of the press. At the outset General Luard attempted to avoid answering questions in the usual way by submitting a written account of his story: an identical *modus operandi* to that adopted by Colonel Charles Warde when he subsequently all but took over the inquest into the General's death. The Chief Constable interfered in the organisation of both the first and second inquests into the death of Mrs Luard, and his presence overshadowed the entire affair. None of this reflected well on General Luard, in spite of the fact that he may not have been the instigator of any of it. (Even his attempt to confine himself to a written statement at the first inquest may have been on the advice of others.)

No wonder the General appeared to many to be a guilty man sheltering behind his powerful allies – but was he?

16

An Unhappy Chance

The British reading public has always had an appetite for murder, and the popularity of murder mysteries was at a new high during the Edwardian age. Some of the very pages which contained details of the summerhouse murder coincidentally carried advertisements for a brand new Sherlock Holmes story, shortly to be serialised in the *Strand* magazine.

Sir Arthur Conan Doyle had taught the public to expect standards of detection which were far in advance of anything likely to be achieved by Scotland Yard itself, still less the rural county forces. It was easy enough to criticise the attempts of the Kent force to solve the Luard case, but in truth they had little to go on and were hampered by appalling weather conditions, lack of manpower and few modern resources. Until supplied with the 'yellow car' by a Tonbridge garage, they did not even have a motor car in which to follow up clues.[1]

The 'Holmes factor' had a separate and more damaging influence on the Luard case, however. In a Sherlock Holmes story the murder has generally been committed by some cunning and dastardly trickery – not merely by someone who happens upon a rich woman walking through the woods and steals her rings. In a Holmes story the General would have been the villain, his unbreakable alibi a cleverly constructed ruse, which ultimately failed to fool the master detective.

Caroline Luard's murder opened up just like a detective story: the summerhouse, the silent wood, the General's perfect alibi – small wonder it was such an immediate hit with the London editors, who built it up into an insoluble mystery. Another element in the tragedy ensured that although Caroline Luard was far from the only victim of murder that summer, no case made bigger headlines.

This second element is best summed up by the *Maidstone & Kentish Journal*. After a long article, all of which emphasised just how remarkable and mysterious the case was, it commented: 'The murdered woman did not belong to that class in which crime of this sort is more or less rife.'[2]

Gilbert and Sullivan had sounded a similar note almost thirty years earlier, when their policemen sang of 'when the coster's finished jumping on his mother'[3] and 18 months later, a Newcastle policeman would express surprise at the class of man he went to interview in connection with the murder of John Nisbet. Murder and mayhem were seen as the preserve of the lower classes.

Thus while coverage was given to anything minutely connected to the death of Caroline Luard, the murders of numerous other 'less important' citizens went almost unmentioned. There was a brief flutter of national interest in the case of Margaret Kirby, a child from an ordinary working-class home in Liverpool, whose remains were discovered some months after she had originally disappeared. Like the murder of Caroline Luard, the murder of Maggie Kirby was never solved. The case had a number of unusual, mysterious – indeed sensational – elements, but it simply did not attract the same prolonged national coverage as did the Luard case and unlike the Luard case, it is now largely forgotten.

This contrast is again illustrated by the *Maidstone & Kentish Journal*, whose 15 October edition carried a report about the late General Luard's gift to the Patriotic Society, including the full text of the letter to the society in which he explained that the gift was made in memory of his wife. On the same page, the paper briefly reported the murder of another woman in Kent. She was a mother of four, stabbed to death by her husband, who was a labourer. The amount of coverage given to this woman's death and the arrest of her killer was identical in length to that afforded the General's gift to the Patriotic Society. The paper could not even be bothered to get her name right – referring to her variously as Elizabeth Bauldry and Margaret Bauldry within the space of the few lines devoted to her.

The press elevated Caroline Luard's murder into something remarkable, mysterious and unusual. Initial suspicions that the killer had been motivated by a desire to possess Mrs Luard's extremely valuable rings were quickly lost in the stream of over-excited adjectives employed to describe the case. In the end even Coroner Buss seems to have become caught up in this collective hysteria, describing the case as one of the most mysterious he had ever come across. Buss had been a coroner for twenty-five years, so he must have known the frequency with which citizens of Kent and indeed of the rest of the country met with violent death, often as a result of robbery – and yet by mid-September even he seems to have forgotten that robbery was the most obvious motive of all.

The coroner seems to have shared the almost universal belief that the chances of meeting a gun-toting criminal were utterly remote. During the Edwardian age there seems to have been a collective blindness about the availability of firearms. In the four weeks which were dominated by intensive coverage of the Luard case, the press reported deaths by shooting every week. It was not just General Luard who kept a revolver casually stashed in his bathroom cupboard, or failed to recall where he had put his ammunition. During the first week of September 1908, a solicitor's wife shot herself in the bedroom of her home using a gun kept in the house,[4] and before the end of the month the Revd Clement Todd Davies, who had been vicar at Northop in Flintshire for almost a decade, shot himself in the vicarage garden using his own revolver for the purpose.[5] Guns were so commonplace that even an impoverished tramp might occasionally be found carrying one, as in the case of David Woodruff.

This singular form of blindness also afflicted people's perceptions of criminality. Those who assumed Mrs Luard had been murdered for her rings automatically equated her killer with a member of the lower orders. Tramps were number one on the list of suspects, closely followed by hop-pickers. The type of 'respectable' thief represented by John Dickman, a man who lived by his wits and took whatever opportunity presented itself when the need arose, for example stealing bags from trains when short of cash after an unsuccessful visit to the races, does not seem to have entered the thinking of the police or the press at all.

The press and wider public had also convinced themselves that the remoteness of the summerhouse was a huge factor in the case. Either Mrs Luard had met her killer there by appointment, or else she had been deliberately followed there with murder in mind. Apparently no one could conceive of a prospective thief simply stumbling across the summerhouse by accident and meeting Mrs Luard there: an unhappy chance in which the victim had the misfortune to be in the wrong place at the wrong time.

Here the role of the building known as the Casa becomes crucial. Horace Wilkinson, the owner of the Casa, built Frankfield House in 1869. The house was at the heart of a large estate, surrounded by gardens, parkland and the woods which would achieve brief notoriety as the location of the summerhouse murder. Like many Victorian landowners, Wilkinson took his responsibilities to the local community seriously: while the house was still under construction, work also began on a new church, a quarter of a mile away. Dedicated to St Lawrence, the church was endowed in memory of a Wilkinson daughter who died tragically young. The intention was to provide a place of worship not only for the staff and tenants of the Frankfield estate, but also for those members of the wider local community who had previously faced a 2-mile walk to attend church at Ightham or Seal. A schoolroom for the benefit of local children was provided the same year, and this still forms the core of the existing primary school which stands a few yards down the hill from the church.[6]

Some time later Wilkinson decided to erect a summerhouse, so a spot was chosen on a wooded promontory about half a mile from the main house. When this first building was destroyed by fire in the mid-1890s, it was replaced by another on the same site, known as La Casa. Summerhouses were extremely popular throughout the Victorian period, usually as places to take tea or rest after tennis or croquet. They were often fancifully rustic, with thatched roofs and timbered verandas, and many stood a considerable distance from the main house and could only be accessed on foot. The Casa was on an altogether more ambitious scale than most: although frequently used for picnics, it had been designed for overnight occupation. With at least half a dozen rooms, including bedrooms, kitchen and scullery, it was substantially larger than many of the cottages on and around the estate. For a dozen years it had provided the Wilkinsons with a peaceful retreat from the formality of the big house, and a comfortable refuge while the servants engaged in a thorough 'spring clean' at Frankfield. In the summer months it was not unknown for members of the family to spend up to a fortnight there, and friends such as the Luards were sometimes invited to enjoy this rural idyll.

When the summerhouse achieved national fame in 1908, much was written about the inaccessibility and isolation of the building, and the sheer unlikelihood of anyone coming upon it by accident. In truth this was a somewhat distorted picture. While it is true that the building stood on private land and many locals had no reason to be aware of its existence, in reality the Casa was not at all difficult to locate. On the night of the murder, the reporter for the *Sevenoaks Chronicle* parked his car near St Lawrence Church and managed to walk straight to it without any guidance whatever. Nor is there any mystery about how he achieved this.[7]

When Mr Wilkinson had the Casa built, the site was not randomly chosen merely on account of its lovely views: there were also some practical considerations. While the family were in residence at the Casa, some means of servicing their needs had to be arranged: preferably one which did not involve carrying every necessity of life through sloping wooded terrain, via narrow footpaths. The main house stood about half a mile away across a steep valley, but the problem was solved by clearing a broad track which curved through the woods, following the contour of the land, all the way from the Casa to a point where it joined one of the main carriage drives near Frankfield House. This enabled a pony and trap to be driven between the two along a level route. A small stable was built close to the Casa and whenever any of the family were staying there, the pony and trap negotiated the winding route between the summerhouse and the family's main residence at least once a day, carrying supplies.

261

The presence of this track enabled the *Sevenoaks Chronicle*'s man to find the Casa on the night of the murder and even today, although nothing of the bungalow is left standing and the spot where it stood is all but impossible to locate without a knowledgeable guide, the start of the track which once led to the Casa is still clearly visible, at the point where it crosses the bridle path.

Nor was the site anything like so isolated from public byways as it has sometimes been described. There were two public bridleways nearby, one running south from Crown Point towards St Lawrence Church and school (the 'lane' which passed the Wickham's cottage) and another virtually at right angles to the first, running south-east from St Lawrence School, in the direction of Ivy Hatch. Both of these tracks came within 300–400 yards of the Casa, and the gated pony drive crossed the first of these two bridleways, within sight of the place where it met the second.

The pony drive was a broad grassy track, some 8 feet wide, which often bore marks of use by horse-drawn vehicles. In appearance it was no different from many of the unmade tracks which led to isolated homes throughout the district at the time, and its very width was sufficient to suggest that it might lead to a dwelling of some sort.

Quite aside from the public rights of way which led to the pony drive, it was also possible for anyone using the St Lawrence to Ivy Hatch bridle path simply to ignore the law of trespass and head off into the woods. Today it would be unlikely in the extreme that anyone who did so would find themselves at the site of the Casa, but in 1908 there was a factor which increased that likelihood significantly.

Anyone who follows the bridle path along the southern edge of Fish Ponds Wood today will be confronted all along its northern aspect by dense woodland. A very observant walker might notice a single gatepost incorporated in the fence at one point, its fellow post and gate long gone and its purpose long forgotten. In 1908 that gate led into a large triangular area of rough pasture, presumably cleared to provide grazing for the pony when it was stabled at the Casa. The large-scale 1909 OS sheet shows the stable clearly, standing at the extreme point of this triangular field. The briefest exploration of this unexpected clearing, accessed via an inviting gate, would have revealed the presence of the stable and, adjacent to it, a second gate leading to the Casa, which stood a matter of yards away, just inside the wood. A contemporary photograph shows a policeman hunting along the boundary of this field, with the roof of the Casa clearly visible above the hedge. Every other picture of the Casa suggests that it was completely surrounded by dense woodland – the map and this solitary snapshot prove otherwise. It would not have been difficult for a thief on the lookout for a soft target to have discovered the isolated bungalow.

In his excellent essay on the Luard case published in 1987, Bernard Taylor came to the conclusion that Mrs Luard's murderer was a stranger to her:[8] someone who had taken the opportunity to rob and murder a middle-aged lady who had the misfortune to cross his path in a lonely spot, away from human aid. The present writer has independently reached the same conclusion.

A great deal of nonsense has been written about the isolation of the summerhouse and the unlikelihood of anyone in possession of a firearm coming across Mrs Luard there. In fact small arms of the sort employed to kill Caroline Luard were common currency among the criminal classes, easily obtainable by both legitimate and dishonest means. The sort of man who carried one was not an impoverished hop-picker or gypsy, but someone who dabbled in petty crime and would not scruple to rob a wealthy lady of her purse and jewellery and murder her too, if his back was to the wall.

Mrs Luard's killer was probably not a local man. Not local, that is, to Seal Chart and Ightham, where everyone knew everyone. He may have come from no further afield than one of the larger Kentish towns, but could equally have been from almost anywhere: someone whose business had brought him down to Kent, where he had run out of cash and was looking for any opportunity to pick up some money as he worked his way back to London or beyond.

Near the Casa the police discovered torn scraps of paper bearing the names of local villages, by which it was conjectured that someone was navigating their way through Kent. This was dismissed as irrelevant to the case. It was suggested that these fragments might have been dropped by some touring cyclists. The glaring illogicality of this apparently failed to occur to anyone. No holidaying cyclist was liable to visit the Casa, whose access was less than convenient for bicycles – nor in truth was anyone going to accidentally arrive there when navigating from village to village by means of their list and the roadside signposts. A visit to the Casa implies someone who has deliberately left the better-frequented lanes, perhaps looking for a house to rob, or a solitary traveller to hold up.

In all likelihood, an intending burglar spotted the gate into the stable field and decided to investigate. He cannot have approached along the pony track without the Luards having seen him and it seems unlikely that he had been randomly wandering through Fish Ponds Wood, so an initial approach from the bridleway at the southern side of the woods seems most likely.

We know that when General and Mrs Luard passed the summerhouse together it was deserted. Their dog Scamp was with them and the General was convinced he would have reacted to the presence of anyone else nearby. A few minutes later, Mrs Luard returned alone, walking in the opposite direction. During that few minutes, by the direst of misfortunes, the man who was to kill Mrs Luard must have arrived at the little house in the clearing. The Casa gave the initial appearance of an isolated dwelling house, so the man would have approached cautiously, uncertain whether there was anyone about, checking doors and windows – and suddenly become aware of someone approaching.

It was suggested that had a stranger been lurking near the summerhouse, Mrs Luard must have seen him. A number of reports recorded that the veranda was devoid of any feature behind which he could have concealed himself. This was over-simplistic to the point of downright silliness. The Casa was a substantial building, capable of concealing half a dozen determined assailants, in the event that they should choose to hide behind it. In addition, photographs taken on the day after the murder show waist-high bracken only a matter of feet from the path along which Mrs Luard approached.

It is reasonable to surmise that whereas Mrs Luard walked towards the summerhouse without the slightest suspicion that there might be anyone there, the man who had been checking out the building remained cautiously alert and therefore became aware of her approach; no doubt silently withdrawing, probably behind a corner of the building, so that Mrs Luard continued along the path in complete ignorance of his presence.

In the meantime the man had perhaps taken the precaution of arming himself with a short length of wood, possibly a handy billet from the wood pile which stood outside and which might not have been remarked upon, had he later tossed it from the veranda to lie among other fallen branches. Or perhaps he drew his revolver, prepared to shoot if needs be. As Mrs Luard walked out on to the veranda, someone advancing swiftly along the western side of the building would take her completely by surprise, her assailant felling her from behind with a single blow to the head. The position in which her body was found, a little way on to the veranda with her feet pointing in the direction of the path, makes this scenario highly likely – the blow to the back of her head which damaged her hat further supports it.

The blow only stunned her, perhaps not even rendering her unconscious. From the point of view of her assailant, the situation now stood on a dangerous fulcrum. The excessive savagery of shooting a woman for the sake of a few coins and her jewellery has often been cited as an argument against the murder being motivated by robbery; but murders are sometimes the result of a robbery in which, for various reasons, the violence employed escalates beyond the robber's original intentions.

This was an opportunistic crime which had unfolded on the spur of the moment. It is entirely possible that in spite of carrying a revolver, the man who took Mrs Luard's rings and purse that afternoon did not originally intend to kill her. The plan was to hit her over the head, then make off with her valuables while she lay unconscious: but before he managed to carry this through the woman started to come round.

He had split seconds in which to assess the situation. His gut feeling was probably one of sheer panic. Whether or not he was familiar with the area, he could not guarantee that there was no one else nearby. Suppose the woman was to start screaming for help? He could not risk it. So he took out his gun and shot her in the head. Shots heard in the countryside will not bring anyone running, whereas a woman screaming might produce half a dozen people from any or every direction within minutes.

Rich ladies wear jewellery and a cursory examination of her hands revealed the presence of rings under her left glove. It may have been while he was removing the glove and wrenching the rings from her fingers that he realised to his horror she was stirring. Thoroughly alarmed he straightens up and shoots twice more, one of the shots missing his victim altogether, in spite of his immediate proximity to the target – another indication of panic perhaps. This hypothesis too is borne out by the evidence of Mrs Luard's position, the entry points of the bullets and the close proximity in which they were fired.

Mrs Wickham remarked to her daughter, 'They meant to kill that thing well', but it is probable that when this man first saw Mrs Luard approach he had no thought of killing her at all. It is even possible that the vomit, always assumed to have been Mrs Luard's as she regained consciousness at some point during the attack, actually emanated from her killer, who in spite of his revolver and criminal intent may have been shocked and nauseated by the spectacle of the dying woman and her blood flowing copiously across the veranda floor.

Collecting himself, he completed the task he had set out to do, relieving Mrs Luard of her rings and her purse. In his haste he may inadvertently or deliberately have kicked Mrs Luard's hat further along the veranda.

The lady's purse was located in the infamous dress pocket, which would generate so much confusion later. Why did the killer cut the pocket out, instead of just putting his hand in and extracting the purse? The answer is that he probably did not. Whereas modern forensic experts would be able to assert with confidence whether something had been detached by cutting or tearing, Dr Mansfield and Superintendent Taylor were merely hazarding guesses, based on their observations of normal everyday life, in which making comparisons between material which had been cut or torn presumably did not form a very great part. In his medical evidence, Dr Mansfield could not say with confidence precisely what had caused the effusion to the back of Mrs Luard's head – and we must assume his medical knowledge outstripped his experience of ladies' dress material.

If robbery was the motive, the killer would have been in a very great hurry. One elderly lady had just happened along the path and, for all the murderer knew, a whole posse of others might shortly arrive in her wake. Mrs Luard was lying face down and the dress pocket would have been at the front or side of her skirt, not at the back. This necessitated reaching under her body to locate it. It is easy enough to extract something from a pocket under normal circumstances, but altogether more difficult to fumble about under a dead weight, amid the folds of a long skirt. So the man dragged furiously at the pocket, ripping it clean off the dress: it would not have required a massive amount of force to tear against the grain because most of the fabric was trapped under the weight of Mrs Luard's body.

With revolver, rings and purse in his pockets, he would put as much distance between himself and the scene of the crime as possible. He may have set off the way he had come, across the paddock and towards Ivy Hatch, steering clear of the bridleway until he reached a road sufficiently distant so as not immediately to associate him with the terrible deed. (It may be significant that the bloodhounds followed a trail that suggested this method of escape.) He could easily have emerged close to the Ash Grove estate, where Mrs Taylor encountered the ginger-haired man who so frightened her that afternoon. On the other hand, the police observed that someone had forced their way through the bracken which grew near the stable just yards from the Casa. This trail headed in the direction of Crown Point, where again the killer could have cautiously emerged from the woods on to a main road, just like the man described by the witness who volunteered a statement at Tonbridge police station.

Having put a mile or so between himself and the summerhouse, the man could settle into a steady walk, reasonably confident he would not be apprehended. He would not necessarily have been seen at all – twice that same afternoon, first with his wife and later with Mrs Stewart, General Luard walked almost a mile along the main Maidstone to Sevenoaks Road without being passed by anyone on foot or in a vehicle.

Mrs Luard's purse has generally been described as containing a few coins. The truth is that no one knows how much money she was carrying that day. Everything is relative. What amounted to a 'few coins' to the General and his lady could have represented a week's wages to one of Mr Wilkinson's labourers – or a train fare to a chancer looking for an easy way home. From the Casa, a walk of a few miles in almost any direction would bring a man to a railway station, from whence it was possible to take a train to London and from there to any part of the country. By the time Caroline Luard's death had been reported to the police, her killer could have put many miles between himself and the crime merely by stepping aboard one of the numerous trains which ran through the area that afternoon.

Charles Edward Luard did not murder his wife. The existence or lack of a genuine alibi is not an indicator of his innocence or guilt. The available evidence points to the fact that Caroline Luard was killed for her rings. Everything that was known about her relationship with the General told of a loving marriage and a complete absence of motive.

On the Saturday before she died, Caroline and her husband had attended a garden party in Ightham, where they talked happily of their plans for a forthcoming holiday. There would be some shooting and golf and afterwards a trip to Cumberland. At this there had been some teasing remarks about how cold it would be in the north, but Caroline only laughed and reminded everyone that for her, going up to Cumberland was going home.[9]

In the days after her death, General Luard exhibited signs of shock and grief which only the most consummate actor could have faked. He told a friend, 'She is not gone from me. She is there, telling me to bear up . . . and I am trying to bear up.' When decisions had to be made, the General referred to what 'she would have wanted'. His wife quite simply was as he himself described her – all his happiness.[10]

Her death would have been a terrible blow in any circumstances, but the General's situation in life made it doubly hard. He became a victim of his own class: a sufficiently important figure that his personal tragedy would be elevated into a nationwide sensation – attracting the attention of cranks and theorists, whose letters helped drive him to his death – and so well connected that it would engender suspicions where none needed to exist.

His close relationship with the Chief Constable ultimately did him more harm than good – Henry Warde clearly intended to suppress speculation about the General's role in the affair, but mostly managed to achieve the opposite. At the furthest end of the scale, the horrifying possibility exists that the Warde brothers did entertain suspicions of General Luard and tacitly encouraged him to take his own life. The apparent lack of police interest in leads such as the one provided by Mrs Taylor, and their descent upon Ightham Knoll on the morning of the General's death are certainly suggestive. Many years later, Superintendent Taylor would tell his family that the police 'knew' the killer's identity, but had been unable to bring him to justice.[11] Was this mere braggadocio? Surely Taylor was not referring to Woodruff – someone the police undoubtedly would have been able to proceed against, had they genuinely been in possession of the evidence to do so.

Two small mysteries remain. The first is the General's strange behaviour in calmly taking afternoon tea with Mrs Stewart when his wife was missing from home, and the second is Mrs Luard's 'lost ten minutes' at the summerhouse.

In the case of Mrs Stewart, it was again a combination of class and circumstances which conspired to place the General in a difficult position. Caroline Luard had many close friends and if her visitor that afternoon had been one of them, the General might have skipped the formalities of tea in the face of a mutual concern over Mrs Luard's whereabouts. Unfortunately, Mrs Stewart was not that sort of visitor at all.

At the inquest Mary Alice Stewart explained that she and her husband had come to Ightham for the summer. On their arrival the

Stewarts had followed the usual conventions of the time: calling on their neighbours (or rather the people of their class who resided in the neighbourhood) and leaving a visiting card for those who were out. To omit this formality would have been considered very ill bred. Mr and Mrs Stewart had accordingly called on the Luards and finding them out, left their card in the usual way. They would have been surprised and not a little offended when this courtesy was apparently ignored, with neither a return visit, nor an invitation to call again materialising.

In the meantime when Mrs Luard heard that the Stewarts had arrived for the summer, she expressed surprise that they had not called. In the strict etiquette of the day, it was up to Mrs Stewart to make the first move. (Mrs Luard and Mrs Stewart were evidently not close friends; it is not even certain that they ever met.) The whole situation became somewhat embarrassing when Mrs Stewart heard of her apparent social gaffe via a third party. She was no doubt a trifle indignant and wrote to Mrs Luard, explaining that she *had* called and left a card. Mrs Luard responded by writing back to say that the card had evidently been mislaid and invited Mrs Stewart to tea. This invitation was all part of the elaborate formalities of contemporary social intercourse. Tea would normally be served at 4.30. The invited guest would arrive at 4.15 and stay no more than an hour, which we can see was Mrs Stewart's original intention, because she was expecting a friend shortly after 5.15.

Whatever had been said privately, this correspondence would have been conducted with the utmost politeness. It may well be that by 24 August both ladies felt the situation had been satisfactorily restored, and neither bore the other any ill will for the misunderstanding. However, Mrs Stewart must have been somewhat disconcerted when she arrived at 4.15 and was escorted into the drawing room by the maid, who informed her that the General and Mrs Luard had gone out for a walk. If it was bad manners to omit to leave a calling card, it was far worse to invite someone for tea and then fail to be at home to receive them.

Mrs Stewart was left waiting in the drawing room for at least 15 minutes until the General arrived; when he did so, the atmosphere may have been a trifle cool. General Luard was undoubtedly aware of the history of Mrs Stewart's invitation, and no doubt felt embarrassed to find her sitting alone in the drawing room. Under the circumstances he swallowed his mounting concern about his wife's whereabouts, doing his best to observe the social niceties with Mrs Stewart by offering her some tea while helplessly explaining that he expected his wife at any moment.

When he looked at his watch and decided he must go in search of Mrs Luard, Mrs Stewart offered to accompany him – not apparently out of any overriding concern about what might have befallen her hostess, but rather because she 'desired to speak with Mrs Luard'. It is possible that Mrs Stewart was so preoccupied with what lay behind this strange behaviour that it never occurred to her to wonder what had really become of her absent hostess. Certainly, her determination to at least set eyes on Mrs Luard may have been an attempt to divine whether some sort of deliberate insult was intended. It might be added that Mrs Stewart was not quite Mrs Luard's social equal. She was the wife of a retired solicitor and their address was not one of the grander houses in the neighbourhood. When asked if she knew the location of the Casa, she stated that she did not and had never walked that way – so invitations to take tea at the Casa and meander along the footpaths of the Frankfield estate had evidently never come her way.

One can imagine the baffled and frustrated Mrs Stewart on her return home that afternoon, wondering how she would explain to her husband that having responded to Mrs Luard's invitation, she had still not actually seen her. Being called as a witness at the inquest must have seemed like the final straw. There is no record of the Stewarts attending Mrs Luard's funeral, or sending a wreath.

The second mystery is the timing of Mrs Luard's death. The standard version of the Luards' walk has them parting at the wicket gate at 3.00. From there it was a mere 4 or 5 minutes level walk back to the Casa. If Mrs Luard had been heading home at a normal pace, she would have got some distance beyond the summerhouse by 3.15, a fact which naturally led to all manner of speculation about Mrs Luard's lost time, ranging from a prolonged pause to admire the view, to secret assignations with a blackmailing John Dickman.

One tempting solution lies in the theory that Mrs Luard was not shot at exactly 3.15, the testimony of Mr Wilkinson's obliging tenants notwithstanding. However, the real solution is provided by the evidence of Superintendent Taylor, who stated that it took him 61 minutes to walk the General's route between Ightham Knoll and the clubhouse at Godden Green. (Superintendent Taylor and General Luard evidently walked at the same pace, because other witnesses confirmed that the Luards left the house at 2.30 and the General reached the golf club at 3.30.) Taylor also timed the distance between the Casa and the clubhouse, which took him exactly 30 minutes.

When specifically asked about the timings on his route, General Luard said that he did not know them, because he never looked at his watch at any point during his walk. Yet the accepted version of the afternoon invariably has the General and Mrs Luard parting at the wicket gate at 3.00. Since the General did not check his watch, where did this time come from?

The General knew the route very well. He knew they had left the house at 2.30 and that it took an hour to walk to the clubhouse – the wicket gate was approximately the half-way point. Indeed, one might even surmise that on the fatal afternoon Mrs Luard had said, 'I'll come half way with you.' This is the free and easy use of language and estimations of distance which we all habitually use, when the calculation of precise yards and minutes is not in question.

From Superintendent Taylor's timed experiments however, it is clear that the wicket gate was not the exact half-way point – this was the Casa, at 31 minutes from Ightham Knoll and 30 minutes from the club house. The wicket gate is another 5 minutes further along the route: so the General parted from Mrs Luard not at 3.00, as has always been accepted, but at around 5 or 6 minutes past. It would then have taken Mrs Luard around 5 minutes to get back to the Casa. In the meantime, her husband had been walking for the same amount of time, mostly downhill, and would thus have just passed the cottages at Stone Street. By a trick of the geography, although he was not much further from Mrs Luard as the crow flies than Mrs Wickham in her garden would have been, his route had actually taken him on to the opposite side of the hill, thereby muffling the sound of the shots which were clearly heard on the Frankfield side.

This places Mrs Luard's arrival on the veranda of the Casa at about 10 or 12 minutes past 3.00. Here her assailant struck the initial blow, and a moment or two later the first shot rang out, fitting almost perfectly with the testimony of the two witnesses at the inquest – and ruining all those speculative theories about why Mrs Luard lingered at the Casa for a quarter of an hour.

The General must have disappeared down the lane below St Lawrence Church barely a minute before Daniel Kettel and Frank Wickham came out of the churchyard. Had they been a minute earlier, or he a minute later, the General's alibi would have been strengthened by these two men seeing him heading away from the scene, several minutes before they heard the gunshots. If any independent witness had testified to hearing the shots *after* seeing the General, his innocence must surely have been demonstrated beyond question.

Ironically, there may have been two people who could have provided this crucial missing link, if the police had only been interested in following up what they had to say. On the day after the murder a local youth called George Skeer approached the investigating officers with what was, on the face of it, an unpromising story. Skeer was the witness who said a black man had asked directions for the railway station, coupled with a claim that he had just shot someone. The police failed to take Skeer seriously for obvious reasons – not only was it highly unlikely that anyone would blurt out that they had just shot a woman, but the black man of George's story would have been suspected as at best a practical joke and at worst an imaginary bogyman.

As late as the 1950s, children in some communities were warned to behave well or else 'the black man' would come and get them. Far from conjuring up the image of a man with Afro-Caribbean origins, the term black man in this context was associated with ancient superstitions about Old Nick or the Devil himself. In 1908 a genuine encounter with a man of Asian or Afro-Caribbean origin (a rare event in rural Kent) would be more likely to provoke one of the several descriptive terms which are no longer in acceptable use, such as darkie or nigger. The black man of legend and superstition lurked where evil had been committed – when frightened by the wire diviners up at the Casa, Frank Wickham claimed that the final straw was seeing 'a black man' standing silently in the woods nearby.

Whether there were any flesh-and-blood black men in Ightham before or after the murder – and there is little to support this idea in any reputable contemporary sources – the police were unimpressed by Skeer's story and told him to clear off. By doing so, they presumably never heard the really important evidence he could have given them.

Many years later George Skeer told a local newspaper reporter that on the afternoon of the murder he and his father, who were both farm workers, were mending a hedge within sight of the lane which passes St Lawrence Church. They saw General Luard heading down the lane towards Stone Street, and an estimated 10 to 15 minutes later they heard the three shots, which Skeer Snr remarked upon, saying, 'They're not from a shotgun.'[12]

The police presumably dismissed George Skeer as a daft young lad (he was 17 at the time), but his father Thomas Skeer was then 52, and perhaps just the sort of steady chap who could have elevated the General's alibi to a genuinely unbreakable status.[13]

Postscript

If these two cases illustrate anything, it is that simple solutions are often the correct ones and that the victims of a murder extend well beyond the original corpse. Each of the principal characters in these stories turns out to have been a complex and fascinating individual. John Dickman was possessed of both charm and intellect, and in spite of the terrible act of which he was convicted he emerges as anything but the cardboard cut-out villain of the 'Train Murder'. Dickman enjoyed the love and loyalty of his children and in particular of his wife Annie, an apparently brave, determined woman whom it is difficult not to admire. While her husband stood condemned and the crowds spat and threw missiles in her direction, Annie typically declared that she would not be driven out of Newcastle – and nor was she. She continued to live in the city until her death in 1949. She never remarried. Her descendants currently reside in the south of England.[1]

After her husband's murder, Cicely Nisbet was forced to take his employers to court in order to gain compensation under the Workmen's Compensation Act of 1906. The insurance company which provided cover for Messrs Rayne & Burn insisted on fighting the claim, since they argued that Nisbet's death had not occurred as a direct result of his employment. The county court disagreed and found in Mrs Nisbet's favour. A subsequent appeal against the judgement failed and Cicely Nisbet was awarded compensation and costs.

When letters criticising Nisbet's employers appeared in the press, Cicely responded by publicly defending the firm, explaining that they had not wished to contest the case, but had been prevented from paying out by their insurers. She went on to mention that Messrs Rayne & Burn had shown her every kindness. One cannot but feel she had missed the point.

Almost a century later, it is impossible to contemplate a situation in which a lone, slightly built employee would be required to transport the equivalent of several thousand pounds of the company's cash by public transport, following a regular routine so well established that his errand was known to half his fellow passengers. In his summing up at Dickman's trial, Lord Coleridge noted the fact that Hall and Spink accompanied one another while transporting the colliery wages and remarked: 'Perhaps if the poor man into whose death we are enquiring had had a companion this would not have happened.'

Cicely Nisbet remarried in 1913. It has proved impossible to discover what happened to either her or her daughters after this.[2]

Captain Charles Elmhirst Luard returned to his regiment and began to remake his life after his tragic double bereavement. He had already served with distinction, winning a DSO in 1901 for gallant conduct during the battle of Abassi. (Claims that he played first-class cricket for Hampshire were erroneous – that distinction belongs to one Arthur John Hamilton Luard.) By the outbreak of the First World War, Charles Luard had risen to the rank of major and was a married man. He was killed in action on 15 September 1914 and is commemorated on the La Ferté-sous-Jouarre memorial. The substantial legacy left by his father (over £7,000) was all but gone, and his widow Dorothy was left with a baby son – also called Charles Luard – who did not survive into adulthood.[3]

Clarence Henry Norman died on 17 February 1974 in a council administered nursing home. No relative or friend came forward to deal with the formalities and his death was registered by a council employee.[4]

Major Edwin Hautenville Richardson continued to promote the use of bloodhounds and various other breeds for military and police work. His services were eventually so much in demand that he travelled extensively throughout Europe in the early decades of the twentieth century, where his assistance was sought by governments and monarchs as far afield as Russia and Turkey. He is credited with the introduction of police dogs both in Britain and abroad, and oversaw the training of animals used by Allied armies and the Red Cross in two world wars.[5]

Chief Constable Captain Fullarton James served with the Northumberland force until his retirement in 1935. He was then 70 years old and had spent half his life in the post. He was awarded the King's Police Medal in 1916, followed by a CBE in 1925, presumably based on duration of service rather than actual achievement. Under Fullarton James's leadership, the Northumberland force became trapped in a time warp, having no motorised vehicles until 1930 and no trained detective branch until one was formed by his successor. His methods were frequently questioned and his disastrous personal involvement in the Foster murder in 1931 was the subject of complaints to the Home Office. Seven years after his retirement he succeeded his elder brother to a baronetcy. He died in 1955 at the age of 91.[6]

Lieutenant Colonel Henry Murray Ashley Warde, ex-Chief Constable of Kent, died in March 1940 aged 89. His reputation does not appear to have been in very high standing around the time of the Luard case, but his stock had risen considerably by the time he retired in 1921. Warde was responsible for introducing numerous improvements to the Kent force and took a keen interest in the welfare of his men. The total manpower had grown from 450 officers at Warde's appointment in 1895 to 650 when he retired, and he was universally commended for the way he ran the force during the First World War, when thousands of men and hundreds of tons of equipment passed through Kent *en route* to and from the war zone.[7]

Many of the places mentioned in this book still exist and some have changed very little. The houses inhabited by Major General and Mrs

Luard, John and Annie Dickman, Mr Horace Wilkinson and the cottages of the Wickhams and the Kettels are all still family homes.

Squerryes Court, birthplace of the Warde brothers, now the home of one of their distant relatives, is regularly open to the public. Ightham Mote is now in the care of the National Trust and welcomes hundreds of visitors every year. Barham Court is currently a business centre. Armathwaite Hall became a hotel after narrowly avoiding demolition on the death of Thomas Hartley. Much of its Victorian grandeur survives and a visit only underlines what it was to be a member of 'the gentry'.

All trace of the Casa vanished long ago. The Wilkinson family had it boarded up after the murder of Caroline Luard and it was never used again. Although initially announcing that he intended to pull the building down, Horace Wilkinson seems to have left it to fall into gradual disrepair until the dangers it posed made complete demolition necessary. The site is now completely overgrown.

Trials are still held in the Moot Hall in Newcastle, just a short walk from the cathedral where John Dickman married Annie Bainbridge in happier times. At the present time those who wish to place a bet with a bookmaker in the Bigg Market can do so legitimately at a branch of Ladbrokes. Newcastle Central station, where John Nisbet and John Dickman caught their train, is still recognisable, if much changed since 1910, as is the station at Morpeth. Most of the stops in between are defunct, including Heaton and Stannington which played such an important part in the story.

The Wildernesse Golf Club replaced its clubhouse at Godden Green with a modern structure on a different site. The George & Dragon in Ightham and the Padwell Arms at Stone Street are still open for business.

Notes

ABBREVIATIONS

Criminal Cases: John Alexander Dickman HO 144/4202, National Archives

Law: Recovery of Costs awarded against C.H. Norman T 161/46, National Archives

CHAPTER 1

1. Nigel Nicholson, *Ightham Mote* (London, National Trust, 1998), p. 48.
2. The appalling weather conditions and devastating effect on the harvest are fully described in numerous contemporary accounts.
3. A.M. Parkin, *The Seal Chart Murder* (Kemsing, Parkin, 1995), p. 24.
4. C.H. Norman's 1950 Submission to the Royal Commission on Capital Punishment has been reproduced many times, but was almost certainly first published in C. Wilson and P. Pitman's *Encyclopaedia of Murder* (London, Arthur Barker, 1961), pp. 561–4.
5. HO 144/4202.
6. HO 144/4202 191.957/51.

CHAPTER 2

1. The details of the Dickman and Nisbet families which appear in this chapter have been confirmed by reference to the General Register Office of England records of births, deaths and marriages; the Calendar of Wills held by the Principal Probate Registry, and census records held by the National Archives.
2. Physical descriptions of both men were given in evidence at the trial. HO 144/4202 191.957/51.
3. John Dickman's early life is described by his wife in the *Illustrated Chronicle* (Newcastle upon Tyne), 2 August 1910. Where possible these details have been confirmed by reference to census returns and birth, death and marriage records.

279

4. *Illustrated Chronicle* (Newcastle upon Tyne), 2 August 1910.
5. *Illustrated Chronicle* (Newcastle upon Tyne), 2 August 1910.
6. *Illustrated Chronicle* (Newcastle upon Tyne), 2 August 1910.
7. HO 144/4202 191.957/51. Statements made to the police make it possible to reconstruct a fairly comprehensive picture of John Dickman's business interests in the period leading up to his arrest.
8. Statement of John Dickman. HO 144/4202 191.957.51.
9. This and the following account of John Dickman's movements on 18 March 1910 are taken from his own statement. HO 144/4202 191.957.51.
10. Statement made by Andrew Tait. HO 144/4202 191.957.51.
11. *Illustrated Chronicle* (Newcastle upon Tyne), 3 August 1910.
12. *Illustrated Police Budget*, 2 April 1910.
13. S.O. Rowan-Hamilton (ed.), *The Trial of John Alexander Dickman* (Glasgow, William Hodge, 1914), p. 11.
14. Statement made by Superintendent John Weddell. HO 144/4202 191.957/51.
15. *Illustrated Police Budget*, 2 April 1910.
16. HO 144/4202 191.957/51.
17. HO 144/4202 191.957/51.
18. At time of writing, photographs of the now defunct station at Heaton can be viewed via the University of Newcastle upon Tyne's SINE project at www.ncl.ac.uk (images 4835, 4839 and 4840).
19. *The Times*, 21 March 1910.
20. *Illustrated Police Budget*, 2 April 1910; and in respect of a subsequent court appearance, *The Times*, 23 May 1910.
21. HO 144/4202 191.957.51.
22. Report of Prison Medical Officer, 6 July 1910; HO 144/4202 191.957/2.

CHAPTER 3
1. S.O. Rowan-Hamilton (ed.), *The Trial of John Alexander Dickman* (Glasgow, William Hodge, 1914), p. 3.
2. *Ibid.*
3. *Illustrated Chronicle* (Newcastle upon Tyne), 6 August 1910.
4. *Illustrated Chronicle* (Newcastle upon Tyne), 5 July 1910.
5. *Evening Chronicle* (Newcastle upon Tyne), 4 July 1910.
6. The source for the account of the trial in this chapter is the trial transcript contained in HO 144/4202 supplemented by reference to the *Evening Chronicle* (Newcastle upon Tyne), 4, 5 and 6 July 1910.
7. *Illustrated Chronicle* (Newcastle upon Tyne), 6 August 1910.

8. *Evening Chronicle* (Newcastle upon Tyne), 28 March 1910 and 25 June 1910.
9. *Evening Chronicle* (Newcastle upon Tyne), 18 July 1910.
10. The boy was the son of John Amos, who later the same day shot dead Mrs Sarah Ellen Grice, Sergeant Barton and Police Constable Mussell. *Newcastle Daily Chronicle*, 16 April 1913.
11. *Illustrated Chronicle* (Newcastle upon Tyne), 10 June 1910.

CHAPTER 4

1. The source for the account of the trial in this chapter is the trial transcript contained in HO 144/4202, supplemented by reference to the *Evening Chronicle* (Newcastle upon Tyne), 4, 5 and 6 July 1910.
2. Rowan-Hamilton, S.O. (ed.), *The Trial of John Alexander Dickman* (Glasgow, William Hodge, 1914), p. 20.
3. The closing speeches of counsel do not form part of the evidence and are thus not recorded in the original trial transcript. They were reproduced in the *Newcastle Daily Chronicle*, 6 July 1910.
4. *Evening Chronicle* (Newcastle upon Tyne), 6 July 1910.
5. *Evening Chronicle* (Newcastle upon Tyne), 6 July 1910.

CHAPTER 5

1. *Illustrated Chronicle* (Newcastle upon Tyne), 6 August 1910.
2. Several of these letters are reproduced in the *Illustrated Chronicle* (Newcastle upon Tyne), 9 August 1910.
3. Undated statement made by Cicely Nisbet. HO 144/4202 191.957/22. A letter from the Office of the Director of Public Prosecutions dated 12 July 1910 states that the prosecution counsel were aware that Mrs Nisbet knew John Dickman by sight, but failed to disclose this to the defence. HO 144/4202 191.957/16.
4. Statement made by Percival Hall dated 18 July 1910. HO 144/4202 191.957/30.
5. Unless otherwise stated, the source for all references to the appeal in this chapter is the Report of Hearing by Court of Criminal Appeal HO 144/4202 191.957/51.
6. These complaints not only received wide circulation in the press but are repeated in Annie Dickman's letters in HO 144/4202.
7. *Evening Chronicle* (Newcastle upon Tyne), 11 July 1910.
8. *Evening Chronicle* (Newcastle upon Tyne), 12 July 1910.
9. *Newcastle Daily Chronicle*, 11 and 12 July 1910.
10. *Evening Chronicle* (Newcastle upon Tyne), 12 July 1910.

11. *Illustrated Chronicle* (Newcastle upon Tyne), 12 July 1910.
12. *Illustrated Chronicle* (Newcastle upon Tyne), 30 July 1910. This advertisement appears to have originated in the Personal Column of the *Daily News*, 28 July 1910.
13. *Illustrated Chronicle* (Newcastle upon Tyne), 10 August 1910.
14. *Evening Chronicle* (Newcastle upon Tyne), 25 July 1910.
15. *Illustrated Chronicle* (Newcastle upon Tyne), 9 August 1910.
16. *Daily News*, 9 August 1910.
17. *Illustrated Chronicle* (Newcastle upon Tyne), 15 August 1910.
18. *Evening Chronicle* (Newcastle upon Tyne), 9 August 1910.

CHAPTER 6

1. *Daily News*, 10 August 1910 and *The Times*, 10 August 1910.
2. Letters on the subject continued to appear in the *Illustrated Chronicle* and the *Daily News* among others throughout August 1910.
3. The *People*, 14 August 1910.
4. The best account of the Cohen murder appears in the *Sunderland Daily Echo*, 9 and 30 March 1909.
5. *Sunderland Daily Echo*, 30 March 1909.
6. *Sunderland Daily Echo*, 11 March 1909.
7. *Sunderland Daily Echo*, 17 March 1909.
8. Trial transcript HO 144/4202.

CHAPTER 7

1. The debate and strength of feeling are well reflected in the readers' letters which appeared in the *Daily News* throughout July and August 1910.
2. Report from Prison Medical Officer dated 6 July 1910. HO 144/4202 191.957/2.
3. Trial transcript. HO 144/4202.
4. HO 144/4202 191.957/51.
5. Wilson Hepple (1853–1937) is best known for his oils and watercolours of animals. Examples of his work are held in private and public collections, including those belonging to the cities of Newcastle upon Tyne and Manchester. A brief description of his life and work can be found at www.sellingantiques.co.uk.
6. HO 144/4202 191.957/90.
7. HO 144/4202 191.957/90.
8. Statements by John Spink and Percival Hall dated 18 July 1910. HO 144/4202 191.957/30.

9. Report by Chief Constable Fullarton James dated 19 July 1910. HO 144/4202 191.957/30.
10. HO 144/4202 191.957/22.
11. HO 144/4202 191.957/181.
12. HO 144/4202 191.957/95.
13. HO 144/4202 191.957/181.
14. All letters and petitions referred to in this chapter can be found in HO 144/4202.
15. HO 144/4202 191.957/148.
16. HO 144/4202 191.957/183.
17. HO 144/4202 191.957/90.
18. HO 144/4202 191.957/9 and 191.957/41.
19. HO 144/4202 191.957/2.
20. HO 144/4202 191.957/51 and 191.957/30.
21. HO 144/4202 191.957/39.
22. HO 144/4202 191.957/51.
23. HO 144/4202 191.957/16.
24. HO 144/4202 191.957/51.
25. HO 144/4202 191.957/9.
26. *Newcastle Daily Chronicle*, 22 March 1910.

CHAPTER 8

1. Details of the Norman family are derived from the 1901 census RG13/672 fo. 8, the will and probate of Clarence Charles Norman 1959, Principal Probate Registry and death certificate of Clarence Henry Norman 1974, General Register Office for England.
2. Clarence Henry Norman's various London addresses derive from correspondence published in *The Times*, electoral rolls held at London Metropolitan Archives, and correspondence in HO 144/4202 and T 161/46.
3. *The Times*, 22 October 1906 provides an example of an early C.H. Norman crusade, in this instance a protest to the Colonial Office regarding alleged ill-treatment of troops.
4. For an insight into the left-wing press in this period see Stephen Koss, *Rise and Fall of the Political Press in Britain, Vol. 2* (London, Hamish Hamilton, 1981).
5. *New Age*, 11 March 1909.
6. *New Age*, 4 March 1909.
7. *The Times*, 1 September 1911. (The full text of this correspondence appeared in a single issue of *The Times*, to which it had presumably been submitted by C.H. Norman.)

8. *The Times*, 1 September 1911.

9. *The Times*, 1 September 1911.

10. *The Times*, 7 April 1915.

11. *The Times*, 14 April 1915.

12. *The Times*, 20 April 1916.

13. *The Times*, 27 April 1916.

14. *The Times*, 24 May 1916.

15. *The Times*, 27 June 1916.

16. *The Times*, 28 July 1916.

17. *The Times*, 28 March 1918.

18. Memo to the Treasury Secretary dated 12 April 1920. T 161/46. A rule nisi for habeas corpus compels a gaoler to bring his prisoner to court and justify his continued detention, or show good reason for failing to do so.

19. *The Times*, 7 June 1917, 27 July 1917, 28 July 1917, 30 July 1917 and 31 July 1917.

20. *The Times*, 28 March 1918.

21. Memo to the Treasury Secretary dated 12 April 1920. T 161/46.

22. Undated memo. T 161/46.

23. Memo dated 30 April 1920. T 161/46.

24. Memo from G.L. Barstow dated 28 August 1920. T 161/46.

25. Police: Metropolitan Force: allegations of unfair dismissal by Inspector John Syme. HO 45/24589, National Archives.

26. *The Times*, 4 June 1929 and 13 March 1962.

27. *The Times*, 10 April 1962.

28. *The Times*, 3 February 1962.

29. HO 144/4202 191.957/41.

30. Orage's links with Norman are discussed in an undated internal memo written in 1925. HO 144/4202 191.957/186.

31. HO 144/4202 191.957/161.

32. HO 144/4202 191.957/175.

33. HO 144/4202 191.957/186.

34. Letter dated 7 October 1925. HO 144/4202 191.957/186.

35. Internal memo, October 1925. HO 144/4202 191.957/186.

36. Internal memo, October 1925. HO 144/4202 191.957/186.

37. HO 144/4202 191.957/67.

38. Rowan-Hamilton, S.O. (ed.), *The Trial of John Alexander Dickman* (Glasgow, William Hodge, 1914).

39. Norman's memorandum refers to *Great Unsolved Crimes* (London, Hutchinson, 1935), a compilation by various authors including Percy Savage. Savage had also published similar remarks about the Luard case in

his widely advertised memoirs, *Savage of Scotland Yard* (London, Hutchinson, 1934).

40. Bernard Taylor and Stephen Knight, *Perfect Murder* (London, Grafton Books, 1987), p. 157.

41. *The Times*, 29 April 1949.

42. Colin Wilson and Patricia Pitman, *Encyclopaedia of Murder* (London, Arthur Barker, 1961), p. xv.

43. *Second Verdict – Murder on the 10.27* written by John Lloyd, first transmitted by BBC Television on 17 June 1976, starring Stratford Johns and Frank Windsor.

44. In spite of strenuous efforts via the BBC and beyond, it has proved impossible to trace June Leech. However, the timing and content of the programme strongly indicate that June Leech had access to C.H. Norman's personal papers.

45. *Illustrated Chronicle* (Newcastle upon Tyne), 15 August 1910.

46. H.L. Adam, *CID: Behind the Scenes at Scotland Yard* (London, Sampson Low, Marston, 1931), pp. 240–3.

47. The items found on John Dickman at the time of his arrest are on record as one pair of tan gloves, one silk handkerchief, leather cigarette case, gun-metal cigarette case, snuffbox, matchbox, case with railway guide and canvas money bag. Statements of John Weddell and Andrew Tait. HO 144/4202 191.957/51. This list was enlarged upon by the receipt issued for the items taken from the prisoner which clarifies that the cases were a cigarette case, cigar case and card case, and mentions in addition a pencil, watch and chain, house keys and two ½d stamps. It is unlikely that a list which minutely records the value of two postage stamps would fail to mention the presence of a letter. HO 144/4202 191.957/9.

48. Adam, *CID: Behind the Scenes at Scotland Yard*, p. 239.

49. H.L. Adam, *Murder by Persons Unknown* (London, Collins, 1931), pp. 17–39.

50. In September 1908 the *Penny Illustrated Paper* ran a story alleging that unsupervised lunatics were roaming abroad. They made no attempt to connect this to the murder of Mrs Luard, but the two stories appear in close juxtaposition and it is possible that Adam derived inspiration for his 'inside information' from this source.

51. Adam, *CID: Behind the Scenes at Scotland Yard*, pp. 237–44.

52. J.M. Parrish and J.R. Crossland (eds), *The Fifty Most Amazing Crimes of the Last 100 Years* (London, Odhams Press, 1936).

53. Westminster County Council Appointeeship Section confirmed this policy to the author in 2005. They no longer hold C.H. Norman's papers.

CHAPTER 9

1. The details about the Luard, Selby-Luard and Hartley families which appear in this chapter have been drawn from diverse sources. Many newspapers published potted histories of the Luard family in August/September 1908, the most reliable of which appeared in *The Times* and the *Maidstone & Kentish Journal*. This information has been confirmed, clarified, expanded upon and corrected with reference to Births, Deaths and Marriages, General Register Office of England; Census Records, National Archives; parish registers of Ightham and Plaxtol, Centre for Kentish Studies; Calendar of Wills, National Probate Registry; West Kent Poll Books, Centre for Kentish Studies; WO 76/363 Fo. 366 and WO 3913 Fo. 322, National Archives; successive editions of *Kelly's Directory for Kent*; *The National Army List*, and monumental inscriptions at Ightham, Kent.

2. *Sevenoaks Free Press*, 10 July 1875.

3. This phrase appeared frequently, in particular in a letter from Thomas Kennion reproduced in numerous newspapers, including the *Tunbridge Wells Advertiser*, 9 October 1908.

4. Details of Major General's Luard's military career can be found in WO 3913 Fo. 322, National Archives, successive editions of the *National Army List*, and *The Times*, 19 September 1908.

5. *Maidstone & Kentish Journal*, 27 August 1908.

6. *Maidstone & Kentish Journal*, 27 August 1908.

7. *Kent Messenger & Sevenoaks Telegraph*, 29 August 1908. The 1901 census records four patients aged from 1 to 14 years, cared for by a matron and general servant.

8. Admiralty & Shipping Agent, charges: Removal of Remains of Lt Luard. MT 23/197, National Archives.

9. C.E. Luard, *Ightham Mote Kent, Description & Plan* (privately published 1893 by permission of the *Builder* where it had originally appeared).

10. All reports are consistent on this point.

11. *Sevenoaks Chronicle & Kentish Advertiser*, 28 August 1908.

12. *Sevenoaks Chronicle & Kentish Advertiser*, 28 August 1908.

13. Details of Colonel Warde's career derive from Roy Ingleton, *Policing Kent 1800–2000* (Chichester, Phillimore, 2002), R.L. Thomas (ed.), *Kent Police Centenary* (Maidstone, Kent, 1957), the *Kent Messenger*, 16 March 1940 and *The Times*, 12 and 15 March 1940.

14. *Maidstone & Kentish Journal*, 27 August 1908.

15. *Maidstone & Kentish Journal*, 27 August 1908.

16. *Kent Messenger & Sevenoaks Telegraph*, 29 August 1908.
17. *Kent Messenger & Sevenoaks Telegraph*, 29 August 1908.
18. *Kent Messenger & Sevenoaks Telegraph*, 29 August 1908.
19. *Daily Chronicle*, 26 August 1908.
20. *Kent Messenger & Sevenoaks Telegraph*, 29 August 1908.
21. *Daily Chronicle*, 26 August 1908.
22. *Daily Telegraph*, *Star* and *Daily Mail*, 26 August 1908.
23. *Daily Telegraph*, 26 August 1908.
24. *Daily Chronicle*, 26 August 1908.
25. *Daily Telegraph*, 26 August 1908 and many others.
26. *Daily Mirror*, 26 August 1908.

CHAPTER 10

1. *Sevenoaks Chronicle & Kentish Advertiser*, 28 August 1908, has one of the most comprehensive descriptions of the day's events – their reporter was one of the few to gain access to the inquest and is the source for this chapter unless otherwise stated.
2. The Surrey police were the first to avail themselves of Scotland Yard's expertise. In June 1906 they called for assistance to investigate the murder of Mary Hogg – the case remains unsolved. Percy Savage, *Savage of Scotland Yard* (London, Hutchinson, 1934), pp. 53–8.
3. A particularly scathing report appears in the *Maidstone & Kentish Journal*, 27 August 1908.
4. *Kent Messenger & Sevenoaks Telegraph*, 29 August 1908.
5. *Maidstone & Kentish Journal*, 27 August 1908.
6. *Kent Messenger & Sevenoaks Telegraph*, 29 August 1908.
7. *Daily Chronicle*, 27 August 1908 – their reporter was present at the inquest and in the evidence that follows, their account is used to supplement that of the *Sevenoaks Chronicle & Kentish Advertiser*.
8. *Kelly's Directory for Kent*, 1907 and 1909 editions.
9. A.M. Parkin, *The Seal Chart Murder* (Kemsing, Parkin, 1995), p. 15.
10. By the time of the 1881 census Daniel Kettel was already living at his cottage on the Sevenoaks road, employed as a gardener. The birthplaces of his children indicate that he had been living in the district since 1869, the year the Wilkinsons came to Frankfield. RG11 0904/70 Fo. 2, National Archives.
11. *Sevenoaks Chronicle & Kentish Advertiser*, 28 August 1908.
12. *Daily Chronicle*, 26 August 1908.
13. *Sevenoaks Chronicle & Kentish Advertiser*, 16 October 1908.

14. Details of the Wickham family are derived from 1881, 1891 and 1901 census for Ightham, Centre for Kentish Studies.
15. *Sevenoaks Chronicle & Kentish Advertiser*, 28 August 1908.
16. *Sevenoaks Chronicle & Kentish Advertiser*, 28 August 1908.
17. *Sevenoaks Chronicle & Kentish Advertiser*, 28 August 1908.
18. *Daily Chronicle*, 27 August 1908.

CHAPTER 11
1. *Sevenoaks Chronicle & Kentish Advertiser*, 28 August 1908.
2. *Sunderland Daily Echo*, 10 March 1909.
3. *Sunderland Daily Echo*, 11 March 1909.
4. Accounts of the route taken are confused and endlessly varied, but the reports which make most geographical sense have the dogs taking a line to the south-east (for example *The Times*, 28 August 1908). The *Maidstone & Kentish Journal* (3 September 1908) displays what appears to be first-hand knowledge of the event, mentioning that the dogs 'circled Mr Stagg's house'. The Electoral Roll, Centre for Kentish Studies, confirms that a Roland Stagg lived at Beacons Mount, Ivy Hatch.
5. *Daily Telegraph*, 28 August 1908.
6. *Daily Telegraph*, 29 August 1908.
7. *Maidstone & Kentish Journal*, 10 September 1908.
8. *Penny Illustrated Paper*, 5 September 1908.
9. *Daily Chronicle*, 28 August 1908.
10. *Sevenoaks Chronicle & Kentish Advertiser*, 4 September 1908.
11. *Daily Mail*, 26 August 1908.
12. *Daily Chronicle*, 29 August 1908.
13. *Maidstone & Kentish Journal*, 3 September 1908.
14. *Tunbridge Wells Advertiser*, 4 September 1908.
15. *Tunbridge Wells Advertiser*, 4 September 1908.
16. *Kent Messenger & Sevenoaks Telegraph*, 29 August 1908.
17. *Maidstone & Kentish Journal*, 3 September 1908.
18. *Illustrated Police Budget*, 5 September 1908.
19. The *People*, 30 August 1908.
20. *Kent Messenger & Sevenoaks Telegraph*, 5 September 1908, is among the most comprehensive of numerous accounts of Mrs Luard's funeral and is the principal source for this episode.
21. Sybil Constance Bigge, daughter of Marianne Selby Bigge and her first husband Charles John Bigge, married William Church on 14 July 1875. Ightham parish registers, Centre for Kentish Studies.

22. Beatrice Selby Luard married Alfred Willink, nephew of James Cropper the paper magnate, whose family-run business is still at Burneside, Cumbria.

23. *Kent Messenger & Sevenoaks Telegraph*, 5 September 1908.

24. *Kent Messenger & Sevenoaks Telegraph*, 5 September 1908.

25. *Sevenoaks Chronicle & Kentish Advertiser*, 11 September 1908.

26. *Westminster Gazette*, quoted in *Sevenoaks Chronicle & Kentish Advertiser*, 4 September 1908.

27. *Westerham Herald, Kent & Surrey Gazette*, 5 September 1908.

28. The letter appears in the *Tunbridge Wells Advertiser*, 4 September 1908, among others.

29. *Tunbridge Wells Advertiser*, 4 September 1908.

30. *Sevenoaks Chronicle & Kentish Advertiser*, 4 September 1908.

31. *The Times*, 4 September 1908. False confessions continued for several months. In November 1908 a youth walked into a police station in Manchester and confessed, claiming he had killed Mrs Luard with an axe and a dagger. *Daily Chronicle*, 18 November 1908.

32. *Tunbridge Wells Advertiser*, 4 September 1908.

33. *Kent Messenger & Sevenoaks Telegraph*, 5 September 1908.

34. *Tunbridge Wells Advertiser*, 28 August 1908.

35. *Maidstone & Kentish Journal*, 3 September 1908.

36. *The Times* (28 August 1908) accurately reported the circumstances of the discovery – other newspaper coverage was vague and variable.

37. All these stories were picked up and repeated in varying forms by numerous papers. The *Tunbridge Wells Advertiser* carried them all at various times in August and September 1908.

38. *Daily Graphic*, 1 September 1908.

39. *The Times*, 10 September 1908.

40. *Daily Telegraph*, 31 August 1908.

41. *Daily Chronicle*, 26 August 1908.

42. A.M. Parkin, *The Seal Chart Murder* (Kemsing, Parkin, 1995), pp. 23–4.

43. *Penny Illustrated Paper*, 26 September 1908.

44. The letter appears in the *Tunbridge Wells Advertiser*, 11 September 1908, among others.

CHAPTER 12

1. Details of the inquest in this chapter are derived from *The Times*, 10 September 1908, unless otherwise stated.

2. *Sevenoaks Chronicle & Kentish Advertiser*, 11 September 1908.

3. *Kelly's Directory for Kent*, 1907 edition and 1901 census RG 13/744 Fo. 16, National Archives.

4. *Sevenoaks Chronicle & Kentish Advertiser*, 11 September 1908.
5. *Sevenoaks Chronicle & Kentish Advertiser*, 28 August 1908.
6. *Sevenoaks Chronicle & Kentish Advertiser*, 28 August 1908.
7. *Kent Messenger & Sevenoaks Telegraph*, 12 September 1908.

CHAPTER 13

1. *Westerham Herald, Kent & Surrey Gazette*, 12 September 1908.
2. *Sevenoaks Chronicle & Kentish Advertiser*, 18 September 1908.
3. *Sevenoaks Chronicle & Kentish Advertiser*, 16 October 1908.
4. The photograph reproduced in the majority of newspapers depicts a stern-faced woman of indeterminate age and was in fact a heavily retouched copy of a photograph which had been taken some years previously, a reasonable copy of which appears in *Daily Graphic*, 19 September 1908. The poor quality copies bear so little resemblance to the original it is difficult to believe they are of the same woman.
5. These theories are all aired in A.M. Parkin, *The Seal Chart Murder* (Kemsing, Parkin, 1995).
6. Memoir written by Revd Bertram Winnifrith. Parkin, in *ibid.*, pp. 13–15.
7. *Ibid.*, p. 17.
8. *Daily Graphic*, 19 September 1908.
9. *Tunbridge Wells Advertiser*, 11 September 1908.
10. *Kent Messenger & Sevenoaks Telegraph*, 12 September 1908.
11. This account of the final days of Major General Luard's life and the inquest into his death is drawn from the statements issued by Colonel Warde and others as reported in *The Times*, 19 and 21 September 1908.
12. This quote was picked up by numerous newspapers, e.g. *Birmingham Post*, 19 September 1908. It had been circulated by a bona fide press agency according to the *Dover Express*, 28 September 1908.
13. *The Times*, 21 September 1908.
14. *Tunbridge Wells Advertiser*, 25 September 1908.

CHAPTER 14

1. *Tunbridge Wells Advertiser*, 25 September 1908.
2. *Tunbridge Wells Advertiser*, 25 September 1908.
3. *The Times*, 19 September 1908.
4. *The People*, 20 September 1908.
5. *The Times*, 21 September 1908.
6. *Daily Graphic*, 19 September 1908.
7. The source for the account of the General's funeral in this chapter is the *Tunbridge Wells Advertiser*, 25 September 1908, unless otherwise stated.

8. The source for the account of the inquest in this chapter is *The Times*, 24 September 1908, unless otherwise stated.

9. *Maidstone & Kentish Journal*, 24 September 1908.

10. *Dover Express*, 25 September 1908.

11. *Maidstone & Kentish Journal*, 24 September 1908.

12. *Daily News*, 3 October 1908.

13. *Maidstone & Kentish Journal*, 1 October 1908.

14. *Maidstone & Kentish Journal*, 15 October 1908.

15. *Tunbridge Wells Advertiser*, 6 November 1908.

16. *Kent Messenger & Sevenoaks Telegraph*, 25 September 1909.

17. The account of the Woodruff affair in this chapter derives from *The Times*, 21 September 1909, and the *Kent Messenger & Sevenoaks Telegraph*, 25 September 1909.

18. *Kent Messenger & Sevenoaks Telegraph*, 25 September 1909.

19. It is evident that at least some citizens in Kent were unhappy with the way the enquiry was conducted: a Mr Fisher of Sundridge complained of police harassment, specifically mentioning Chief Constable Warde. Fisher said that the police's suspicions centred on the fact that he had left some luggage in store at Brasted railway station for several weeks, and had coincidentally spent several years in South Africa – and the police considered there might be 'an overseas link'. *People*, 15 November 1908.

20. *Kent Messenger & Sevenoaks Telegraph*, 25 September 1909.

21. *Kent Messenger & Sevenoaks Telegraph*, 2 October 1909.

22. Further details of the Slater case and the various books devoted to the subject can be accessed via the www.

CHAPTER 15

1. A.M. Parkin, *The Seal Chart Murder* (Kemsing, Parkin, 1995), p. 16.

2. See Jane Pugmore's inquest evidence in Chapter 12.

3. Parkin, *The Seal Chart Murder*, pp. 17–18. The present writer cross-checked the names of gardeners known to have been employed by the Luards with local death and marriage records, and the subsequent occupations of their sons where they had any. Nothing emerged to substantiate this story.

4. *Kelly's Directory for Kent*.

5. *Medical Directory 1911* (A.M. Churchill, London, 1911).

6. A brief resumé of the fascinating life and career of Admiral George Stanley Bosanquet (1835–1914) can be found in *Who Was Who 1897–1916* (London, A.C. Black, 1916).

7. *Daily Graphic*, 19 September 1908.

8. A full version of Edith Wickham's tale appears in Parkin, *The Seal Chart Murder*, pp. 19–23.
9. W.H. Johnson, *Kent Tales of Mystery and Murder* (Newbury, Countryside Books, 2003), p. 123.
10. *Sevenoaks Chronicle & Kentish Advertiser*, 28 August 1908.
11. *Sevenoaks Chronicle & Kentish Advertiser*, 28 August 1908.
12. *Sevenoaks Chronicle & Kentish Advertiser*, 28 August 1908.
13. 1901 census RG13/746 Fos 15–16, National Archives.
14. Reports on the parliamentary discussions regarding the introduction of an old age pension can be found in *The Times* throughout the autumn of 1908.
15. *Penny Illustrated Paper*, 10 October 1908.
16. *Tunbridge Wells Advertiser*, 4 September 1908.
17. *Kent Messenger & Sevenoaks Telegraph*, 12 September 1908.

CHAPTER 16

1. The Kent police were loaned the yellow motor car (nicknamed 'the Butterfly') by Messrs H.E. Hall & Co, of Tonbridge. *Tunbridge Wells Advertiser*, 4 September 1908. Even the most advanced force in the country, the Metropolitan Police, did not normally have motor cars at their disposal in 1908. Divisional superintendents and above had a horse and trap, lower ranks relied on horse-drawn buses, tramcars, bicycles and shank's pony. Percy Savage, *Savage of Scotland Yard* (London, Hutchinson & Co, 1934), p. 34.
2. *Maidstone & Kentish Journal*, 24 September 1908.
3. *The Pirates of Penzance* by Gilbert and Sullivan, first performed 1880.
4. *Westerham Herald, Kent & Surrey Gazette*, 5 September 1908.
5. *Sevenoaks Chronicle & Kentish Advertiser*, 2 October 1908.
6. I am indebted to Mrs and Mrs John Lewis of Frankfield for information regarding the history of the estate, which is substantiated by census records, electoral rolls, directories and various editions of the Ordnance Survey map.
7. *Sevenoaks Chronicle & Kentish Advertiser*, 28 August 1908.
8. Bernard Taylor and Stephen Knight, *Perfect Murder* (London, Grafton Books, 1987).
9. *Daily Graphic*, 19 September 1908.
10. *Daily Graphic*, 19 September 1908.
11. A.M. Parkin, *The Seal Chart Murder* (Kemsing, Parkin, 1995), p. 24.
12. *Ibid.*, pp. 23–4.
13. In 1901 Thomas Skeer was a farm carpenter living with his wife and seven

children, one of whom was 10-year-old George. 1901 census, National Archives.

POSTSCRIPT

1. Annie Dickman died on 30 March 1949 at 189 Simonside Terrace, Heaton. Calendar of Wills, Principal Probate Registry.
2. For a summary of *Nisbet* v. *Rayne & Burn* see S.O. Rowan-Hamilton (ed), *The Trial of John Alexander Dickman* (Glasgow, William Hodge, 1914), pp. 204–7. Coleridge's remarks are included there and in the trial transcript. Cicely Nisbet's letter defending Rayne & Burn appeared in the *Illustrated Chronicle* (Newcastle upon Tyne), 30 July 1910. Her second marriage was registered in 1913, General Register Office for England.
3. *The National Army List 1913*; The Commonwealth War Graves Commission; Regimental History & Officers Book held at the Royal Norfolk Regimental Museum; Calendar of Wills 1916, Principal Probate Registry.
4. Death certificate of C.H. Norman, General Register Office for England.
5. Thomas F. Newton, *A Biography of E.H. Richardson* www.community-2.webtv.net.
6. *The Times*, 21 July 1955; *Morpeth Herald & Reporter*, 6 September 1935; Jonathan Goodman, *The Burning of Evelyn Foster* (Newton Abbot, David & Charles, 1977).
7. *Kent Messenger*, 16 March 1940; *The Times*, 12 and 13 March 1940; Roy Ingleton, *Policing Kent 1800–2000* (Chichester, Phillimore, 2002); R.L. Thomas (ed.), *Kent Police Centenary* (Maidstone, Kent Constabulary, 1957).

Select Bibliography

Adam, H.L., *CID: Behind the Scenes at Scotland Yard*, London, Sampson Low, Marston, 1931

——, *Murder by Persons Unknown*, London, Collins, 1931

Ingleton, Roy, *Policing Kent 1800–2000*, Chichester, Phillimore, 2002

Johnson, W.H., *Kent Tales of Mystery and Murder*, Newbury, Countryside Books, 2003

Koss, Stephen, *The Rise & Fall of the Political Press in Britain, Volume 2*, London, Hamish Hamilton, 1981

Luard, C.E., *Ightham Mote*, published privately, 1893

Nicholson, Nigel, *Ightham Mote*, London, National Trust, 1998

Parkin, A.M., *The Seal Chart Murder*, Kemsing, Parkin, 1995

Parrish, J.M. and Crossland, J.R. (eds), *The Fifty Most Amazing Crimes of the Last 100 Years*, London, Odhams Press, 1936

Rowan-Hamilton, S.O., *The Trial of John Alexander Dickman*, Glasgow, William Hodge, 1914

Savage, Percy, *Savage of Scotland Yard*, London, Hutchinson, 1934

Taylor, Bernard and Knight, Stephen, *Perfect Murder*, London, Grafton Books, 1987

Thomas, R.L. (ed.), *Kent Police Centenary*, Maidstone, Kent Constabulary, 1957

Wilson, Colin and Pitman, Patricia, *Encyclopaedia of Murder*, London, Arthur Barker, 1961

Index